THE CHANGING FACE OF CONFLICT AND THE EFFICACY OF INTERNATIONAL HUMANITARIAN LAW

International Humanitarian Law Series

VOLUME 2

The *International Humanitarian Law Series* is a series of monographs and edited volumes which aims to promote scholarly analysis and discussion of both the theory and practice of the international legal regulation of armed conflict.
The series explores substantive issues of International Humanitarian Law including,

- protection for victims of armed conflict and regulation of the means and methods of warfare

- questions of application of the various legal regimes for the conduct of armed conflict

- issues relating to the implementation of International Humanitarian Law obiligations

- national and international approaches to the enforcement of the law and

- the interactions between International Humanitarian Law and other related areas of International law such as Human Rights, Refugee Law, Armed Control and Disarmament Law and International Criminal Law.

IHUL.ser

The Changing Face of Conflict and the Efficacy of International Humanitarian Law

edited by

HELEN DURHAM
National Manager, International Humanitarian Law,
Australian Red Cross

and

TIMOTHY L.H. McCORMACK
Australian Red Cross Professor of International Humanitarian Law,
Faculty of Law, The University of Melbourne

MARTINUS NIJHOFF PUBLISHERS
THE HAGUE / LONDON / BOSTON

A C.I.P Catalogue record for this book is available from the Library of Congress.

ISBN 90-411-1180-8

Published by Kluwer Law International,
P.O. Box 85889, 2508 CN The Hague, The Netherlands

Sold and distributed in North, Central and South America
by Kluwer Law International,
675 Massachusetts Avenue, Cambridge, MA 02139, USA

In all other countries, sold and distributed
by Kluwer Law International, Distribution Centre
P.O. Box 322, 3300 AH Dordrecht, The Netherlands

Printed on acid-free paper

Printed and bound in Great Britain by Antony Rowe Limited.

to two special little women in our lives

Lucinda Claire Durham Floyd

and

Miriam Elisabeth McCormack

Table of Contents

Foreword

You will not be surprised perhaps to know that Vice-Chancellors, for a cluster of motives, some noble, some less so, some down right mercenary, are fond of quoting that aphorism of H.G. Wells: 'History is more and more a race between education and catastrophe.'

At the most crass (and essentially ineffective level) the implication is 'Give us money or risk catastrophe.' It is ineffective, not because it is untrue, because education is costly and is of critical and increasing importance in a knowledge-rich world, but simply because every lobby group in the world tells every politician precisely the same thing about their particular enterprise.

There is nothing sadder for humankind than the need for the Red Cross, nor anything more noble than the work it does. The same kind of thing may be said of International Humanitarian Law. That *homo sapiens* needs 'the law of war' at all is a hideous reminder of a great contradiction embedded in the very essence of our humanity.

On the one hand, that so many of the best minds, best managers, finest leaders, and most creative, innovative, sophisticated developments in human history, have been motivated by the compunction to make war with more and more terrible effect, is enough to make any sapient, self-conscious species fear for its very future.

Yet on the other hand, that so many of our best-trained minds have always turned to the challenge of ameliorating the suffering associated with war, still humankind's greatest self-inflicted disaster, and that so many of the most generous, self-sacrificing, heroic acts of human kindness regularly are taken to protect those injured, threatened or dispossessed by war, offers arguably the best grounds for hope that *homo sapiens* may learn a better way to conduct life on earth.

The stakes get higher and higher.

It is over 36 years since John F. Kennedy reminded the world at his inauguration that: 'Man holds in his mortal hands the power to destroy all forms of human poverty and all forms of human life.' *Man* was, of course, the wrong word; so was *hands*. Other animals have delicately prehensile hands. What makes humankind different is the human brain, and it is the

Helen Durham and Timothy L.H. McCormack (eds.), The Changing Face of Conflict and the Efficacy of International Humanitarian Law, xiii–xv.
© 1999 *Kluwer Law International. Printed in Great Britain.*

vast, if somewhat mysterious superiority of that organ which makes our species the great custodian and predator of the earth.

Some of the most interesting research on the human brain is already being done in Australia by scientists working on the boundaries between psychology and neuroscience. I still recall being horrified by the dramatic way in which a former colleague in the University of New South Wales, George Paxinos, drew attention to the results of his own research. Is it possible, he argued, that the human brain is simply the wrong size?

Extinction occurs because something destabilises the relationship between a species and its environment. Many things can do it. Perhaps the appearance of a new predator or a more efficient competitor; perhaps a change of climate; possibly a degradation of the environment resulting from a cataclysmic event (such as that massive meteor impact on the earth 65 million years ago which destroyed the planet as a habitat for dinosaurs) or from some more gradual deterioration.

The extinction of humankind, if it happens, will be unique because we, of all species, have acquired the capacity to manipulate our own environment, to anticipate its development and adapt in advance to new conditions. The irony is that the most likely cause of fatal destabilisation in our environment will be our own fault. We will 'intelligently' engineer the circumstances of our own extinction.

Which means that humankind has the unique potential to be fatally stupid, at the same time as being arrestingly intelligent. Bright enough to be able to destroy the whole world; and just possibly dumb enough to actually do it! That is the paradox of being human.

Nor is it a modern paradox. Let me remind you of the Greek creation myth about Epimetheus and Prometheus, two gods whose task it was to equip all creatures with the kinds of powers and skills that each would need to survive.

Protagarus told the story to Socrates as follows:

> Epimetheus asked Prometheus to let him assign the powers himself ... To some creatures he gave strength, but not speed, while he equipped the weaker with speed. He gave some claws or horns, and for those without them he devised some other power for their preservation. To those whom he made of small size, he gave winged flight, or a dwelling underground; to those he made large, he gave their size itself as a protection.

So far so good. But in Protagoras's words, 'Epimetheus, not being altogether wise, didn't notice that he had used up all the powers on the non-rational creatures; so last of all he was left with humankind, quite unprovided for ...'

This alarmed Prometheus when he reviewed the handiwork of Epimetheus, 'and saw the other creatures well provided for in everyway, while man was naked and unshod, without any covering ... or any fangs or claws'. According to Protagarus, Prometheus:

> was at his wits' end to find a means for the preservation of mankind, so he stole from Hephaestus and Athena, (fellow gods) their technical skill, along with the use of fire ... and that was what he gave to man.

Fire – the command of non-human energy, and godlike technical skills – that, as the Greek philosophers rightly recognised, is what sets humankind apart from all other creatures.

And that is what makes our species so downright dangerous. Epimetheus and the other gods were rightly alarmed by what Prometheus had done. For with these stolen cognitive and technical capabilities the human species had the potential to dominate and ultimately destroy the rest of the natural world.

The pity was that Hephaestus and Athena, whom Prometheus robbed, did not possess the political and social arts of morality and justice, and without them, had neither the power nor the wisdom to establish or maintain just, stable human communities. Zeus did, but the guards of Zeus, in Protagarus's words, 'were terrible'. So Prometheus stole the one and left humankind without the other. Humankind thus became godlike in power and knowledge, but remained frail and flawed in the prudence, wisdom and moral judgment needed to manage their own social and political relationships.

That brings me back to George Paxinos and his fear that the human brain may be the wrong size for long-term human survival. The wrong size! Not too small. Were it smaller, humankind would be less powerful, and have less destructive technologies at its disposal. The power to destroy all forms of human life would be as absent as the power to destroy all forms of human poverty.

Were the brain larger, greater *wisdom* might accompany the control of the 'fire of the gods'. We then really could tackle human poverty. We would be sufficiently prudent to control our species' aggression. We would have the sense to nurture the planet instead of simply using our advanced technical capabilities to deplete its resources and pollute its environment for short-term satisfactions.

The trouble is that there are no Greek deities from whom to steal the moral and political arts humankind desperately needs to become wise as well as merely powerful. Homo sapiens is terribly alone when it comes to this great problem. History, to paraphrase H. G. Wells, is more and more a race between the increasingly terminal disaster of war and the effective realisation of International Humanitarian Law – the subject matter of this volume and the new series of which it is a part.

Alan D. Gilbert
Vice-Chancellor, The University of Melbourne

Editors' Preface

There is nothing controversial in suggesting that the nature of armed conflict has changed considerably – particularly in the second half of the Twentieth Century. Until the outbreak of World War II most conflicts were international in character, the overwhelming majority of victims were combatants, and technological developments in the creation of new weapons systems were still relatively rudimentary. In 1977 the international community felt compelled to respond to new realities in the conduct of armed conflict. Two new Protocols Additional to the Geneva Conventions of 1949 were adopted and these instruments strengthened the protection of civilians, dealt in some detail with internal armed conflicts and codified principles relating to the conduct of armed hostilities. In the last two decades of the Twentieth Century changes in the nature of armed conflict have been even more dramatic. We have witnessed an increasing incidence of enthno-national conflict often fought in the context of so called "disintegrating" or "collapsed" States, the blurring of distinctions between combatants and civilians and the proliferation of, and unparalleled access to, ever more lethal weaponry.

The reality of the changing nature of armed conflict, a concept reflected in the title to this volume, is taken as given. It is the second aspect, *The Efficacy of International Humanitarian Law* in the light of changes to the way warfare is conducted, that is the focus of the various contributions. 1977 is a critical date because the chapters in this volume are a substantially revised set of selected papers from a conference to mark the 20th Anniversary of the adoption of the Additional Protocols held at the University of Melbourne in 1997. It is with the passing of now more than 20 years since the Protocols that the volume raises questions about the efficacy or otherwise of international humanitarian law.

The more controversial issue is the question of how best to respond to these new challenges. One recurrent theme throughout various contributions to this volume is precisely this question of how to maximise the efficacy of international humanitarian law. Some authors advocate the need to consider new treaty regimes – that international humanitarian law is not effective enough – whilst others argue for more effective implementation

Helen Durham and Timothy L.H. McCormack (eds.), The Changing Face of Conflict and the Efficacy of International Humanitarian Law, xvii–xx.
© 1999 *Kluwer Law International. Printed in Great Britain.*

of existing norms – that international humanitarian law has not been sufficiently tested to adequately judge its efficacy. New treaties since 1977 have encompassed both approaches. On one hand, there have been significant new regimes to prohibit specific weapons categories. Key examples include chemical weapons, blinding and laser weapons and anti-personnel landmines. On the other hand, there has been an unprecedented development in the codification of existing principles. Nowhere is this more apparent than in institution building for the enforcement of international humanitarian law with the establishment of the two *ad hoc* international criminal law tribunals and the international criminal court.

The volume commences with an incisive critique of the Additional Protocols by Christopher Greenwood. In undertaking a realistic analysis of the relative strengths and weaknesses of these instruments, Greenwood cautions against a presumption that new situations automatically require new law. Rather, he urges the international community to more effectively implement existing international humanitarian law. In comparison, Christine Chinkin's chapter calls for consideration of a new legal instrument. This conclusion flows from a persuasive analysis of the experiences of women in armed conflict which exposes the limitations of the existing law and the reticence of the international community to take serious stock of these issues.

This apparent disparity of approach is encapsulated again in other chapters. Michael Kelly, for example, argues for the creative application of existing Geneva Convention IV to non-belligerent occupation during peace operations. In a similar approach, albeit in relation to different subject matter, Robin Coupland's chapter focusses exclusively on the long-standing prohibition on weapons which cause superfluous injury or unnecessary suffering. In an innovative approach, he uses medical data to propose a legal definition to this general principle. Contrasting this, Robert Mathews and Tim McCormack's detailed contribution on the relationship between arms control and international humanitarian law recognises the inevitable need for new comprehensive treaty regimes for the prohibition of specific weapons categories.

Upon reflection, these two apparently disparate responses may not necessarily be mutually exclusive. Whilst recent developments in the enforcement of international humanitarian law constitute attempts to flesh out existing principles, there is also an aspect involving the development of new norms. The helpful chapter by Gillian Triggs uncovers the patchy nature of national prosecutions for alleged violations of international humanitarian law as an argument for the establishment of a truly global and effective international criminal law regime. Both Geoff Skillen's and Helen Durham's chapters demonstrate the inextricable link between respect for the law and enforcement of it. Durham also highlights the need for new international institutions to set strong precedents of fair prosecution to rectify the poor image of previous processes. In addition, Skillen identifies the aspects of the Rome Statute for the International Criminal Court which extend the parameters of existing international criminal law.

Another major theme dealing with the effectiveness of international humanitarian law revolves around the need for this area of law to move beyond an isolationist position. In an after-dinner speech at the conference in 1997, Hilary Charlesworth called for "bridge-building" with related fields of law such as human rights and peacekeeping. Professor Charlesworth also encouraged those interested in this important area of law to communicate with colleagues in other related professions. It is interesting to note the extent to which her calls are heeded, at least in part, even in the range of authors and in the writings they contribute to the current volume. In relation to professional background, this volume features chapters from members of the medical profession, scientific community and the military in addition to academic lawyers. Furthermore, several of the contributors alert us to the fact that for international humanitarian law to be effective, it is necessary to harness the skills of other professionals such as psychologists, diplomats, politicians and journalists.

In relation to the need for international humanitarian law to interface with related areas of law, a number of writers pick up this theme. Daniel Thürer's contribution correctly identifies the increasingly adverse impact of armed conflict on ethnic minorities. He considers it necessary for international humanitarian law to combine with human rights law to understand the complexities of protecting these groups in times of armed conflict. In a similar vein, Garth Cartledge is critical of a simplistic approach to peace operations which assumes that the only relevant law is international humanitarian law. He points out that in most operations, peace-keeping contingents do not participate in the hostilities and undertake a range of tasks requiring resort to a broader source of obligations. A number of other papers also follow this theme of the importance of relating international humanitarian law to other areas of international law such as arms control and disarmament and international criminal law.

It is true that, in the past, international humanitarian law has tended to be viewed as external to "mainstream" issues in international law and, indeed, in international affairs. Whatever the reasons for this situation, there is no doubt that a seachange in attitude towards international humanitarian law is occurring. Dramatic recent developments include the entry into force of the Ottawa Anti-Personnel Landmines Convention, the establishment of the two *ad hoc* tribunals for the Former Yugoslavia and Rwanda, the first international convictions of war criminals for 50 years, the successful negotiation of the Rome Statute for an ICC and the unprecedented decision of the House of Lords that Augusto Pinochet does not enjoy foreign head of State immunity for certain alleged acts of torture. All of these developments are indicative of a new expectation that international humanitarian law ought to be effective; that efforts to make it more effective in the past have been inadequate; and that the law will be enforced by

States either individually, through domestic criminal law systems, or collectively, through multilateral processes. The international community seems to be in the process of moving beyond the passive acceptance of minimum standards without a corresponding commitment to ensure respect for those standards.

In reflecting on the changing face of conflict and the efficacy of international humanitarian law, we would be dissatisfied if this volume only commemorated the twentieth anniversary of the Additional Protocols without setting its sights firmly on a future involving greater respect for international humanitarian law. If the positive developments throughout the period of preparation of this volume for publication are any indication, the future for efforts to strengthen the regulation of armed conflict is an encouraging one indeed.

Helen Durham
Timothy L.H. McCormack
Law School
The University of Melbourne
1 March 1999

Acknowledgments

Having taken the significant step of establishing a new Chair in International Humanitarian Law at the University of Melbourne in 1996, the Victorian Division of the Australian Red Cross Society decided to mark the establishment of the chair with a major Asia-Pacific regional conference. The twentieth anniversary of the 1977 Protocols Additional to the Four Geneva Conventions of 1949 was an opportune occasion to gather leading academics and practitioners to question the efficacy of international humanitarian law. The various contributions to this volume are based largely upon papers delivered at that conference. There has, of course, been a substantial amount of revision and updating of virtually all the papers – particularly in the light of developments in the jurisprudence of the two *ad hoc* international criminal tribunals for the Former Yugoslavia and Rwanda and in response to the conclusion of negotiations for the Rome Statute of the International Criminal Court.

As with any edited volume of essays such as this, many individuals have contributed to the final product. First we wish to thank the Victorian Division of the Australian Red Cross Society for their commitment to the organisation of a successful international conference. Richard Morgan, Kate Redwood and Noreen Minogue all enthusiastically supported both the concept and the organisation of the conference. The IHL Department at the Victorian Division, in particular Paula Irani, Sam Knox, Bev Patterson and Helen Vaughan, worked tirelessly to ensure the Conference reflected the importance of the anniversary and ran smoothly. It was the success of the conference which convinced us of the viability of this volume.

We were encouraged by support for the conference from the private sector including Arthur Robinson and Hedderwicks, First Pacific Stockbrokers and AON. The Commonwealth Attorney General's Department, the Department of Defence and the Department of Foreign Affairs and Trade also provided generous economic support. AUSAid's assistance enabled many regional Red Cross and Red Crescent members to participate in the conference and greatly enrich our discussions.

The success of the 1997 conference was guaranteed by the quality of the speakers and their presentations. We are indebted to each of the contributors to this volume for their efforts in the initial preparation of their papers and for their willingness to contribute to this volume. As editors, we have

Helen Durham and Timothy L.H. McCormack (eds.), The Changing Face of Conflict and the Efficacy of International Humanitarian Law, xxi–xxii.
© 1999 *Kluwer Law International. Printed in Great Britain.*

also appreciated their patience with us and their willingness to undertake considerable work up-dating their original papers. It is often a dilemma to determine the optimum amount of re-writing and up-dating. Whilst it is exciting to be living in an era in which international humanitarian law is a dynamic and ever changing subject, at times it is hard to identify where to draw the line. Almost every piece in this publication deals with a topic which has recently experienced an explosion of new developments and to our delight the authors have responded accordingly.

We have also enjoyed the privilege of working with a large number of willing and competent volunteers who have given freely of their time and skills to see this book materialise. In particular, Ram Doraiswamy has provided outstanding assistance in final editing and footnoting, along with Nick Anson, Penelope Gleeson, Matthew Harding, Tonia Hieronymi, Jessica Howard, Martin Joy and Narda Sango-Stanisic. Our wonderful colleague at the International Humanitarian Law Department of the National Office of Australian Red Cross, Elizabeth Grant, kept us both focussed and encouraged with her superb administrative skills and intelligent suggestions. We remain deeply grateful to her.

We are also indebted to Alan Stephens and Lindy Melman of Kluwer Law International. They have consistently remained enthusiastic for the publication of this volume despite our failure to meet successive deadlines. Their commitment to the publication of a new series on international humanitarian law, and for the inclusion of this volume in it, has been a great source of professional and personal encouragement to us.

Two of the contributions here have also been published elsewhere and we take this opportunity to acknowledge permission to reproduce them. Daniel Thürer's chapter entitled 'Protection of Minorities in General International Law and in International Humanitarian Law' has already been published in Karel Wellens (ed), *International Law Theory and Practice: Essays in Honour of Eric Suy* (1998), 533-548 and appears in this volume with the permission of Kluwer Law International. Robin Coupland's chapter entitled 'The SirUS Project: Towards a Determination of Which Weapons Cause Superfluous Injury or Unnecessary Suffering' has previously been published by the International Committee of the Red Cross, Geneva and is included here with the permission of the ICRC.

In a personal sense Helen would like to dedicate this publication to her niece Lucinda Claire Durham Floyd. In holding Lucinda in my arms minutes after she was recently born I gained a flash of understanding as to why I dedicate much of my energies to this area of law – in the hope that children will grow up in a world which is at peace with itself.

For Tim, it is a pleasure to dedicate my contribution to the editing of this volume to my daughter Miriam Elisabeth McCormack. She was truly longed for and from the moment she came into our lives she has provided an irrepressible source of joy and fulfilment. Her beautiful life is a constant source of motivation for me to work to make a difference in the world.

Notes on Contributors

Garth J. Cartledge
Lieutenant Colonel (ret.) Garth Cartledge is currently South East Regional
Counsel for the Australian Civil Aviation Safety Authority. In 1994-1996
inclusive he was Director of International and Operational Law for the
Australian Defence Force. He has several publications in the area of the
law of armed conflict. His Ph.D., currently in progress, deals with the laws
that govern the actions and operations of soldiers who deploy on operations short of armed conflict, such as peacekeeping and legal issues associated with crossing the threshold into armed conflict.

Christine Chinkin
Professor Christine Chinkin is Professor of International Law at the London School of Economics and Political Science. She was previously Dean
and Head of Department in the Faculty of Law, at the University of South-
ampton. Professor Chinkin has also taught in Law Schools in the United
States, Asia, Australia and is a member of the Board of Editors of the
American Journal of International Law. She has authored many articles on
various aspects of international law and human rights and her most recent
book is entitled *Third Parties in International Law*. She has a particular
research interest in the application of feminist theories to international law
and recently submitted an *amicus curiae* brief to the International Criminal
Tribunal for the Former Yugoslavia on the issue of protection for witnesses
in proceedings before the Tribunal.

Robin Coupland
Dr Robin Coupland is Chief Surgeon in the Medical Division of the International Committee of the Red Cross Geneva. He has extensive field
hospital experience in the surgical treatment of victims of armed conflict
and is now involved in the development of medical criteria for the definition of 'superfluous injury or unnecessary suffering'. Dr Coupland has
authored a number of publications on the surgery of war wounds and is a
Fellow of the Royal College of Surgeons, London.

*Helen Durham and Timothy L.H. McCormack (eds.), The Changing Face of Conflict and the Efficacy of International
Humanitarian Law*, xxiii–xxvi.
© 1999 *Kluwer Law International. Printed in Great Britain.*

Helen Durham

Helen Durham is the National Manager of International Humanitarian Law for the Australian Red Cross. She is also an SJD candidate in the Faculty of Law at the University of Melbourne. In 1997 she was awarded the Evans-Grahmeyer Travelling Scholarship to New York and The Hague to research her doctoral dissertation which is provisionally entitled 'The Role of Non-Governmental Organisations in International Criminal Law'. Helen was a member of the ICRC Delegation to the Rome Diplomatic Conference for the Establishment of the International Criminal Court.

Christopher Greenwood

Professor Christopher Greenwood is Professor of International Law at the London School of Economics and Political Science. He has appeared as Counsel for the UK in several cases before the International Court of Justice and was recently appointed Queen's Counsel in Essex Court Chambers in London. He co-edits the *International Law Reports* and is a member of the editorial boards of several journals including the *British Yearbook of International Law* and the *Yearbook of International Humanitarian Law*. Professor Greenwood is a leading international authority on International Humanitarian Law and has been appointed Rapporteur on that topic by the Dutch and Russian Governments for the commemoration of the centenary of the First Hague International Peace Conference of 1899.

Michael J. Kelly

Lieutenant Colonel Michael Kelly currently serves in the Directorate of Operations and International Law, Defence Legal Office, Australian Department of Defence, Canberra. In 1995 he was made a Member in the Order of Australia in recognition of his contribution as Legal Adviser to the Australian contingent to Operation 'Restore Hope' in Baidoa, Somalia. He was also seconded from the Australian Defence Force to work for the International Committee of the Red Cross in dissemination of International Humanitarian Law to armed forces in the Former Yugoslavia in 1996. Lt Col Kelly recently graduated with a Ph.D. for his dissertation entitled 'Public Security in Peace Operations: The Interim Administration of Justice in Peace Operations and the Search for a Legal Framework'.

Robert J. Mathews

Robert Mathews is Principal Research Scientist in the Australian Defence Science and Technology Organisation's Aeronautical and Marine Research Laboratories in Melbourne. He has been involved in chemical and biological defence issues for more than 20 years and has represented the Australian Government in multilateral arms control and disarmament negotiations throughout that period. In 1996 he was awarded the Medal in the Order of

Australia for his contributions to Australia's efforts to conclude negotiations for the Chemical Weapons Convention. He is a Visiting Fellow and a candidate for Ph.D. in the Faculty of Law at the University of Melbourne. Robert is also a member of the Australian Red Cross National Advisory Committee on International Humanitarian Law.

Timothy L.H. McCormack
Professor Tim McCormack is the Foundation Australian Red Cross Professor of International Humanitarian Law and the Associate Dean (Research) in the Faculty of Law at the University of Melbourne. He chairs the Australian Red Cross National Advisory Committee on International Humanitarian Law and is also a member of the Australian Foreign Minister's National Consultative Committee on Peace and Disarmament. Professor McCormack is a member of the editorial board of the *Yearbook of International Humanitarian Law* and his most recent book, co-edited with Gerry Simpson, is entitled *The Law of War Crimes: National and International Approaches.*

Geoffrey J. Skillen
Air Commodore (ret.) Geoff Skillen is currently Legal Officer in the Human Rights Branch in the Australian Department of the Attorney-General. He was the Director-General of Defence Force Legal Services in the Australian Department of Defence. In that position, Air Commodore Skillen participated in successive Australian delegations to preparatory negotiating sessions and the Rome Diplomatic Conference for the Establishment of an International Criminal Court.

Daniel Thürer
Professor Dr Daniel Thürer is the Professor of International, European, Constitutional and Administrative Law and the Dean of the Faculty of Law at the University of Zurich. He is a Member of the International Committee of the Red Cross (ICRC) and the President of the ICRC's Legal Commission. Professor Thürer is also a member of the Constitutional Court of the Principality of Liechtenstein and an alternate member of Court of Conciliation and Arbitration of the Organisation for Security and Co-operation in Europe. He is also co-founder of the Europa Institut Zurich, a member of the International Commission of Jurists and a member of the editorial boards of the journals *Revue de droit suisse, Revue Suisse de droit international et de droit européen* and *Archiv des Völkerrechts.* Professor Thürer has published widely in the fields of International, European and Public Law. His latest book is *Perspektive Schweiz – Übergreifendes Verfassungsdenken als Herausforderung* (1998).

Gillian Triggs

Professor Gillian Triggs is Professor of Law and Associate Dean (Undergraduate Studies) in the Faculty of Law at the University of Melbourne. She chairs both the UNESCO-Equipe Cousteau Working Group on Environmental Decision Making and the International Human Rights Committee of the Law Council of Australia. Professor Triggs is a consultant to the law firm Mallesons Stephen Jacques and in that capacity has been involved in the development of international commercial practice in South East Asia. She also manages a number of AUSAid and Asian Development Bank funded training programs in Vietnam and Mongolia. She has authored a number of publications on national approaches to the prosecution of war crimes with a particular emphasis on the Australian experience.

PART I

Overview

CHRISTOPHER GREENWOOD

1. A Critique of the Additional Protocols
to the Geneva Conventions of 1949

1. INTRODUCTION

Since the two themes of this conference are the changing face of conflict
and the effectiveness of international humanitarian law, it is appropriate to
start with a critique of the two 1977 Protocols Additional to the Geneva
Conventions.[1] Those Additional Protocols – the first dealing with international armed conflicts and the second with civil wars – represent the international community's most ambitious attempt to escape from the shadow
of the Second World War and to legislate for a new generation of armed
conflicts, more often internal than international and frequently conducted
by irregular, guerrilla methods rather than by set piece battles between
opposing bodies of regular, uniformed armed forces. The Additional Protocols also involve a serious attempt to make international humanitarian law
more effective by strengthening the machinery of enforcement and closing
what have been seen as gaps in the legal regime.

The Additional Protocols stand as the latest in a long line of Geneva
agreements on international humanitarian law sponsored by the International Committee of the Red Cross (ICRC) and beginning, in effect, with

---

[1] See *Geneva Convention for the Amelioration of the Condition of the Wounded and the
Sick in Armed Forces in the Field*, 75 UNTS 31 ('*First Geneva Convention*'); *Geneva
Convention for the Amelioration of the Condition of Wounded, Sick and Shipwrecked
Members of Armed Forces at Sea*, 75 UNTS 85 ('*Second Geneva Convention*'); *Geneva
Convention Relative to the Treatment of Prisoners of War*, 75 UNTS 135 ('*Third Geneva
Convention*'); *Geneva Convention Relative to the Protection of Civilian Persons in Time of
War*, 75 UNTS 287 ('*Fourth Geneva Convention*'). All Conventions entered into force on
21 October 1950, and as at 24 March 1999, there were 188 States Parties. See also *Protocol
Additional to the Geneva Convention of 12 August 1949, and Relating to the Protection of
Victims of International Armed Conflict*, 1125 UNTS 3; 16 ILM 1391 ('*Additional Protocol
I*') (entered into force 7 December 1978), as at 24 March 1999, there were 153 States
Parties; and *Protocol Additional to the Geneva Convention of 12 August 1949, and Relating
to the Protection of Victims of Non-International Armed Conflicts*, 1125 UNTS 609; 16
ILM 1442 (*Additional Protocol II*) (entered into force on 7 December 1978), as at 24 March
1999, there were 145 States Parties.

*Helen Durham and Timothy L.H. McCormack (eds.), The Changing Face of Conflict and the Efficacy of International
Humanitarian Law*, 3–20.
© 1999 *Kluwer Law International. Printed in Great Britain.*

the first Geneva Convention of 1864. They differ from their predecessors, including the 1949 Geneva Conventions, however, in that they address not only the traditional 'Geneva' concern of the protection of victims of war but also the conduct of hostilities themselves, the preserve of what was once known as 'the law of The Hague'. They also differ from the earlier Geneva Conventions in the degree of controversy that they have attracted. To their supporters, especially in the Red Cross movement, the Additional Protocols are a major step forward in the drive to achieve what Geoffrey Best termed 'humanity in warfare'.[2] To their critics, however, they have appeared in an entirely different light, charged with being militarily unrealistic or worse. Additional Protocol I must be the only international humanitarian law agreement to have been described by a member of the then US Government as 'law in the service of terror'.[3]

The rhetoric of the Reagan years has given way to a more sober analysis and the Protocols have now achieved majority acceptance in the international community. Majority acceptance, however, is still a far cry from universal acceptance. The Geneva Conventions now have 188 parties and only two UN Member States (only one of which, Eritrea, has armed forces of any size) have not yet become party to them. Twenty years after they were signed, Additional Protocol I has 153 States Parties and Additional Protocol II 145. More serious still is the fact that the forty or so States that have so far avoided becoming party to Additional Protocol I include some of the biggest military powers both in the West (the United States, France and Israel) and the Third World (India, Pakistan, Indonesia, Iran and Iraq).[4] In addition, a number of States which have – or are likely to have – internal conflicts taking place on their territory have refrained from becoming parties to Additional Protocol II.

The twentieth anniversary of the adoption of the Additional Protocols is thus a good time to draw up a balance sheet of their achievements and failures, to examine the arguments of their critics and to attempt to assess their effect upon international humanitarian law. Such an assessment is particularly timely, because the Additional Protocols have now been tested in a number of major conflicts. Although Additional Protocol I has been recognised as formally applicable in only one conflict (that between Peru

---

[2] Geoffrey Best, *Humanity in Warfare* (1980) ('*Best 1980*'). See also Geoffrey Best, *War and Law Since 1945* (1994) ('*Best 1994*').

[3] Douglas J Feith, 'Law in the Service of Terror' (1985) 1 *National Interest* 36. See also Sofaer, 'Terrorism and the Law' (1986) 94 *Foreign Affairs* 901; and the letter from President Reagan to the Senate, dated 29 January 1987, reprinted in (1987) 81 *American Journal of International Law* 910. For a convincing reply to these arguments, see Waldemar A Solf, 'A Response to Douglas J Feith's Law in the Service of Terror - The Strange Case of the Additional Protocol' (1986) 20 *Akron Law Review* 261; Hans-Peter Gasser, 'An Appeal for Ratification by the United States' (1987) 81 *American Journal of International Law* 912.

[4] The United Kingdom became a party on 28 January 1998. The Additional Protocols came into force for the United Kingdom on 28 July 1998. At the time of press, France was reconsidering its position.

and Ecuador), it should have been treated as applicable to at least some aspects of the fighting in the former Yugoslavia[5] and many of its most important provisions were applied as rules of customary international law in the Kuwait conflict.[6] Additional Protocol II was applicable to internal conflicts in El Salvador, the Philippines, Rwanda[7] and other aspects of the fighting in the former Yugoslavia. It is now possible, therefore, to make a more realistic assessment of the strengths and weaknesses of the Additional Protocols.

2. THE 1974-77 NEGOTIATIONS AND THEIR BACKGROUND

Any assessment of the Additional Protocols must begin with an understanding of the aims that those agreements were intended to achieve. In embarking upon the project that led to the adoption of the two Additional Protocols, the ICRC had two declared goals. One was the development of international humanitarian law. By 1974, it was clear that this was much needed. The 'Hague Law' had become seriously out-dated. The last attempt at codification had been in 1907[8] and the rules adopted then were based upon a series of nineteenth century projects.[9] In addition, the con-

---

[5] The applicability of Additional Protocol I to the fighting in the former Yugoslavia is, of course, dependent upon the characterisation of the various conflicts there as international rather than internal conflicts, a matter considered by the International Criminal Tribunal for the Former Yugoslavia in *Prosecutor v Dusko Tadic* (Jurisdiction) (Decision of the Appeals Chamber, 2 October 1995) 105 ILR 419, 453; and *Prosecutor v Dusko Tadic*, IT-94-1-T (Decision of 7 May 1997); 36 ILM 908; summarised in (1997) 97 *American Journal of International Law* 718. See also Peter Rowe, 'The International Criminal Tribunal for Yugoslavia: the Decision of the Appeals Chamber on the Interlocutory Appeal on Jurisdiction in the *Tadic Case*' (1996) 45 *International Comparative Law Quarterly* 691, 691-701; Christopher Greenwood, 'International Humanitarian Law and the *Tadic* Case' (1996) 7 *European Journal of International Law* 265. A Trial Chamber of the Tribunal referred to Additional Protocol I in its decision in Rule 61 proceedings in *Prosecutor v Martic*, 108 ILR 39, 44-5.

[6] See Christopher Greenwood, 'Customary International Law and the First Geneva Protocol of 1977 in the Gulf Conflict' in Peter Rowe (ed), *The Gulf War 1990-91 in International Law and English Law* (1993), 63.

[7] *Statute of the International Tribunal for the Prosecution of Persons Responsible for Genocide and Other Serious Violations of International Humanitarian Law Committed in the Territory of Rwanda and Rwandan Citizens Responsible for Genocide and Other Violations Committed in the Territory of Neighbouring States, Between 1 January 1994 and 31 December 1994*, UN Doc S/RES/955 (1994), 49 UN SCOR (3453rd mtg); 33 ILM 1598 (*'Statute of the ICTR'*), art 4, gives the Tribunal jurisdiction in respect of violations of Additional Protocol II.

[8] See *Convention Concerning The Laws and Customs of War on Land* (*'Hague Convention IV'*), signed at The Hague, 18 October 1907, 205 CTS 277. The Regulations are Annexed to the Convention (*'The Hague Convention'*).

[9] In particular, the Lieber Code, issued by the United States Government in 1863; the Brussels Project, adopted by the international conference in 1874; and the Oxford Manual

flicts of the years since 1949 had highlighted a number of lacunae in the protection afforded by the Geneva Conventions, in particular, the inadequacy of those conventions for dealing with the problems of guerrilla warfare[10] and the almost complete absence of provisions for the protection of the environment.[11]

Just as important, however, and all too often overlooked, was the other aim of the ICRC – to reaffirm existing principles of international humanitarian law which were already part of customary international law but which had been neglected or ignored in the practice of States both in the Second World War and afterwards. The principle that civilians are not legitimate targets in warfare is a particularly important example. In assessing the importance of this goal of reaffirmation of existing principles, it should be remembered that the Geneva Conventions and the earlier international humanitarian law treaties had been negotiated before the great era of decolonisation that led to a tripling in the number of States. The reaffirmation of basic international humanitarian law principles by the wider international community of the 1970's was an important goal in itself.

If the goals of the ICRC were purely humanitarian, however, others who participated in the 1974-7 Diplomatic Conference had different agendas. A large lobby of Third World States, with support from the then socialist bloc, were determined to achieve recognition of the legitimacy of armed struggle against colonial powers, even though the conflicts which resulted were not conflicts between States and thus were not normally classified as international.[12] The same group also wanted to go much further than the ICRC in relaxing the requirements for attaining the status of combatant, so as to ensure that 'freedom fighters' waging a guerrilla war would be treated as prisoners of war on capture. This group had some notable victories at the Conference. It wrote into Additional Protocol I the controversial Article 1(4), which provides that 'armed conflicts in which peoples are fighting

---

published by the *Institut de droit International* in 1880. See especially, Dietrich Schindler and Jiri Toman (eds), *The Laws of Armed Conflicts: A Collection of Conventions, Resolutions, and Other Documents* (2nd ed, 1988) 3-35.

[10] J Verwey, *Guerrilla et droit Humanitaire* (1985). See also G I A D Draper, 'The Status of Combatants and the Question of Guerilla Warfare' (1971) 45 *British Yearbook of International Law* 173.

[11] *The Convention on the Prohibition of Military or any Hostile Use of Environmental Modification Techniques*, opened for signature 18 May 1977, 1108 UNTS 151 (entered into force 5 October 1978). The Convention, adopted under United Nations auspices, was the result of a separate initiative designed to prevent the manipulation of the environment as a method of warfare, not to protect the environment against the incidental effects of war. For an analysis of the environmental provisions of Additional Protocol I and the concerns which lay behind them, see the essays in Grunawalt, King and McClain (eds), *Protection of the Environment During Armed Conflict*, US Naval War College International Law Studies, (1997) vol 69.

[12] On these aspects of the negotiations, see Keith D Suter, *An International Law of Guerilla Warfare: The Global Politics of Law-Making* (1984).

against colonial domination and alien occupation and against racist regimes in the exercise of their right of self-determination' are to be characterised as international armed conflicts, to which the full body of international humanitarian law rather than the skeletal provisions on internal conflicts, would be applicable.[13] It succeeded in securing new rules on combatant status broad enough to include resistance fighters who had always been excluded in the past (Article 44),[14] while also obtaining a provision (Article 47) which outlawed mercenaries, albeit in terms which are so narrowly drawn that, as one commentator put it, 'any person who cannot avoid being characterized as a mercenary under this definition deserves to be shot and his defence lawyer with him'.[15]

With hindsight, it was probably naive of the ICRC and the Swiss Government not to anticipate this 'hijacking' of their agenda, one result of which was that the Conference lasted four years instead of the one which had been envisaged. The world of 1974 was a very different place from that of 1949, and the 1970's were perhaps the high water mark of an approach to international negotiations which gave rhetoric pride of place over substance. It was also naive of the Third World not to see that some of these very triumphs at the Conference would attract controversy that would threaten the attempt to secure an agreement capable of commanding universal acceptance.

Moreover, the successes scored by those who wanted to bring national liberation movements within the scope of Additional Protocol I had serious and near disastrous effects on Additional Protocol II. Having achieved their goal of characterising wars of national liberation as international armed conflicts, many of those States had no further interest in developing the law applicable to the conflicts that would still be treated as internal in character. Additional Protocol II only survived in a much truncated form and even then only by the skin of its teeth, as the result of an eleventh hour

---

[13] See Heather A Wilson, *International Law and the Use of Force by National Liberation Movements* (1988); Georges Abi-Saab, 'Wars of National Liberation in the Geneva Conventions and Protocols' (1979-IV) 165 *Recueil des Cours de l'Académie de droit International* 353.

[14] See Christopher Greenwood, 'Terrorism and Additional Protocol I' (1989) 19 *Israel Yearbook of Human Rights* 187.

[15] See Best 1980, above n 2, 374-5. According to art 47(2),

A mercenary is any person who: (a) is specially recruited locally or abroad in order to fight in an armed conflict; (b) does, in fact, take a direct part in the hostilities; (c) is motivated to take part in the hostilities essentially by the desire for private gain and, in fact, is promised, by or on behalf of a Party to the conflict, material compensation substantially in excess of that promised or paid to combatants of similar ranks and functions in the armed forces of that Party; (d) is neither a national of a Party to the conflict nor a resident of territory controlled by a Party to the conflict; (e) is not a member of the armed forces of a Party to the conflict; and (f) has not been sent by a State which is not a Party to the conflict on official duty as a member of its armed forces.

compromise.[16] If the struggle for Statehood was to be treated as an international matter, the defence of that Statehood against rebels and secessionists was to be viewed as a simple assertion of national sovereignty subject to few limitations even of a humanitarian character. That same assertion of state sovereignty also led a majority of States to reject most proposals for strengthening the enforcement machinery of international humanitarian law in any type of conflict.

Another feature of the 1974-7 negotiations that requires some comment is the so-called 'nuclear understanding'. In broaching the subject of the law governing the conduct of hostilities, the ICRC knew that it would have to accommodate the position of the nuclear weapons States if those States, the biggest military powers in the world, were to become parties to the Protocols. Yet many of the innovations which the ICRC wanted to make in this area of the law, if applied to nuclear weapons, would have had the effect that almost any use of such weapons would have become illegal. While there were many humanitarian lawyers then – as there are now – who would have welcomed such a result, it would have been utterly unrealistic to imagine that States that had built their defence strategies around the possession of nuclear weapons would agree to provisions that outlawed those weapons. A similar exercise by the ICRC in the 1950's had failed on precisely this point.[17] The ICRC therefore took the decision not to allow the reform of the law on conventional warfare to fail because of the intractable problem of nuclear weapons. Before the Conference opened, it announced that it was not intending to broach the subject of the law relating to nuclear weapons.[18] As Professor Kalshoven put it, 'the ICRC had consciously discarded not only the question of a categorical prohibition on the use of nuclear weapons but all questions specifically relating to possible restrictions on such use.'[19]

---

[16] See David P Forsythe, 'Legal Management of Internal War – The 1977 Protocol on Non-International Armed Conflicts' (1978) 72 *American Journal of International Law* 272.

[17] The Draft Rules presented by the ICRC to the XIX International Conference of the Red Cross in New Delhi in 1957 failed to achieve support from governments on this ground. See Yves Sandoz, Christophe Swinarski and Bruno Zimmermann (eds) *Commentary on the Additional Protocols of 8 June 1977 to the Geneva Conventions of 12 August 1949* (1987) xxix.

[18] The ICRC's comments attached to the Draft Protocols which were circulated to States in June 1973 contained the following passage:

> Problems relating to atomic, bacteriological and chemical warfare are subjects of international agreements or negotiations by governments, and in submitting these draft Additional Protocols the ICRC does not intend to broach those problems. It should be borne in mind that the Red Cross as a whole, at several International Red Cross Conferences, has clearly made known its condemnation of weapons of mass destruction and has urged governments to reach agreements for the banning of their use.

See International Committee of the Red Cross, *Draft Additional Protocols* (1993) 2.

[19] Frits Kalshoven, 'Arms, Armaments and International Law' (1985) 191 *Recueil des Cours de l'Académie de droit International* 183, 281-2.

A number of States stated on the record that they participated in the Conference on the basis that while the existing rules of customary international law which were to be codified and reaffirmed would continue to apply to nuclear weapons, any new rules adopted at the conference would apply only to the use of conventional methods and means of warfare.[20] There was no serious challenge to these statements at the Conference or to their repetition by a number of States on signing or ratifying the First Additional Protocol.[21] It follows that, while those provisions of Additional Protocol I that codified existing rules of customary international law apply to all types of weaponry, nuclear or conventional, the innovative provisions of Additional Protocol I are not applicable to nuclear weapons.[22]

3. THE BALANCE SHEET

How, then, should we evaluate the Protocols adopted at the end of these tortuous and tortured negotiations?

3.1 Achievements of the Additional Protocols

Let us start with some of the achievements. The aim of reaffirmation of basic principles of international humanitarian law that had been called into

---

[20] For example, the United Kingdom representative stated at the final session of the *Diplomatic Conference on the Reaffirmation and Development of International Humanitarian Law Applicable in Armed Conflicts,* 17 March to 10 June 1977:

> At the first session of Diplomatic Conference, his delegation had expressed in plenary its concurrence in the view that the draft Protocols were not intended to broach problems concerned with atomic, bacteriological or chemical warfare. Nothing in the four years' work of the Conference or in the texts themselves had caused it to depart from that view. It therefore continued to be his government's understanding that the new rules were not intended to have any effect on and did not regulate or prohibit the use of nuclear or other non-conventional weapons.

See VII *Official Records* 303. See also the statements by the United States, at 295; France, at 193; USSR, V *Official Records*, at 121; Sweden, at 145 and Argentina, at 179.

[21] See, however, the statement by India at VI *Official Records* 115.

[22] As Sandoz, Swinarski and Zimmermann, above n 17, put it at 1858:

> Clearly, the hypothesis that States acceding to the Protocol bind themselves without wishing to – or even without knowing – with regard to such an important question as the use of nuclear weapons is not acceptable. The desire not to broach it during the CDDH [Diplomatic Conference] is a determining factor in this respect.

This is also the view of a number of other respected commentaries. See, eg, M Bothe, K J Partsch and W A Solf, *New Rules for Victims of Armed Conflicts: Commentary on the Two 1977 Protocols Additional to the Geneva Conventions of 1949* (1982) 192; Rauschning in Rudolf Bernhardt (ed) *Encyclopedia of Public International Law* (1981) vol 4 49; O E Bring and H B Reimann, 'Redressing a Wrong Question' (1986) 33 *Netherlands International Law Review* 99, 103; Kalshoven, above n 19.

question by the practice of States is in many ways the most important achievement of Additional Protocol I. Particularly significant is the fact that the Additional Protocol (in Articles 48-52 and 57-8) codifies the principles, already part of customary law, that civilians and civilian objects are not legitimate targets of attack (the principle of distinction) and that even military objectives should not be attacked if to do so would be likely to cause civilian casualties or damage to civilian property which would be disproportionate to the concrete and direct military gain expected from the attack (the principle of proportionality).[23] Those principles had been almost completely ignored in the latter stages of the Second World War when they had been openly questioned by many military theorists who inveighed against those who held the 'ridiculous notion' that it was wrong to attack enemy workers but acceptable to kill them in the course of an attack upon something else.[24]

One of the most significant achievements of Additional Protocol I is that that notion, which is far from ridiculous (to anyone except an historian with an axe to grind and a reputation to defend), is now firmly embedded in international law. Article 48 codifies the principle of distinction in these terms:

> In order to ensure respect for and protection of the civilian population and civilian objects, the Parties to the conflict shall at all times distinguish between the civilian population and combatants and between civilian objects and military objectives and accordingly shall direct their operations only against military objectives.

More importantly, Additional Protocol I puts flesh on the bare bones of this principle by defining what is meant by a military objective in Article 52(2):

> Insofar as objects are concerned, military objectives are limited to those objects which by their nature, location, purpose or use make an effective contribution to military action and whose total or partial destruction, capture or neutralization, *in the circumstances ruling at the time*, offers a definite military advantage. (emphasis added)

This definition avoids the pitfalls of the approach taken in, for example, the 1923 Draft Rules on Air Warfare[25] of seeking to list categories of

---

[23] See Christopher Greenwood, 'The Customary Law Status of the Protocols' in Astrid J M Delissen and Gerard J Tanja (eds), *International Humanitarian Law: Challenges Ahead* (1991) 93,108-11.

[24] For an excellent discussion of these issues in the context of the RAF bombing of Germany, see Max Hastings, *Bomber Command* (1979). See also Charles K Webster and Noble Frankland, *The Strategic Air Offensive against Germany* (1961) vol 1,15-6, offering a different perspective generally critical of IHL's insistence on the distinction between civilian and military targets.

[25] Adam Roberts and Richard Guelff, *Documents on the Laws of War* (2nd ed, 1989) 121.

military objectives.[26] Instead, it lays down a two stage test: (1) does the object make an effective contribution (actual or potential) to the enemy's military action; and if so (2) is the object, in the circumstances ruling at the time, one whose destruction, capture or neutralisation would offer a definite military advantage. The reference to the circumstances ruling at the time is particularly important as it should avoid the approach of treating entire categories of items (such as bridges) as military objectives in all circumstances.[27]

The Protocol also codifies the principle of proportionality, although it does not use that term. Article 51(5)(b), defines as an indiscriminate attack, and thus one prohibited by Article 51(4):

> An attack which may be expected to cause incidental loss of civilian life, injury to civilians, damage to civilian objects, or a combination thereof, which would be excessive in relation to the concrete and direct military advantage anticipated.

Similarly, Article 57(2)(a)(iii), in laying down the duties of a commander in deciding to launch an attack, requires the commander to refrain from launching any attack which might be expected to produce excessive civilian casualties or damage. These provisions were welcomed at the time as a useful codification of the principle of proportionality.[28] While any attempt to determine the content of this principle is problematic, not least because the principle requires that a balance be struck between two such different considerations as military advantage and civilian losses,[29] the approach taken in Additional Protocol I represents an advance in that it emphasises that the military advantage must be 'concrete and direct'.

---

[26] For criticism of the text in Article 52(2) as too vague and open-ended, see A Randelzhofer, 'Civilian Objects' in Bernhardt, above n 22, vol 3, 93.

[27] Frits Kalshoven, 'Reaffirmation and Development of International Humanitarian Law Applicable in Armed Conflict: The Diplomatic Conference, 1974-1977 (Pt 2)' (1978) 9 *Netherlands Yearbook of International Law* 107, 111.

[28] See, eg, the statement by the United Kingdom Representative, VI *Official Records* 164.

[29] The test is always a relative one in which the harm to the civilian population must be weighed against the military advantage. There is no justification for the attempt in the ICRC *Commentary* to introduce an absolute ceiling beyond which civilian casualties can never be justified. The passage in Sandoz, Swinarski and Zimmermann, above n 17 at1980,

> The idea has also been put forward that even if they are very high, civilian losses and damages may be justified if the military advantage at stake is of great importance. This idea is contrary to the fundamental rules of the Protocol; in particular it conflicts with Article 48 '(*Basic rule*)' and with paragraphs 1 and 2 of the present Article 51. The Protocol does not provide any justification for attacks, which cause extensive civilian losses and damages. Incidental losses and damages should never be extensive ...

is misleading because it appears to confuse the term 'extensive', which suggests an absolute test, with 'excessive', a term which is clearly relative. However attractive the view may be from a humanitarian viewpoint, it does not accurately reflect the text of Additional Protocol I or the underlying principle of customary law.

Nebulous factors such as 'breaking the morale of the enemy State' are not enough.[30]

While this is not the place for a detailed assessment of the application of international humanitarian law in the 1990-1 Gulf conflict, it is interesting to note that the coalition forces there considered themselves bound by the principles of distinction and proportionality as defined in Additional Protocol I, on the basis that those provisions of the Additional Protocol were declaratory of customary international law. The experience of that conflict suggests that these principles are workable in practice.[31] Thus, the coalition distinguished between bridges and railways that linked the Iraqi forces to their supply centres or otherwise assisted the Iraqi military from those that did not and attacked only the former. They also distinguished between oil refining and storage facilities, which made an important military contribution and were thus treated as targets, and oil production facilities, which, in the context of a short conflict, were not regarded as making a sufficiently direct contribution and were not attacked.

Nevertheless, some of the difficulties inherent in the principles of distinction and proportionality are illustrated by the controversy surrounding coalition attacks on Iraqi power stations during that conflict. The coalition treated as a legitimate target 'electrical production facilities powering military systems'.[32] Put that way, nobody could deny that such facilities constituted military objectives within Article 52(2).[33] The majority of Iraqi electrical production facilities, however, were part of an integrated national power grid, which provided electrical power for both civilian and military use. Although the coalition attacks on power stations appear to have killed or injured few civilians and the immediate damage to civilian objects from these raids could not be said to have been excessive in relation to the military advantage of destroying most of the Iraqi national grid, the result of destroying most of the Iraqi power supply was that the infrastructure of civilian life ground to a halt as hospitals, sewerage plants, water purification facilities and the like ceased to be able to operate. The resulting collapse of infrastructure vital to civilian life caused far greater civilian loss and damage than the bombing itself.

Were the attacks on the power stations therefore unlawful? Human Rights Watch has attacked the coalition for violating the principle of distinction on the ground that the power stations were 'dual use facilities'

---

[30] Breaking the morale of the enemy's armed forces, so that they will be less able to resist an attack is a different matter.

[31] See Greenwood, above n 6, 70-9.

[32] US Department of Defense, *Conduct of the Persian Gulf Conflict: An Interim Report to Congress* (1991), para 4-2.

[33] The ICRC had included in its 1956 list of military objectives (submitted to the 1957 New Delhi Red Cross Conference) 'installations providing energy mainly for national defence, e.g. ... plants producing gas or electricity mainly for military consumption': see Sandoz, Swinarski and Zimmermann, above n 17, at 2002.

and should not, therefore, have been treated as military objectives.[34] Article 52, however, has no separate provision for 'dual use objects' – either something is a military objective or it is not. Applying the criteria in Article 52(2), there is no doubt that the Iraqi national grid, and therefore the power stations which supplied it, made an effective contribution to Iraqi military action and that their destruction offered a definite military advantage to the coalition.[35] The attacks on the power stations were not, therefore, a violation of the principle of distinction. Whether they violated the principle of proportionality is a more difficult question. The tendency has been to apply that principle by comparing the immediate military advantage resulting from an attack with the immediate civilian losses. In the case of the power stations, however, both the military advantage and the harm to the civilian population were less immediate. That should not, however, prevent the proportionality test from being applied, even if it does make it more difficult.[36] The purpose of attacking the power stations was to reduce the supply of electrical power to the Iraqi forces and the incidental damage was the reduction in supply to the civilian population. Just as the military advantage can be assessed only by reference to the effects of a lack of electricity upon the military, so the humanitarian side of the proportionality equation requires an analysis of the effects of the reduction of power upon the civilian population.[37]

Another important aspect of the reaffirmation of customary international humanitarian law principles in Additional Protocol I is the insistence, in Article 49(3), that the principles on targeting stated in Additional Protocol I apply to any warfare which may affect the civilian population on land. Although usually discussed in the context of air bombardment and the use of regular forces, the duty to distinguish between the civilian population and the military and the requirement to observe the principle of proportionality apply just as much to those conducting guerilla warfare as they do to the air force or artillery of the regular armed forces. Thus, the prohibition in Article 51(2) of attacks 'the primary purpose of which is to spread

---

[34] Middle East Watch, *Needless Deaths* (1991), 317-99.

[35] The British commander in the Gulf, General de la Billiere, gave evidence to that effect to the House of Commons Defence Committee:

> The strategic air campaign was designed to destroy the Iraqi capability supporting his forces in the field and delivering chemical weapons and generally giving aid and succour to his military machine. An important aspect of this was, of course, to destroy his ability to produce power, which, in turn, supported a large area of strategic military support. In my view, I think that to take out the power stations was essential.

House of Commons, *Defence Committee*, 10th Report, No 287/I (1990-1) 24.

[36] See A P V Rogers, *Law on the Battlefield* (1996) para 14-9, which provides an excellent analysis of the law and practice in this area.

[37] Without knowing more about the military advantages that were derived from the reduction in power supplies to the Iraqi military, it is difficult to say whether the damage to the civilian population was excessive.

terror among the civilian population' applies to the planting of a car bomb by a resistance movement just as much as to the activities of a strategic air force. Those who criticise Additional Protocol I as legitimising terrorist tactics overlook the importance of this broad application of the principles of distinction and proportionality. Although, as discussed below, Additional Protocol I may have the effect of bringing within the scope of international humanitarian law the activities of groups frequently characterised as terrorist and in that sense legitimising their act of waging war, it does not in any way legitimise the use of terrorist tactics.[38]

A second undeniable achievement of Additional Protocol I is that it has developed the law in a number of beneficial ways. For example, Article 75, which draws heavily on the law of human rights as well as international humanitarian law, lays down a valuable set of fundamental guarantees on which anyone in the hands of an adverse party to the conflict, irrespective of their exact status, may rely. Articles 35(3) and 55 introduce a new principle of environmental protection that requires belligerents to have regard to the incidental damage that may be caused to the environment by military operations. Articles 8 to 34 of Additional Protocol I improve the legal regime for the protection of the wounded, sick and medical personnel and, in particular, contain a valuable code for ensuring respect for medical aircraft evacuating the wounded. Articles 61 to 71 make important changes in the law for the benefit of relief operations and civil defence activities.

Finally, any list of the achievements of the Additional Protocols must take account of Additional Protocol II. Although the ICRC failed to obtain all that it proposed by way of a code for the regulation of non-international armed conflicts, Additional Protocol II goes a long way to putting flesh on the bare bones of common Article 3 of the 1949 Geneva Conventions. In particular, Additional Protocol II contains the first attempt to regulate by treaty the methods and means of warfare in internal conflicts. Articles 13 to 16 may not be as extensive or as detailed as the provisions of Articles 48 to 58 of Additional Protocol I but they represent an important step forward from what went before. Moreover, while a great opportunity was missed in Additional Protocol II to develop a treaty law on the enforcement of the *ius in bello interno*, in 1994 the Security Council considered that criminal responsibility for violations of Additional Protocol II was implicit in the obligations which it contained, notwithstanding that there was no equivalent to the grave breaches provisions of Additional Protocol I, and gave the International Criminal Tribunal for Rwanda jurisdiction over such violations.[39] The following year, the ICTY held in the famous *Tadic* decision [40]

---

[38] Hans-Peter Gasser, 'Prohibition of Terrorist Acts in International Humanitarian Law' (1986) 26 *International Review of the Red Cross* 200.

[39] See Statute of the ICTR, above n 7.

[40] See above n 5.

that individual criminal responsibility also existed in respect of violations of the customary law of internal armed conflicts.

Of even greater potential significance is the fact that the international community has provided the International Criminal Court (ICC) jurisdiction over war crimes committed in non-international conflicts.[41] Article 8(2)(c) of the Statute of the ICC extends the Court's jurisdiction to serious violations of Common Article 3 to the Four Geneva Conventions of 1949, while Article 8(2)(e) of the Statute covers other 'serious violations of the laws and customs applicable in conflicts not of an international character.' Although this latter provision is not as extensive as Article 8(2)(b), which is the corresponding provision dealing with international armed conflict, it does take international penal sanctions against violations of the law in non-international armed conflict to unprecedented lengths. In 1977 such developments would have been unthinkable and it is unlikely that they would have taken place today had it not been for the groundbreaking work done in Additional Protocol II.

3.2 Grounds for Criticism

That is one side of the balance sheet but there is also much to be found on the other side. Criticisms of Additional Protocol I have tended to revolve around three main points. First, the provisions of Articles 1(4) and 96(3) regarding 'wars of national liberation'[42] have been criticised as introducing into international humanitarian law the highly politicised considerations of

---

[41] *Rome Statute of the International Criminal Court*, adopted by the United Nations Diplomatic Conference of Plenipotentiaries on the Establishment of an International Criminal Court on 17 July 1998; 37 ILM 1002. The whole of the Statute is located at <http://www.un.org/icc/romestat.htm> ('*Statute of the ICC*').

[42] Article 1(4) provides that the concept of international armed conflict, to which the Protocol and the 1949 Conventions are applicable should henceforward include

> armed conflicts in which peoples are fighting against colonial domination and alien occupation and against racist regimes in the exercise of their right of self-determination, as enshrined in the Charter of the United Nations and the Declaration on Principles of International Law concerning Friendly Relations and Co-operation among States in accordance with the Charter of the United Nations.

Article 96(3) adds that

> The authority representing a people engaged against a High Contracting Party in an armed conflict of the type referred to in Article 1, paragraph 4, may undertake to apply the Conventions and this Protocol in relation to that conflict by means of a unilateral declaration addressed to the depositary. Such declaration shall, upon its receipt by the depositary, have in relation to that conflict the following effects: (a) the Conventions and this Protocol are brought into force for the said authority as a Party to the conflict with immediate effect; (b) the said authority assumes the same rights and obligations as those which have been assumed by a High Contracting Party to the Conventions and this Protocol; and (c) the Conventions and this Protocol are equally binding upon all Parties to the conflict.

the *ius ad bellum*.[43] This writer agrees that the provisions on wars of national liberation are less than ideal and the language in which Article 1(4) is cast is particularly inappropriate. Nevertheless, if one examines the practical aspects of these provisions, they turn out to be very limited. The provisions on wars of national liberation were very much a product of the decolonisation era that came to an end not long after the adoption of the Additional Protocols. They are an example of how international agreements on international humanitarian law always focus upon the last conflict rather than the next one. As one commentator puts it, if Article 1(4) 'opens up a "Pandora's box" at all, it is an unexpectedly small one',[44] for the conditions of application of Article 1(4) are drawn so narrowly that very few conflicts are likely to fall within them and the procedural provisions of Article 96(3) come into operation only if the substantive requirements of Article 1(4) are satisfied. Indeed, there is a certain irony in the fact that if Article 1(4) is to be interpreted as applying outside the colonial situations for which it was intended, as is frequently suggested, then it will be some of the very States which were the most enthusiastic supporters of this provision which will be adversely affected.

Secondly, there has been criticism – much of it justified – of the provisions in Additional Protocol I on combatant status. Articles 43 to 47 of Additional Protocol I attempted to make it easier for guerilla fighters to qualify as legitimate combatants by introducing a relaxation of the very stringent rules of Article 1 of the Hague Regulations 1907, and Article 4A of the Fourth Geneva Convention relating to prisoners of war. Under the 1907-49 test, fighters who were not members of a State's regular armed forces qualified as legitimate combatants and were therefore entitled to prisoner of war status on capture only if they were:

> Members of other militias and members of other volunteer corps, including those of organized resistance movements, belonging to a Party to the conflict and operating in or outside their own territory, even if this territory is occupied, provided that such militias or volunteer corps, including such organized resistance movements, fulfil the following conditions:
> (a) that of being commanded by a person responsible for his subordinates;
> (b) that of having a fixed distinctive sign recognizable at a distance;
> (c) that of carrying arms openly;

---

[43] For an example of such criticism, see G I A.D Draper, 'Wars of National Liberation and War Criminality' in Michael Howard (ed), *Restraints on War: Studies in the Limitation of Armed Conflict* (1979) 135.

[44] Wilson, above n 13, 168. See also, the discussion in Greenwood, above n 14, 191-5.

(d) that of conducting their operations in accordance with the laws and customs of war.[45]

That test was in practice one with which it was impossible for a resistance movement or other group of irregulars to comply.[46] The ICRC had proposed to relax the test by laying down the same requirements for regular and irregular combatants, namely a requirement that they distinguish themselves from the civilian population at all times when engaged in an attack or in a deployment preceding an attack. The ICRC's proposal, however, did not go far enough for the majority of States at the Conference who wanted to see all irregulars treated as legitimate combatants. The result was the unhappy compromise of Article 44(3) of Additional Protocol I, which provides that:

> In order to promote the protection of the civilian population from the effects of hostilities, combatants are obliged to distinguish themselves from the civilian population while they are engaged in an attack or in a military operation preparatory to an attack. Recognizing, however, that there are situations in armed conflicts where, owing to the nature of the hostilities an armed combatant cannot so distinguish himself, he shall retain his status as a combatant, provided that, in such situations, he carries his arms openly:
> (a) during each military engagement, and
> (b) during such time as he is visible to the adversary while he is engaged in a military deployment preceding the launching of an attack in which he is to participate.
> Acts which comply with the requirements of this paragraph shall not be considered as perfidious within the meaning of Article 37, paragraph 1 (c).

The second sentence of this Article was the product of a last minute compromise negotiated between delegations which otherwise had little in common. It is perhaps the best example in the international humanitarian law texts of the saying that a treaty is 'a disagreement reduced to writing'. Nevertheless, the new Article 44(3) is not unworkable. The lower standard in the second sentence is not of general application, for it operates only in conditions where compliance with the stricter requirements of the first

---

[45] Third Geneva Convention, art 4(A)(2).

[46] The impossibility of a movement in occupied territory complying with these requirements becomes still more apparent when one sees how they were interpreted. Thus, the *British Manual of Military Law* (1958), commenting on the requirement of a fixed distinctive sign, stipulates (at 92) that:

> it is reasonable to expect that the silhouette of an irregular combatant in the position of standing against the skyline should be at once distinguishable from the outline of a peaceful inhabitant, and this by the naked eye of an ordinary individual at a distance from which the form of an individual can be determined.

sentence is impossible.[47] Even where the standard in the second sentence is applicable, it requires that the irregular carry arms openly during an attack and for some time prior to the attack. The suggestion that all that is required is to produce weapons immediately before opening fire has no basis in law and is clearly contrary to the text. Moreover, if the provisions of Article 44(3) go too far in relaxing the requirements of combatancy and may thus be said to endanger the civilian population, the 1907-49 test was also inadequate to protect that population, because it imposed conditions with which irregulars could not comply and thus offered no inducement to comply with other aspects of the law. It must also be borne in mind that, as pointed out above, the new rules on combatancy do not involve any acceptance of terrorist methods of warfare – attacks upon the civilian population and indiscriminate attacks are outlawed by Article 51. It is important not to confuse the question of who may lawfully engage in hostilities with the quite different question of what methods of warfare they may employ when they do so engage.

Finally, Additional Protocol I has been criticised from both sides in respect of its position (or lack of position) on nuclear weapons. To some commentators, the absence of a complete ban on nuclear weapons and the understanding that the innovative provisions of Additional Protocol I (which include, for example, the provisions on the environment) would not apply to the use of nuclear weapons was a betrayal of the fundamental values of international humanitarian law. On the other hand, some of the defenders of nuclear deterrence have been alarmed that the 'nuclear understanding' (which was discussed earlier) was not written into the text of Additional Protocol I and that the innovative provisions of Additional Protocol I might therefore be read as applicable to nuclear as well as conventional weapons. The concerns of the second group were highlighted by submissions made to the International Court of Justice in the recent proceedings on the request by the General Assembly for an advisory opinion on nuclear weapons, where a number of States argued that all of the provisions of Additional Protocol I were applicable to nuclear weapons. The Court, however, placed little emphasis upon Additional Protocol I, apart from referring to the provisions on distinction and proportionality which the nuclear Powers had conceded were applicable, in any event.[48] That may do something to allay the fears of the nuclear Powers and it is noticeable that since the Court's Opinion was delivered the United Kingdom has ratified Additional Protocol I. As for those who think Additional Protocol I

---

[47] The United Kingdom's declaration on signature makes clear that the second sentence applies only in occupied territory and Article 1(4) conflicts, see Roberts and Guelff, above n 25, 467.

[48] *Advisory Opinion on the Legality of the Threat or Use of Nuclear Weapons* [1996] ICJ Rep 225. For discussions on this case, see the special issue (1997) 37 *International Review of the Red Cross* 3-119.

did not go far enough, it can only be said that this was the only basis on which agreement could be obtained at all.

Other criticisms of Additional Protocol I are perhaps more justified than those that have attracted the most attention. The complicated provisions of Article 56 of the First Protocol on protection of dams, dykes and nuclear electrical generating stations will almost certainly prove unworkable in practice. The attempt to ban reprisals against civilians, civilian objects and certain other categories of target may well prove to be too ambitious in a treaty which contains so few enforcement mechanisms which could serve as an alternative to reprisals, particularly since a violation of Additional Protocol I (unlike violations of the Geneva Conventions) may confer considerable military benefits. It is noteworthy that a number of States have made declarations warning that they will react sharply to any violation of Additional Protocol.[49]

The present writer would, however, criticise the Additional Protocols more for what they do not contain than for what they do. By far the most serious defect in Additional Protocol I is the failure to strengthen the enforcement machinery beyond the creation of the Fact Finding Commission in Article 90 of Additional Protocol I and a widening of the scope of grave breaches which all parties undertake to prosecute. In particular, the institution of the protecting power, which offers a far greater chance of preventing violations of international humanitarian law than does the threat of prosecution, remains largely voluntary and thus unlikely to be used.[50] Additional Protocol II survived only in a truncated form, losing a number of provisions that had existed in the draft (including a prohibition on the carrying out of death sentences during a conflict) and being made subject to a definition of internal conflicts which excludes the majority of such conflicts.[51] It is these missed opportunities which are the biggest weaknesses of the two Additional Protocols.

4. CONCLUSION

It must be asked, therefore, whether the effort that went into negotiating the Additional Protocols and the subsequent struggle to achieve the present level of acceptance for them was actually worthwhile. In this writer's view it was. The Additional Protocols are by no means perfect instruments as

---

[49] See, eg, the reservation by the United Kingdom on ratification of Additional Protocol I. For an exchange of views on this subject see Christopher Greenwood, 'Twilight of the Law of Belligerent Reprisals' (1989) 20 *Netherlands Yearbook of International Law* 35. But see Frits Kalshoven, 'Belligerent Reprisals Revisited' (1990) 21 *Netherlands Yearbook of International Law* 43.

[50] See Additional Protocol I, art 5, for the attempt (a very modest one) to render the institution of the protecting power more effective.

[51] See Additional Protocol II, art 1.

this Chapter has endeavoured to show. They were, however, the best that could be obtained in the conditions of the 1970s and there is no realistic prospect of beginning again today. If they were observed faithfully in the various conflicts taking place today, the humanitarian gain would be immense. The prize for which those who value international humanitarian law need to strive today is not the adoption of another treaty, be it a general agreement or a more specific treaty on, for example, the rights of women in armed conflict,[52] but the implementation of the international humanitarian law treaties that already exist. That is where our energies need to be directed now.

---

[52] The author must, however, acknowledge the very powerful case to the contrary made by Judith Gardam in her recent article, 'Women and the Law of Armed Conflict: Why the Silence?' (1997) 46 *International and Comparative Law Quarterly* 55.

PART II

Increasing Protection for Victims of Armed Conflict

CHRISTINE CHINKIN

2. Women: The Forgotten Victims of Armed Conflict?*

1. INTRODUCTION

Events from 1991 onwards surrounding the disintegration of the former Yugoslavia served to demonstrate to the world that women have been among the 'forgotten' victims of the laws of both international and non-international armed conflict. Reports of the massive, widespread and systematic rapes, enforced prostitution and sexual enslavement of women as part of policies of ethnic cleansing led to demands for an effective response from the international community. As the first proposals for a war crimes tribunal were being made in 1992-3 two interlocking observations were possible. First, despite the long history of rape and sexual assault against women during armed conflicts, these offences had not figured significantly in war crimes prosecutions. Second, it was even possible to argue that their scant treatment in the Four Geneva Conventions and the 1977 Protocols meant that these offences did not legally amount to grave breaches of the Geneva Conventions, or even as war crimes. This paper will outline the legal responses to the catastrophe in the former Yugoslavia, and subsequently Rwanda, from the perspective of the inclusion of women. It will then consider whether these responses have been sufficient to re-dress the situation, or whether women in fact remain forgotten by international humanitarian law.

---

* This chapter draws closely upon Chapter 10 of H Charlesworth and C Chinkin, *The Boundaries of International Law: a Feminist Analysis* (forthcoming). Since it was written the decision of the ICTY in *Prosecutor v Anto Furundzija*, 10 December 1998, has added significantly to the substantive jurisprudence on rape as a war crime. Procedural challenges throughout the case have also highlighted the obstacles found in bringing a successful prosecution for such offences.

Helen Durham and Timothy L.H. McCormack (eds.), The Changing Face of Conflict and the Efficacy of International Humanitarian Law, 23–44.
© 1999 *Kluwer Law International. Printed in Great Britain.*

2. Sexual Assault in the Tribunals for the Former Yugoslavia and Rwanda

2.1 *Jurisdiction*

In late 1991 and 1992 the Security Council was faced with having to respond to allegations of war crimes in the territory of the former Yugoslavia. It condemned violations of the laws of war, requested information on the commission of war crimes and established a Commission of Experts to undertake an independent investigation.[1] After receiving the conclusions of the Commission, the Security Council, by Resolution 808 dated 22 February 1993, requested the Secretary-General of the United Nations to submit proposals for the establishment under Chapter VII of the United Nations Charter of an ad hoc tribunal for the prosecution of war crimes in the former Yugoslavia.[2] The Secretary-General's Report[3] was adopted on 2 May 1993 by Resolution 827, and the Tribunal for the Former Yugoslavia was created.[4] In 1994, events in Rwanda led the Security Council to establish a second International Tribunal 'to prosecute persons for genocide and other serious violations of international humanitarian law'.[5]

The report of the Secretary-General emphasised that the proposed international tribunal should apply rules of international humanitarian law 'which are beyond doubt part of customary law so that the problem of adherence of some but not all States to specific conventions does not arise.'[6] The report concluded that the Geneva Conventions of 12 August 1949,[7] the Hague Convention (IV) 1907,[8] the Genocide Convention 1948[9]

---

[1] *Final Report of the Commission of Experts Pursuant to Security Council Resolution 780 (1992)* 47 UN SCOR (3119th mtg), UN Doc S/Res/780 (1992); 31 ILM 1476, UN Doc S/674/1994 Annex (1994) (*'Final Report'*).

[2] SC Res 808, 48 UN SCOR (3175th mtg), UN Doc S/Res/780 (1992); 31 ILM 1476, UN Doc S/674/1994 Annex (1994) (*'Final Report'*).

[3] *Report of the Secretary-General Pursuant to Paragraph 2 of Security Council Resolution 808* (1993), UN Doc S/25704 (1993); 32 ILM 1159 (*'Secretary-General's Report'*).

[4] *Statute of the International Tribunal for the Prosecution of Persons Responsible for Serious Violations of International Humanitarian Law Committed in the Territory of the Former Yugoslavia since 1991*, SC Res 827, 48 UN SCOR (3217th mtg), UN Doc S/Res/827 (1993); 32 ILM 1203 (*'Statute of the ICTY'*).

[5] *Statute of the International Tribunal for the Prosecution of Persons Responsible for Genocide and Other Serious Violations of International Law Committed in the Territory of Rwanda and Rwandan Citizens Responsible for Genocide and Other Violations Committed in the Territory of Neighbouring States, Between 1 January 1994 and 31 December 1994*, UN Doc S/RES/955 (1994), 49 UN SCOR (3453rd mtg); 33 ILM 1598 (*'Statute of the ICTR'*).

[6] Paragraph 34 of the Secretary-General's Report, above n 3.

[7] See *Geneva Convention for the Amelioration of the Condition of the Wounded and the Sick in Armed Forces in the Field*, 75 UNTS 31 (*'First Geneva Convention'*); *Geneva Convention for the Amelioration of the Condition of Wounded, Sick and Shipwrecked Members of Armed Forces at Sea*, 75 UNTS 85 (*'Second Geneva Convention'*); *Geneva*

and the Nuremberg Charter[10] were without doubt customary international law. The Statute of the Tribunal for the Former Yugoslavia accordingly bestows jurisdiction over grave breaches of the Geneva Conventions, violations of the laws or customs of war, genocide and crimes against humanity.[11] The internal nature of the events in Rwanda meant that the ICTR also had jurisdiction based on Common Article 3 of the Geneva Conventions and Additional Protocol II to the Geneva Conventions[12] that provides a minimum code of conduct for non-international conflicts.[13]

Acknowledgment that the Tribunal's jurisdiction needed to be founded upon pre-existing law and pressure to ensure that rape and sexual abuse of women were included within that jurisdiction necessitated consideration of the extent to which these offences were already incorporated within international humanitarian law. Humanitarian attention was first paid to those who became *hors de combat* through injury or capture – that is members of the fighting forces – who were invariably men. Despite long formal understanding of the prohibition of attacks on non-combatant women, it was not until 1949 that the Fourth Geneva Convention on Civilians was introduced. Even under this Convention attention to rape and sexual assault is minimal. Article 27 provides that States parties are under an obligation to protect women in international armed conflict 'against any attack on their honour, in particular against rape, enforced prostitution, or any form of indecent assault.' This provision does not constitute a forceful prohibition of rape but rather presents women as in need of protection. This draws upon two separate ideas. First, are the concepts of protector and protected that are used both to justify recourse to armed force and to lessen the civil status of those deemed to need protection. Second, the designation of rape as a crime against honour embodies a masculine notion of women as property rather than as victims of violence, humiliation and degradation. The Addi-

---

Convention Relative to the Treatment of Prisoners of War, 75 UNTS 135 (*'Third Geneva Convention'*); *Geneva Convention Relative to the Protection of Civilian Persons in Time of War,* 75 UNTS 287 (*'Fourth Geneva Convention'*). All these Conventions entered into force on 21 October 1950, and as at 24 March 1999, there were 188 States Parties.

[8] *Convention Concerning The Laws and Customs of War on Land (Hague IV),* signed at The Hague, 18 October 1907, 205 CTS 277. The Regulations are annexed to the Convention.

[9] *Convention on the Prevention and Punishment of the Crime of Genocide,* opened for signature 9 December 1948, 78 UNTS 277, (entered into force 12 January 1951) (*'Genocide Convention'*), art 2. As at 24 March 1999, there were 129 States Parties.

[10] *Agreement for the Prosecution and Punishment of Major War Criminals of the European Axis, (London Agreement),* 8 August 1945, 82 UNTS 279. The Charter of the International Military Tribunal is appended to the Agreement (*'Charter of the IMT'*).

[11] Statute of the ICTY, arts 2-5.

[12] *Protocol Additional to the Geneva Convention of 12 August 1949, and Relating to the Protection of Victims of Non-International Armed Conflicts,* 1125 UNTS 609; 16 ILM 1442 (*'Additional Protocol II'*) (entered into force on 7 December 1978). As of 24 March 1999, there were 145 State Parties.

[13] Statute of the ICTR, art 4.

tional Protocols, while updating and extending the Conventions, make no reference to the honour of women but retain the objective of protection of women. Thus Article 76 of Additional Protocol I, states that 'women shall be the object of special respect and shall be protected in particular against rape, forced prostitution, and any other form of indecent assault.' [14] Other references to women in the Geneva Conventions tend to emphasise their roles as child bearers and carers rather than as individuals with their own rights. For example, Article 76(2) of Additional Protocol I states, 'pregnant women and mothers having dependent infants who are arrested, detained or interned for reasons related to the armed conflict, shall have their cases considered with the utmost priority.' Judith Gardam has concluded from an analysis of 34 provisions within the Geneva Conventions that purportedly provide safeguards for women, 19 in fact primarily protect children.[15] This makes the position of women without children problematic, and also obscures the fact that female children are especially vulnerable to various forms of sexual attack. Armed attackers are not generally particular about the age of their female victims.

The ICTY has jurisdiction over grave breaches of the Geneva Conventions.[16] Rape was not explicitly designated a grave breach of the Geneva Conventions, although grave breaches include acts wilfully committed and causing great suffering or causing injuries to body or health. Sexual violence can be easily read into this definition, but a specific reference to these offences would have closed the possibility of contrary argument. Additional Protocol I among its list of grave breaches, *inter alia* included, 'degrading practices involving outrages on personal dignity based on racial discrimination', but makes no reference to gender-based discrimination.[17] Although non-grave breaches are nevertheless violations of the Conventions, the distinction between grave and other breaches may lead to the latter being perceived of as unimportant and as not meriting enforcement. Certainly rape and other forms of sexual violence against women, 'are not rigorously punished in international humanitarian law partially because they are not sufficiently protected or punished by either domestic law or international human rights law.' [18] The consequences of this somewhat equivocal language is that the Geneva Conventions create what Judith Gardam has termed a 'gender hierarchy' in that the provisions concerning

---

[14] *Protocol Additional to the Geneva Convention of 12 August 1949, and Relating to the Protection of Victims of International Armed Conflict,* 1125 UNTS 3; 16 ILM 1391 (*'Additional Protocol I'*). As at 17 March 1999, there were 153 States Parties.

[15] Judith Gardam, 'Women and the Law of Armed Conflict: Why the Silence?' (1997) 46 *International and Comparative Law Quarterly* 55, 57.

[16] Additional Protocol I, art 2.

[17] Additional Protocol I, art 85(4)(c).

[18] Kelly Dawn Askin, *War Crimes Against Women: Prosecution in International War Crimes Tribunals* (1997) 257.

women are not regarded as seriously as those concerning other protected persons.[19]

Common Article 3 to the Geneva Conventions provides a minimum standard of behaviour that applies to both government and non-government forces in non-international (internal) armed conflict, although the threshold of applicability is quite high. Prohibited actions include violence to life and the person, cruel treatment and torture, and humiliating and degrading treatment. Sexual violence can be understood within these terms. However Article 4(e) of the Statute of the ICTR makes this explicit in that it expressly includes: 'outrages upon personal dignity, in particular humiliating and degrading treatment, rape, enforced prostitution, and any form of indecent assault.'[20]

The Geneva Conventions and Protocols are not the only legal regime applicable to sexual violence in armed conflicts. A second category is that of crimes against humanity. Crimes against humanity were defined in the Nuremberg Charter as:

> Murder, extermination, enslavement, deportation, and other inhumane acts committed against any civilian population before or during the war, or persecutions on political, racial, or religious grounds in execution of or in connection with any crime within the jurisdiction of the Tribunal whether or not in violation of the domestic law of the country where perpetrated.[21]

The omission of rape from the list of acts constituting crimes against humanity was rectified in the Allied Control Council Law No 10 that was adopted by the four occupying powers in Germany.[22] The inclusion of 'other inhumane acts' meant that the Nuremberg Charter did not provide an exhaustive definition of the elements for a crime against humanity and so the Tribunal for the former Yugoslavia needed to give careful consideration to the elements of the offence in the first case involving charges of

---

[19] Gardam, above n 15, 56.

[20] Statute of the ICTR, art 4(e).

[21] Charter of the IMT, art 6.

[22] *Allied Control Council Law No 10 Punishment of Persons Guilty of War Crimes, Crimes Against Peace and Humanity*, 20 December 1945, Official Gazette of the Control Council for Germany, No 3, Berlin, 31 January 1946, art VI.c ('*Control Council Law No 10*'). The prohibition of crimes against humanity was subsequently affirmed by the General Assembly in its resolution entitled *United Nations General Assembly Resolution in Affirmation of the Principles of International Law Recognized by the Charter of the Nuremberg Tribunal*, 11 December 1946, UN GA Res 95, 1 UN GAOR (Part II) at 188; UN Doc A/64/Add.1 (1946), and thereafter confirmed in the *Principles of International Law Recognized in the Charter of the Nurenberg Tribunal and in the Judgement of the Tribunal*, adopted at Geneva, 29 July 1950; 5 UN GAOR Supp (No 12), 11; UN Doc A/1316 (1950); (1950) 4 *American Journal of International Law* 126 (Supp). Principle VI.c provides that a crime against humanity is punishable as a crime under international law.

crimes against humanity. This was the trial of Dusko Tadic.[23] According to the Tribunal there must be evidence of systematic government planning for the commission of crimes against a civilian population, not just against individual civilians, but the acts need not occur during an armed conflict.[24] Where rape is used as a deliberate instrument of war intended to cause physical harm, to spread terror and to degrade women and children, it is appropriately categorised as a crime against humanity. Women are dehumanised by this treatment, as indeed are all members of the community and perpetrators of the crimes. As such, the crime is perceived as destructive of humanity, not just of individual victims.

At first sight rape does not appear to fall within the legal definition of genocide contained in the Genocide Convention and replicated verbatim in the Statutes of both war crimes tribunals. Genocide requires:

An intention to destroy, in whole or in part, a national, ethnical, racial or religious group through the commission of such acts as killing or causing serious bodily or mental harm to members of the group; deliberately inflicting on the group conditions of life calculated to bring about its physical destruction in whole or in part; imposing measures to prevent births within the group; forcibly transferring children of the group to another group.[25]

It has been forcefully asserted by the United Nation's General Assembly that where rape has been carried out on a massive and systematic basis for the purposes of destroying the family and community life of the victims and of 'cleansing' the vicinity of all other ethnicities by causing mass flight, and births of a tainted bloodline, it becomes genocidal.[26] In review-

---

[23] *Prosecutor v Dusko Tadic (Decision of Trial Chamber II, 7 May 1997)* IT-94-1-T; 36 ILM 908. It has also recognised that a single act of the perpetrator, when committed within a context of widespread or systematic attack against a civilian population, entails individual criminal responsibility (at [649]) ('*Tadic*').

[24] Ibid [618]-[657].

[25] Genocide Convention, art 2.

[26] *Rape and Abuse of Women in the Areas of Armed Conflict in the Former Yugoslavia,* GA Res 49/205 (Sess XLIX), UN GAOR, UN Doc A/Res/49/205 (1995). See also Catharine A MacKinnon, 'Rape, Genocide and Women's Human Rights' (1994) 17 *Harvard Women's Law Journal* 5, 12-13; Christine Chinkin, 'Rape and Sexual Abuse of Women in International Law' (1994) 5 *European Journal of International Law* 326, 333; Koenig, 'Women and Rape in Ethnic Conflict and War' (1994) 5 *Hastings Women's Law Journal* 129. On sexual violence against women in the conflict in the Former Yugoslavia see Todd A Salzman, 'Rape Camps as a Means of Ethnic Cleansing: Religious, Cultural, and Ethical Responses to Rape Victims in the Former Yugoslavia' (1998) 20 *Human Rights Quarterly* 348; Catherine N Niarchos, 'Women, War, and Rape: Challenges Facing The International Tribunal for the Former Yugoslavia' (1995) 17 *Human Rights Quarterly* 651; Cleiren and Tissen, 'Rape and Other Forms of Sexual Assault in the Armed Conflict in the Former Yugoslavia: Legal, Procedural and Evidentiary Issues' (1995) 5 *Criminal Law Forum* 471. See also Human Rights Watch, *War Crimes in Bosnia-Herzegovina* (1992). On sexual violence against women in the Rwanda genocide see Africa Human Rights Watch Women's

ing the indictments against Karadzic and Mladic, a Trial Chamber of the ICTY invited the prosecution 'to consider broadening the scope of the characterization of genocide to include other criminal acts listed ... '[27] It suggested that 'the systematic rape of women ... is in some cases intended to transmit a new ethnic identity to the child. In other cases, humiliation and terror serve to dismember the group.'[28] It considered this characterisation to be supported by the forced detention of women for impregnation and subsequently to prevent abortion.[29]

Finally the Statute of the International Criminal Court (ICC),[30] agreed in Rome in July 1998, also includes 'other serious violations of the laws and customs applicable in international armed conflict ... '[31] which includes 'intentionally directing attacks against the civilian population ... '[32] Outrages on personal dignity are in a separate paragraph[33] from rape, sexual slavery, enforced prostitution and forced pregnancy.[34] This explicitly includes rape within the Hague provisions, again eliminating the need to show that it is contrary to the 'customs of war'.

Thus the jurisdictional provisions of the Statutes establishing war crimes tribunals for the former Yugoslavia and Rwanda have at least clarified that rape constitutes a crime against humanity when committed in a widespread systematic fashion. However these diverse legal regimes for grave breaches, crimes against humanity and genocide, allow a shifting perception of rape and other violent crimes against women. The emphasis in both crimes against humanity and genocide is on the group and the violence committed against members of the group for its destruction, not upon rape as a gender crime against individual women. Crimes against humanity and genocide take other forms when committed against men, while women are subject to other forms of the offences, as well as to sexual violence. The omission of rapes from the definition of grave breaches allows the perception that it is only where they reach the systematic and widespread level of crimes against humanity that they are punishable as war crimes. Just as a single illegal act towards a prisoner of war violates the Third Geneva Convention (and, depending upon content of the act, potentially a grave

---

Rights Project, *Shattered Lives, Sexual Violence During the Rwandan Genocide and its Aftermath* (1996).

[27] *Prosecutor v Radovan Karadzic and Ratko Mladic*, 108 ILR 85, 136.

[28] Ibid, 135.

[29] Ibid, 118.

[30] *Rome Statute of the International Criminal Court*, adopted by the United Nations Diplomatic Conference of Plenipotentiaries on the Establishment of an International Criminal Court on 17 July 1998; 37 ILM 1002. The whole of the Statute can be accessed at <http://www.un.org/icc/romestat.htm> ('*Statute of the ICC*').

[31] Statute of the ICC, art 8(b).

[32] Statute of the ICC, art 8(b) (i).

[33] Statute of the ICC, art 8(b) (xxi).

[34] Statute of the ICC, art 8(b) (xxii).

breach of that Convention) so too a single act of rape in armed conflict must be regarded as illegal under the laws of war.

2.2 Prosecution Policy

Jurisdictional provisions are of no account if they are not acted upon. In determining when to bring indictments for rape and sexual assault in armed conflicts, the prosecution has had to take account of the Rules of Evidence and Procedure and the adequacy and reliability of available evidence. Investigations of crimes against women in the Former Yugoslavia and Rwanda have raised numerous practical and legal problems: the dispersal of victims and witnesses across all regions of the world; the unwillingness of women to speak of crimes committed against them through humiliation, shame, fear of public or family ostracism or fear of reprisal; the intervention of too many people wanting accounts of their experiences, including media, NGOs, support agencies etc, and, eventually, official investigators; the passage of time and the desire not to relive such atrocities; and the feeling that rape and sexual assault were not in fact of major concern compared with the loss of community, home and possessions and the death or disappearance of family members.[35]

With respect to indictments, the prosecution has had to determine what charges to bring. The lack of any international definition of rape in Article 27 of the Fourth Geneva Convention perhaps assumed a common understanding of the elements of the offence, but perhaps also assumed that it would not be subject to international criminal prosecution. In determining what legally constitutes rape, the ICTY could have relied upon the criminal law applicable in that country to which all those involved were subject. It is however undesirable that the formulation of any international crime should depend upon the happenstance of the location of the first prosecuted offences, especially given the likely precedential impact of any rulings. Further, the criminal law of many States defines rape from the viewpoint of the male perpetrator rather than of the usually female victim.[36] The prosecution has circumvented these problems by first issuing indictments for the crime of forcible sexual intercourse.[37] This formulation allows fresh consideration of the elements of the offence, without importing understandings of rape from any particular legal system, for example, that rape must be penile and is only committed against women. It also emphasises the elements of violence and force.

---

[35] Christine Chinkin, 'Amicus Curiae Brief on Protective Measures for Victims and Witnesses' (1996) 7 *Criminal Law Forum* 179, 185.

[36] See especially, Jocelynne A Scutt, *Women and the Law* (1990) 444-501. See also Catharine A MacKinnon, *Feminism, Marxism, Method and the State: Towards Feminist Jurisprudence* (1983) 636.

[37] *Tadic*, above n 23.

The prosecution for the Tribunal for the Former Yugoslavia has indicted alleged accused for the offence of rape under Articles 2 and 5 of the Statute of the Tribunal. It has, however, gone further and investigated sexual assaults for the specific purpose of prosecution under the rubrics of torture and enslavement as a crime against humanity.[38] In indictments issued in June 1996 against Dragan Gagaovic and others in the *Foca Case* the prosecution alleged 62 counts of crimes committed against women, including crimes against humanity, grave breaches of the Geneva Conventions and violations of the laws and customs of war relating especially to rape, torture, outrages upon personal dignity, persecution, wilfully causing great suffering, enslavement and inhuman treatment.[39] The prosecution has also included charges of rape in indictments against all sides in the various conflicts in the former Yugoslavia, thereby emphasising that such actions are not the preserve of any one faction but have been common to all.[40]

2.3 *Rules of Procedure and Evidence*

The Secretary-General of the Untied Nations proposed that protective measures be 'provided in the rules of procedure and evidence for victims and witnesses, especially in cases of rape or sexual assault.'[41] Protective measures have been implemented through a number of provisions for the protection of victims and witnesses in proceedings before Trial Chambers, and the establishment of the Victims and Witnesses Unit in the Registry.

The understanding of the dilemma faced in court by victims of rape and sexual assault is shown in Article 96 of the Rules of Procedure that warrants citation in full:

In Cases of sexual assault:
(i)   ... no corroboration of the victim's testimony shall be required;
(ii) Consent shall not be allowed as a defence if the victim (a) has been subjected to or threatened with or has had reason to fear violence, duress, detention or psychological oppression, or (b) reasonably believed that if the victim did not submit, another might be so subjected
(iii) Before evidence of the victim's consent is admitted, the accused shall satisfy the Trial Chamber *in camera* that the evidence is relevant and credible;

---

[38] See the Indictment in *Prosecutor v Dragan Gagovic and others* [1996] (the *Foca Case*) IT-96-23-I. The most significant aspect of this case is Judge Vohrah's confirmation of the Prosecutor's allegations of the crime of enslavement, based on the evidence of sexual violence.

[39] Ibid. No arrests have been made to date in this case.

[40] *Prosecutor v Zejnil Delalic and others* [1996] IT-96-21-I.

[41] Secretary-General's Report, para 108.

(iv) Prior sexual conduct of the victim shall not be admitted in evidence.[42]

Dispensing with the need for corroboration shows sensitivity towards both the facts of rape during armed conflict, and its psychological impact. The Special Rapporteur on Violence against Women has explained in her first report some of the reasons why survivors may be reluctant to testify in public criminal proceedings. These include 'severe traumatization, feelings of shame, lack of trust, fear of awakening bad memories as well as fear of reprisals against themselves and their families.'[43] Evidentiary difficulties are accentuated where there is no medical corroboration because victims did not, or could not, seek medical advice through fear, shame or because of its unavailability. Victims may not have discussed what occurred with anyone out of fear of retribution or rejection.

Many domestic rape trials turn on whether or not there was consent to intercourse, especially where the victim knows the alleged attacker.[44] In the fear and horror of armed conflict, the concept of consent is meaningless. Closely connected with the issue of consent is the retraumatisation experienced by women alleging rape through humiliating and rough questioning by defence counsel on their prior sexual conduct in order to present them as 'bad' women and therefore as unreliable witnesses. Rule 96 approaches the question of consent from the viewpoint of the victim. It is her reasonable belief of the consequences if she does not submit that is determinative, not that of the accused as to her consent as is so often the case in domestic law. It is to be hoped that 'reasonableness' will be interpreted in light of the history of sexual violence in armed conflict, from the standpoint of a woman as a victim, and not on the relevance of her sexual history.

2.4 *Trial Process*

Many of the concerns about the trial of rape cases were addressed by the Trial Chamber in pre-trial motions in the first case brought before it, that of *Dusko Tadic*. The prosecution sought confidentiality for certain witnesses from press and media, protection from the potential retraumatisation of

---

[42] *International Tribunal for the Prosecution of Persons Responsible for Serious Violations of International Humanitarian Law Committed in the Territory of the Former Yugoslavia Since 1991, 'Rules of Procedure and Evidence'*, as amended, UN Doc IT/32 Rev 11 (1997).

[43] *Preliminary Report Submitted by the Special Rapporteur on Violence Against Women, its Causes and Consequences, Ms Radhika Coomaraswamy, Submitted in Accordance with Comm'n on Hum Rts Res 45 (Sess XLV)*, UN ESCOR, UN Doc E/CN.4/1995/42 (1995) ('*Preliminary Report on Violence Against Women*'), [13]. See also *Rape and Abuse of Women in the Territory of the Former Yugoslavia: Report of the Secretary-General, Comm'n on Hum Rts (L)*, UN ESCOR, UN Doc E/CN.4/1994/5 (1993) ('*Rape and Abuse Report*').

[44] MacKinnon, above n 36, 636.

confronting the accused in open court and anonymity, including from the accused for as long as possible, for particular witnesses.[45] This application raised important questions about the content of a fair trial in accordance with the European Convention on Human Rights,[46] the International Covenant on Civil and Political Rights (ICCPR) [47] and the Tribunal's own Statute. Article 21 (e) of the Statute of the Tribunal provides that:

> the accused shall be entitled to the following minimum guarantees, in full equality:

> (e) To examine or have examined, the witnesses against him and to obtain the attendance and examination of witnesses ... under the same conditions against him;

This right of the accused must however be balanced against other interests, notably those of victims and witnesses in their security and privacy, and those of the international community in seeing guilty persons brought to justice. In considering these applications, the Trial Chamber emphasised its over-riding preference for a public trial, especially in light of a trial's important educative function.[48] However the Chamber was also mindful of the unique mandate to protect witnesses and victims, that distinguishes its Statute from human rights treaties that contain no such affirmative obligation.[49] The fact that the Tribunal had been established during a continuing conflict that had caused 'terror and anguish' to the civilian population had to be taken into account. The Chamber was also aware that, unlike at Nuremberg, it would be largely dependent upon eyewitness testimony.[50]

The Chamber drew upon national jurisprudence[51] and case law under the European Convention on Human Rights[52] to provide guide-lines for the factors that must be taken into account in determining whether to accord anonymity to witnesses.

---

[45] *Prosecutor v Dusko Tadic* (Decision of the Trial Chamber, 10 August 1995 on Protective Measures for Victims and Witnesses) 105 ILR 599.

[46] *[European] Convention for the Protection of Human Rights and Fundamental Freedoms*, opened for signature 4 November 1950, 213 UNTS 222, (entered into force 3 September 1953), as amended by Protocols Nos 3, 5, and 8 which entered into force on 21 September 1970, 20 December 1971 and 1 January 1990, respectively. As at 28 October 1998, there were 40 States Parties.

[47] *International Covenant on Civil and Political Rights*, opened for signature 19 December 1966, 999 UNTS 171, 6 ILM 368 (entered into force 23 March 1976) ('*ICCPR*'). As at 17 March 1999, there were 144 States Parties.

[48] *Prosecutor v Tadic*, above n 45, 629.

[49] Ibid, 611-12.

[50] Ibid, 609-10.

[51] Ibid, 615-17. The Tribunal made extensive references to United States, Australian and New Zealand case law on confidentiality and to the *Evidence Act (Amendment Act)* 1989 (Qld) that allow additional protection during the testimony of a "special witness" including the exclusion of the public and or the defendant or other named persons from court.

[52] Ibid, 614-15.

First there must be a real fear for the safety of victims and witnesses. Although this requirement was phrased objectively, the Chamber stated that the ruthless character of the alleged crimes justified witnesses fearing the accused and his accomplices. Second, the evidence of the witness must constitute an important part of the prosecution case. Thus, there must be no evidence that the witness is unreliable or untrustworthy, for example, through having a criminal background. Fourth, the Tribunal must be unable to supply adequate protection, and fifth, the measures must be strictly necessary to justify the unavoidable prejudice to the accused of not knowing the identity of witnesses against him.[53]

These guidelines do not provide a blanket expectation of privacy for witnesses but rather a flexibility that allows all the relevant factors in the particular claim to be assessed. In some cases identity will be more important than in others. For example, in a chain of command case where there is no accusation that the defendant was present at the commission of the offences, identity of those testifying is less important than in trials where the accused is the alleged perpetrator. It might be further argued that in many instances the identity of the victims was irrelevant at the time of the commission of the offences. Women have spoken of being taken in turn, or arbitrarily 'selected' for sexual abuse.[54] In these circumstances, it seems somewhat strained to argue that their identity is now crucial to the prosecution case. Nor do the guidelines suggest that anonymity will be permanent but will only last for as long as the decision making.

In *Kostovski v The Netherlands*,[55] the European Court of Human Rights recognised the disadvantages that an accused person faces when answering the allegations of an anonymous witness and suggested that the trial court should ensure that certain safeguards are put into place to provide some counter-balance. The Appeals Chamber of the ICTY in referring to the decision in *Kostovski*, similarly indicated procedural measures to minimise the accused's handicap.[56] The judges must verify the true identity of each witness and must be able to observe the demeanour of all witnesses to assess the reliability of their testimony. In the absence of a trial by jury, the judges are the decision-makers both as to fact and law and confidence in their ability to weigh all aspects of the evidence is crucial to the credibility of the Tribunal. The defence must be given ample opportunity to question all witnesses on issues unrelated to their identity and current whereabouts. This principle conforms to the requirements of Article 21(4)(e) of the Tribunal's Statute that the accused is entitled 'to examine, or have examined, the witnesses against him.' Finally any anonymity accorded is not

---

[53] Ibid, 622-3.
[54] Askin, above n 18, 261-379.
[55] (1989) 166 ECHR (ser A).
[56] *Prosecutor v Tadic*, above n 45, 620-1.

permanent, but will last only as long as there is reason to fear for the witness's security.[57]

The ruling of the Tribunal in *Tadic* on witness anonymity has provoked an extremely hostile response on the grounds that it will deny accused persons a fair trial and may lead to the conviction of accused persons on the basis of tainted evidence. Monroe Leigh has argued, for example, that the well-established rights of the accused should not be undermined by the more recent conception of victims' rights.[58] However focus on the rights of the accused deflects attention from the broader interests of the international community in achieving the three objectives for which the war crimes tribunals were established: to do justice, to deter further crimes and to contribute to the restoration and maintenance of international peace. It also ignores the fact that in national courts too security and policing interests have at times justified the receipt of testimony from anonymous witnesses.

Most importantly, this refusal to see beyond the rights of the accused illustrates precisely the claim made by feminist analysis of human rights law that its principles have been predicated upon the concerns of men and have failed to take account of the life experiences of women.[59] Women typically feature in criminal trials as victims and witnesses, while more men than women feature as accused persons.[60] It is not surprising that the guarantee of a fair trial – that is, to fair treatment by the agents of the State – is seen by many as more fundamental than the right of the victim to equality before the law and of the victim and potential victims to be free from fear of further abuse. It has been asserted that, 'sex crimes against women cannot be effectively controlled or punished by domestic laws during times of armed conflict.'[61] The subsequent refusal of one of the witnesses accorded anonymity by the Chamber to testify in the *Tadic* trial highlights the reality of the fears of witnesses that the Dayton Peace Accords have done little to relieve.

Inclusion of rape and sexual assault within the jurisdiction of war crimes tribunals is an overdue signal to the international community of the unacceptability under international law of atrocities committed against women during armed conflict. If the tribunals are unable to prosecute successfully those who have been indicted of such offences because of the reasonable fears of witnesses who are offered no protective guarantees, that message becomes blurred and its seriousness open to question. For women it means that yet again their suffering is denied and their stories discounted.

---

[57] Ibid, 624.

[58] Monroe Leigh, 'Witness Anonymity is Inconsistent with Due Process' (1997) 91 *American Journal Of International Law* 50, 51. See also, in reply, Christine Chinkin, 'Due Process and Witness Anonymity' (1997) 91 *American Journal of International Law* 75.

[59] MacKinnon, above n 26, 15.

[60] Scutt, above n 36.

[61] Askin, above n 18, 295.

3. Do Women Remain the Forgotten Victims of War?

The Judges and prosecution staff of the War Crimes Tribunals for the Former Yugoslavia and Rwanda have done much to ensure that women are no longer the forgotten victims of war. In particular the long silence about the suffering of women in armed conflict has been broken. Crimes against women have been widely investigated and the inclusion of rape and sexual assault within the jurisdiction of the Tribunals may have conclusively determined that such offences are war crimes that must be subjected to enforcement measures.

The second judgement handed down on 2 September 1998 by the Rwanda Tribunal has resulted in the conviction of the defendant Jean-Paul Akayesu for crimes of sexual violence.[62] The trial chamber in that case made a number of important findings. It defined rape and sexual violence as acts of a sexual nature not limited to domestic definitions of the crime. The Chamber found that sexual violence might constitute a crime against humanity or a breach of article 3 common to the Geneva Conventions and Additional Protocol II as an outrage on personal dignity. It also held that sexual violence constituted serious bodily or mental harm and could constitute genocide. Finally, the judges found that the participation of the accused in the sexual violence need not be restricted to the role of the main offender but could include ordering, instigating, aiding and abetting the commission of such acts by allowing them to take place.[63] These significant findings assist in the creation of jurisprudence that views sexual violence from different perspectives, including that of genocide.

Other recent developments in international law also indicate that the issue of sexual violence against women remains on the agenda. The Statute of the ICC identifies sexual assault and other similar violence as crimes against humanity and under war crimes provision for acts committed during international and internal armed conflict. Article 7(1)(g) states that the following acts are a crime against humanity, when the other constitutive elements are present: 'rape, sexual slavery, enforced prostitution, forced pregnancy, enforced sterilization, or any other form of sexual violence of comparable gravity'.

Article 7(2) assists in the interpretation of the list of crimes under article 7(1). It defines the crime of 'forced pregnancy' as:

> the unlawful confinement, of a woman forcibly made pregnant, with the intent of affecting the ethnic composition of any population or carrying out other grave violations of international law. This definition shall not

---

[62] *Prosecutor v Jean-Paul Akayesu* [1996] ICTR-96-4-T. The decision can be accessed at <http://www. un.org/ictr/english/judgements/akayesu.html>.

[63] Ibid.

in any way be interpreted as affecting national laws relating to pregnancy.

The intent required to prosecute the crime of forced pregnancy is very high, the crime is limited by the purpose of the perpetrator and there is no doubt that it will be extremely difficult for prosecutors to provide such evidence.

Article 8(2)(b) (xxii) of the Statute of the ICC lists war crimes committed during international armed conflict and includes:

> Committing rape, sexual slavery, enforced prostitution, forced pregnancy, as defined in article 7, paragraph 2 (f), enforced sterilization, or any other form of sexual violence also constituting a grave breach of the Geneva Conventions.

It is interesting to note that whilst rape and other such crimes are not articulated under article 8(2)(a) dealing with grave breaches, the statement 'also constituting a grave breach ... ' indicates that crimes of sexual assault may be starting to be recognised as a grave breach as well as a serious violation. The same listing of sexual violence crimes can be found in article 8(2)(e)(vi) pursuant to cases of armed conflict not of an international character. The final part of the sub-paragraph states, ' ... and any other form of sexual violence also constituting a serious violation of article 3 common to the four Geneva Conventions.'

The Statute of the ICC contains the most comprehensive coverage to date of sexual crimes regularly suffered by women during times of armed conflict. The practical elements required to prosecute some of these crimes will create difficulties and no assumptions can be made in relation to the potential prosecution policies with respect to indictments for such crimes.

Steps taken in other arenas have reinforced this progress. For example, the truth about sexual slavery for the benefit of the Japanese military during World War II has at last been revealed, and to some limited extent addressed.[64] Rape in armed conflict was denoted a violation of human rights law by both the World Conference on Human Rights in Vienna in 1993[65] and the Fourth United Nations World Conference on Women in Beijing in 1995.[66] The UN Special Rapporteur on Violence against

---

[64] Askin, above n 18, 73-85.

[65] On 25 June 1993, representatives of 171 States adopted by consensus the *Vienna Declaration and Programme of Action of the World Conference on Human Rights.* The final paragraph of the Vienna Declaration and Programme of Action was adopted by all the States attending the World Conference. The full text of the Vienna Declaration is located at <http://www.unhchr.ch/html/menu5/d/vienna.htm>. On 20 December 1993 the General Assembly of the United Nations endorsed the Declaration: see GA Res 48/121, UN GAOR (85th plen mtg), UN Doc A/Res/48 (1993).

[66] The official documents of the Conference are located at <gopher://gopher.undp.org:70/00/unconfs/women/ off/a--20.en>, UN Doc A/CONF.177/20 (1995); 35 ILM 401. See especially, Annex II: Platform for Action - Women in Armed Conflict [131]-[149]. The

Women, Radhika Coomaraswamy, has given special attention to the subject.[67] The civil jurisdiction of the US courts has been asserted in a class action against Radovan Karadzic brought by women victims of sexual violence in Bosnia and Herzegovina.[68] Perhaps the most significant advance has been at the regional level in the decisions of the Inter-American Commission of Human Rights in *Raquel Marti de Mejia v Perú*[69] and the European Court of Human Rights in *Aydin v Turkey*.[70] The salient facts of the former case for the purposes of this discussion are that soldiers in Perú raped Raquel Mejía after they had abducted her husband, a known political activist. When she learned of her husband's death, Raquel Mejía filed criminal charges in Perú but fearing reprisal, did not mention rape. Some years later when she had received political asylum in Sweden, Raquel Mejía lodged a petition with the Inter-American Commission on Human Rights alleging violations of the American Convention on Human Rights,[71] including, *inter alia*, of Article 5 (the right to be free from torture and other inhumane treatment), Article 11 (the right to private life) and Article 1 (the duty of the State to respect and guarantee the exercise of the rights and freedoms within the Convention).

---

role of the United Nations in making the document available 'on-line' is hereby greatly acknowledged.

[67] Preliminary Report on Violence Against Women, above n 43. See also, *Report of the Special Rapporteur on Violence Against Women, Its Causes and Consequences, Ms Radhika Coomaraswamy, Submitted in Accordance with Commission Resolution 1997/44 (Sess LIV)* UN ESCOR, E/CN.4/1998/54 (1998) ('*1998 Report on Violence Against Women*').

[68] *Kadic v Radovan Karadzic* and *Jane Doe v Radovan Karadzic*, 866 F Supp 734-35 (SD NY 1994), rev'd, 70 F 3d 232 (2d Cir 1995), cert denied, 116 S Ct 2524 (1996) ('*Karadzic Actions*'). See also in this regard, the remarks by Catharine MacKinnon made during the Fourth Hague Joint Conference held in The Hague, 2-5 July 1997, in 'International Human Rights and Humanitarian Law', Wybo P Heere (ed), *Contemporary International Law Issues: New Forms, New Applications* (1998) 150-3, in her capacity as lead council in the case of *Kadic v Karadzic*. The plaintiffs sought compensatory and punitive damages, as well as injunctive relief as a redress for torts including: genocide; summary execution; wrongful death; torture; cruel, inhuman or degrading treatment; rape; assault and battery; war crimes; intentional infliction of emotional distress; forced pregnancy and prostitution; and forced childbirth, the *Karadzic* Actions, 735-7. The actions were instituted pursuant to the *Alien Torts Claims Act*, 28 USC § 1350 (1994). The Supreme Court denied the defendant's writ of certiorari and allowed the plaintiffs to proceed with the case. For a detailed analysis of these cases see Beth Ann Isenberg, 'Comment: Genocide, Rape, And Crimes Against Humanity: An Affirmation of Individual Accountability in the Former Yugoslavia in the *Karadzic* Actions' in (1997) 60 *Albany Law Review* 1051; Theodore R Posner, 'Alien Tort Claims Act-genocide-war crimes-violations of international law by non State actors' in (1996) 90 *American Journal of International Law* 658.

[69] (1996) Report No 5/96, Inter-Am CHR, OEA/Ser L/V/II.91 Doc 7, 157.

[70] (1998) ECHR (ser A), (1998)3 Butterworths Human Rights Cases 300.

[71] *American Convention on Human Rights*, opened for signature 7 January 1970, OAS Treaty Series No 36; 1144 UNTS 123; 9 ILM 673, OEA/Ser.K/XVI/1.1 Doc 65, Rev 1, Corr 2 (entered into force 18 July 1978).

It might be first noted that what had happened to the complainant is not unusual. Her association with a known activist targeted her for violence. Women who themselves have played no political role are singled out in this way and a Human Rights Watch Report with respect to Peru has found that women may well become subject to abuse from both government and anti-government forces.[72] The Inter-American Commission made a number of groundbreaking statements with respect to her allegations of rape. First, they presumed the facts as alleged by Raquel Mejía to be true, although she had not reported it at the time and there was no corroborating evidence. There was strong circumstantial evidence to presume the responsibility of Peruvian army troops in a complaint of violation of human rights, which does not demand the same high standard of proof as a criminal trial. The Commission accepted that the rapist was wearing Peruvian army fatigues and was in the company of soldiers. She was living in an area under emergency legislation where the military 'commonly perpetrate numerous human rights violations.' The Commission found support for her allegations in the abundant information contained in reports of intergovernmental organisations and NGOs of rapes by security forces in Peru as part of their campaign to intimidate, humiliate and punish civilians suspected of collaborating with insurgents.[73] Such rapes were committed with impunity and the Commission noted that there were no effective domestic remedies within Peru for the impartial investigation and prosecution of allegations of sexual abuse by members of the security forces. Accordingly, although the sexual abuse had not been reported in Peru, there was also no failure to seek domestic remedies. In terms of substance, the Commission unequivocally affirmed that:

> Current international law establishes that sexual assault committed by members of security forces, whether as a result of a deliberate practice promoted by the state or as a result of failure by the state to prevent the occurrence of this crime, constitutes a violation of the victim's human rights, especially the right to physical and mental integrity.[74]

The Commission cited Article 27 of the Fourth Geneva Convention and Article 76 of Protocol I to support its pronouncement that 'any act of rape committed individually constitutes a war crime.' It referred to the declaration of the International Committee of the Red Cross that the 'serious offence' of deliberately causing great suffering includes sexual abuse. In the context of non-international armed conflict, Common Article 3 of the Geneva Conventions and paragraph 2 of Article 49 of Additional Protocol

---

[72] Human Rights Watch, *Untold Terror, Violence against Women in Peru's Armed Conflict* (1992).
[73] *Marti de Mejía v Peru*, above n 69.
[74] Ibid.

II include the prohibition of rape and other sexual abuse 'in so far as they are the outcome of harm deliberately influenced (sic) on a person.'[75]

Although its holdings were under the American Convention on Human Rights, the Commission accepted the applicability of both international humanitarian law and human rights law to such events. Rape can therefore constitute the offence of torture under the Geneva Conventions as well as falling within Article 5 of the American Convention. The Commission emphasised that 'rape is a physical and mental abuse that is perpetrated as a result of an act of violence.' It is also a method of psychological torture through the humiliation, victimisation and fear of public ostracism. The purposive element of torture is satisfied by the use of rape for personal punishment and intimidation. In addition, the deliberate outrage to dignity that is caused by rape makes it a violation of the concept of private life within Article 11 of the American Convention on Human Rights. The Commission recommended to the government that it conduct a full investigation into the sexual abuse of Raquel Mejia in order to identify and punish the perpetrators in accordance with national law, and to pay her fair compensation.[76]

This strong statement that rape by security forces constitutes torture that is attributable to the State parallels the indictments by the ICTY in the *Foca Case*. Together they provide strong evidence of a changed understanding of human rights violations that incorporate the violence experienced by women. In Aydin the European Court made important statements about the duty of States to investigate effectively and substantially allegations of rape by government officials.[77]

Despite these important steps forward, I would still argue that women are not yet sufficiently taken account of by international humanitarian law and remain largely forgotten. Indeed there is a risk that these very advances will create the false illusion that the problem of war crimes against women has now been adequately addressed. This remains far from the true position. First, the *ad hoc* tribunals are limited to the conflicts in the former Yugoslavia and Rwanda and there has to date been limited prosecution of rape, despite a number of indictments issued by both Tribunals. There is no general recognition of the reality that violent sexual abuse of women continues with impunity in other internal and international conflicts across the globe. Second, even after the establishment of the ICC, it is unlikely that it will have many cases of violations of international humanitarian law brought before it, at least for several years.[78] As has always been the case,

---

[75] ICRC - Update on Aide-Memoire of 3 December 1992.

[76] *Marti de Mejía v Peru*, above n 69.

[77] *Aydin v Turkey*, above n 70.

[78] Article 126 of the Statute of the ICC provides that the Court will come into existence when 60 States ratify the Statute. The Court will only have prospective jurisdiction after that date and given the limitations of the court's jurisdiction, it is unlikely that the court will be inundated with cases from its inception.

internalised respect for the laws of war must be the first goal and their enforcement through domestic courts enhanced. On one approach, the problems with the incorporation of women's interests are no different from enforcement of international humanitarian law generally. However, similar harms to those suffered by women in armed conflict are committed against women by men from within their own families, communities and States. In many instances these acts are committed with impunity and, even where prosecuted, convictions are hard to secure.[79] Violence against women in armed conflicts, and during peacetime, is not a distinct phenomenon but forms part of the same spectrum of behaviour and each occurs along a continuum of seriousness. The widespread, systematic and brutal nature of the offences committed in the Former Yugoslavia and Rwanda place these offences at the far end of the spectrum, as is recognised by their inclusion as crimes against humanity in the Statute of the two Tribunals. It cannot be assumed that other bodies, including the ICC, will adopt the approach of the Inter-American Commission that all rapes committed individually by all persons in armed conflict constitute war crimes. Further, the legal distinction between these offences emphasises the falsity from the perspective of the lives of women of such dichotomies as war and peace, protector and protected, security and insecurity, human rights law and international humanitarian law. The reaffirmation of the illegality of violence against women in armed conflict by the Statute of the ICC should reinforce recognition that such violence outside armed conflict is a violation of human rights law that incurs State responsibility for failure to take due diligence for its elimination and punishment. The crucial question that needs to be asked in the light of these historic developments is: would future prosecutions be willing to include rape and sexual abuse within indictments, especially where there have been other offences, perceived as more serious, or where witnesses are unwilling to testify?

Third, the adequacy of international legal remedies for victims of rape in armed conflict can be questioned. The focus of the enforcement measures through the Tribunals is on punishing the wrongdoers, not on providing compensation and support to those who have suffered. Admittedly this is a defect shared by municipal criminal legal systems, but these may be backed up by other domestic support services. A war crimes tribunal must be supplemented by long-term financial and practical assistance from governments such as medical care, shelter, support, counselling, resettlement and retraining. It cannot be assumed that all women will share the same needs. Some may feel empowered by the establishment of war crimes tribunals and the opportunity they offer to testify. Others may consider investigation and requests for evidence as further intrusions into their lives and as peripheral to their efforts to rebuild their lives. Available responses under international law must be sensitive to individual needs and choices.

---

[79] Askin, above n 18, 223.

Emphasis must remain upon dissemination, prevention and changing the mindset that sees offences against women civilians as less serious than those, for example, against prisoners of war. For this reason it is important that the provisions with respect to remedies for, and participation by, victims in the ICC statute are given full effect.

The fourth concern comes from quite the other direction. The Geneva Conventions recognise the plethora of offences that might be committed against those subject to their protection and provide a comprehensive code of behaviour during international armed conflict. While the developments discussed above recognise that women are subject to specific abuses in armed conflict, the emphasis remains on their sexual and reproductive identities. Rape, sexual assault, sexual enslavement, enforced prostitution and forced pregnancy have been recognised as gender-specific, violent abuses of the laws protecting civilians. As has been seen, women are also accorded special protection as mothers and carers. But the numerous other ways in which women suffer harms during armed conflict in ways different from men are still not accommodated. Lack of data about the differentiated effects of conflict lays this claim open to challenge. It is unarguable that both men and women non-combatants suffer many diverse forms of hurt during and after armed conflict. The priority accorded by the legal regime to military necessity adversely impacts upon the protection accorded to non-combatants. The construct of societal gender roles combined with the generally subordinate social and economic position of women means that they suffer in particular ways during conflict. Thus, as Judith Gardam expresses, 'women suffer under a double disability in comparison with combatants: their status and treatment are not only inferior as civilians but doubly so as women civilians.'[80]

Many illustrations could be given of this. The struggle for daily survival in the face of price increases for essential foods and health supplies, shortages and the dislocation of services falls most heavily upon those with responsibility for the care of others, including of physically and psychologically injured fighters, the elderly, and traumatised children. Food and health supplies are typically allocated with priority according to military needs. Within a combat zone hardship is exacerbated by the physical danger from sniper or other attack involved in leaving home for routine, but essential, activities such as shopping or finding fuel. Continuation of professional life (and therefore receiving income) might become impossible. Collapse of governmental agencies, including those for maintaining law and order and the concentration of armed men within an area all undermine the usual community restraints on human rights abuses.[81] The use of UN or regional peacekeeping forces does not guarantee security for

---

[80] Judith Gardam, 'Women and International Humanitarian Law' in William Maley (ed), *Shelters From the Storm: Developments in International Humanitarian Law* (1995) 209.

[81] Jeanne Vickers, *Women and War* (1993) 23-6.

women. Research suggests that women also suffer from a higher incidence of violence at home during a period of armed conflict, whether or not they are living within the combat zone.[82] The laws of war do not take account of any of these consequences of armed conflict. Their focus is upon the military operations, not upon the inevitable, but largely ignored repercussions, that fall unequally on different sections of the population. Nor is the role of women in restructuring society and peace building after conflict acknowledged. Women are not routinely included within peace negotiations and plans for the reorganising of society do not take account of the burden upon women. For example, the Special Rapporteur for the human rights situation in the Former Yugoslavia, Elisabeth Rehn, has emphasised in her report the urgency of rehabilitative measures for children traumatised and physically injured by the war and who require expert psychological, educational and medical care.[83] Much of this social burden is likely to fall heavily on women. The potential charge on women of addressing the needs of children could become empowering if the function is respected as a national priority, with provision for appropriate training, and allocation of resources, but could otherwise force women into further domestic roles that are unrecognised as an essential part of reinvesting for the future. Women are an essential human resource in the redevelopment program and in the search for peace. Their leadership, political, organisational and management skills should be harnessed in the identification of priorities and strategies for their achievement. Neither the law nor practices relating to armed conflict include women as agents for the survival of the community or of change, but instead continue to view them as passive victims of international affairs. In this sense the recent developments described earlier have not transformed the position of women within the legal structures of the laws of war.

A suggestion that should receive full deliberation is for a further Protocol to the Geneva Conventions directed to the needs of women in armed conflict comparable with the current proposal for a protocol to the Rights of the Child Convention[84] to increase protection for children in armed conflicts. Such a Protocol would be based upon women's own encounters with armed conflict, not upon assumptions that they experience it in the same ways as men. Gender statistics and data would therefore be an im-

---

[82] ICRC Special Brochure, 'Women and War' No 8/95.

[83] *Report of the UN Special Rapporteur of the Commission on Human rights in the Territory of the Former Yugoslavia, Elisabeth Rehn, Submitted in Accordance with Commission on Human Rights Resolution 1995/89* (Sess *LII*), UN ESCOR, UN Doc E/CN.4/1996/63 (1996) ('*Report on the Situation*'). See further, Christine Chinkin, 'Strategies to Combat Discrimination Against Women' in M O'Flaherty and G Grisvold (eds), *Post-war Protection of Human Rights in Bosnia-Herzegovina* (1998) 173.

[84] *United Nations Convention on the Rights of the Child*, opened for signature 20 November 1989, 28 ILM 1448 (entered into force 2 September 1990). As of 28 October 1998, there were 191 States Parties.

portant requirement. There has been much national debate about the inclusion of women in the military, in particular in combat roles. This would increase the likelihood of women becoming prisoners of war. But many, many more women experience armed conflicts as civilians. A rethinking of international humanitarian law that takes seriously the position of women civilians would be a major contribution to that law.

DANIEL THÜRER

3. Minorities: Their Protection in General International Law and in International Humanitarian Law

> I am life, surrounded by life, which desires to live.
>
> It is good: to preserve life, to promote life, to bring developing life to its highest value; it is bad: to destroy life, to damage life and to hold down developing life.
>
> (Albert Schweitzer)[1]

1. THE TWO WORLDS OF INTERNATIONAL LAW AND THEIR CHALLENGE BY THE MINORITY QUESTION

We are all aware that since the end of the Cold War world society and world order have been caught up in a process of rapid and fundamental transformation. One feature of change is the development and elaboration of new forms of international co-operation and supranational integration. An opposite trend is the emergence on the international scene of ethnic and cultural minorities and other groups searching to realize their own identities. The present article tries to analyze this second, pluralising feature in the evolution of international life.

We may welcome with hope the fact that cultural groups are, to a growing extent, becoming aware of their common 'self'. Is it not so, we might argue, that in history, great cultures grew out of the fertile soil of collective traditions, a common sense of the past and common ambitions for the future?[2] And is it not language as well as other forms of social interaction

---

[1] Quoted in Hans Haug, *Humanity for All* (1993) 454.

[2] A good example is the political culture developed within the Polis in Ancient Greece as described by Jacob Buckhardt, *History of Greek Culture* (Palmer Hilty trans, 1963) 12–13:

> In recent times, apart from philosophical and social thought, it is essentially the individual who demands a state advantageous for his own purposes. For the most part, all that he demands is security, so that he may freely develop his potentialities. To this end he gladly makes well-defined sacrifices, though the less the state bothers him otherwise,

Helen Durham and Timothy L.H. McCormack (eds.), The Changing Face of Conflict and the Efficacy of International Humanitarian Law, 45–62.

such as law, which constitute, so to speak, the living environment or *Lebenswelt* of a community? After all, far from representing mere forms, standards or instruments of communication among strangers, they may form a collective source of creativity and energy and be a focus of common consciousness and identity. Viewed in this light it may well seem legitimate for cultural groups to appeal to the international community if they consider themselves unjustly treated, deprived of a chance to grow, spiritually imprisoned or even threatened in their existence by the rigidities and constraints of institutions within which they are placed.

But there is, unfortunately, also a dark and pathological side to the problem which is much more at the forefront of present-day political opinion: the experience that group identification might easily degenerate into systems of closed societies marked by acts of intolerance or even xenophobia, such as forcible or arbitrary inclusion or exclusion of non-members, excessive self-esteem and regression into idealising myths of an ancient past instead of progressing and facing challenges of the future.[3] Thinking in terms of collective identity might be a source of fear and passion that breeds violence; violence, in turn, engenders hostility, hatred and crime.[4] Fragmentation of State systems or anarchy on the one hand[5]

---

the more content he is. The Greek polis, on the other hand, starts with the whole, which precedes its parts. From an inner logic we may add this: It is not only a matter of giving preference to the general over the particular but also of preferring the permanent over the momentary and transitory.

Whoever governs or is governed here is the citizen of the polis. To govern means, more precisely, to serve on the tribunal or to hold an office. As a rule, the citizen realizes all his capacities and virtues within the state or in its service. The entire Greek spirit and its culture are most intimately related to the polis, and of the poetry and art created during the flowering of Greek genius the loftiest by far was not created for the enjoyment of individuals but for the public, ie, the community.

[3] See Martti Koskenniemi, 'National Self-Determination Today: Problems of Legal Theory and Practice' (1994) 43 *International and Comparative Law Quarterly* 241, 258:

in Eastern Europe, too, the decolonisation of the past is creating nations out of old myths, legends, martyrs and heroes. The movement is not forwards, but backwards into a mythical past. The constitutional process is not about concluding a social contract but about restoration (Footnotes omitted).

[4] See, Carl Gustav Jung, *Two Essays on Analytical Psychology* (R F C Hull trans, 2nd revised edition, 1973) 153–4:

Hence every man is, in a certain sense, unconsciously a worse man when he is in society than when acting alone; for he is carried by society and to that extent relieved of his individual responsibility. Any large company composed of wholly admirable persons has the morality and intelligence of an unwieldy, stupid, and violent animal. The bigger the organization, the more unavoidable is its immorality and blind stupidity (*Senatus bestia, setatores boni viri*). Society, by automatically stressing all the collective qualities in its individual representatives, puts a premium on mediocrity, on everything that settles down to vegetate in an easy irresponsible way. Individuality will inevitably be driven to the wall …

and totalitarian rule on the other hand might be the 'logical' ends of such chains of action and reaction. Most of today's armed conflicts and violent tensions are rooted in this type of identity struggle. All continents are, albeit in varying degrees, affected by such newly emerging nationalistic eruptions. No State is immune.

On the following pages we try to consider how international law as it stands (*lex lata*) responds to these challenges inherent in the changing nature of society. And we ask whether there are ways and means in sight that could be adopted to deal with minority issues in the future (*lex desiderata*).

Two systems of rules are primarily involved: human rights law and humanitarian law. Are there essentially different approaches to be observed within either system? To what degree do they encompass static and dynamic elements? Are there any variations in their ability to evolve? Is the concept of international law itself questioned by these challenges? In fulfilling its aim to secure stability and justice is there an in-built potential in the legal order to experiment and adapt by developing institutions, for example, which could encourage innovation while guarding against decline?

2. STATUS OF MINORITIES UNDER GENERAL INTERNATIONAL LAW

2.1 *The Law as it Stands*

In our contemporary world there are, as we know, some 3000 linguistic groups and 5000 national minorities. It is astonishing that this fact was legally recognized in 'European' international law during the period of the League of Nations but that it was ignored in international law as it emerged after the Second World War. Those who shaped the principles and institu-

---

And in so far as he is normally 'adapted' to his environment, it is true that the greatest infamy on the part of his group will not disturb him, so long as the majority fellows steadfastly believe in the exalted morality of their social organization. Now, all that I have said here about the influence of society upon the individual is identically true of the influence of the collective unconscious upon the individual psyche, But, as is apparent from my examples, the latter influence is as invisible as the former is visible.

See also, as a glimpse to the present-day scene, Jean Rufin, *Le piège humanitaire* (1986) 362:

Dans un monde où ces appuis extérieurs ont disparu, la prime revient aux mouvements qui ont très tôt constitué des structures fermées, totalitaires et criminalisées leur permettant de survivre en situation d'isolement.

[5] Daniel Thürer, Matthias Herdegen and Gerhard Hohloch, *Der Wegfall effektiver Staatsgewalt: 'The Failed State'*, (Berichte der Deutschen Gesellschaft für Völkerrecht, 1995) vol 34.

tions of our post-war international community failed to appreciate that our State societies consist not only of anonymous aggregates of individuals – men, women and children, workers and employers etc – each endorsed with civil and political, social, economic and cultural rights, but that human societies have, in large parts of the world, a highly heterogeneous, pluralistic and diverse character. They are composed of and shaped by national, linguistic, religious and other groups with their own common history, cultural identity, collective consciousness and wishes for their future.

In 1948 national minorities were not mentioned in the Universal Declaration of Human Rights.[6] The Founding Fathers of the present-day international legal order were inspired by the model of liberalism incorporated in the constitution of the United States and other immigration countries. In the light of this philosophy a just and fair society was to be based on two concepts: personal liberty and the equal protection of all under the law. Accordingly, Article 27 of the International Covenant on Civil and Political Rights states:

> In those states in which ethnic, religious or linguistic minorities exist, persons belonging to such minorities shall not be denied the right, in community with other members of their group, to enjoy their own culture, to profess and practice their own religion, and to use their own language.[7]

This provision which, to date, is legally binding on 144 States is the broadest and most widely recognized rule in modern international law concerning the protection of minorities.[8]

---

[6] GA Res 217A, 3 UN GAOR (183rd plen mtg), UN Doc A/Res/217A (1948).

[7] *International Covenant on Civil and Political Rights*, opened for signature 19 December 1966, 999 UNTS 171, 6 ILM 368 (entered into force 23 March 1976) ('*ICCPR*'). As at 17 March 1999, there were 144 States Parties.

[8] The literature concerning the protection of minorities is growing rapidly. See, eg, Russel Barsh, 'The United Nations and the Protection of Minorities' (1989) 58 *Nordic Journal of International Law* 188; Catherine Bröhlmann, René Lefeber, and Marjoeline Zieck (eds), *Peoples and Minorities* (1993); Francesco Capotorti, *Study on the Rights of Persons Belonging to Ethnic, Religious and Linguistic Minorities* (1991); Antonio Cassese, *Self-Determination of Peoples* (1995); Antonio Cassese, 'The Self-Determination of Peoples' in Louis Henkin (ed), *The International Bill of Rights* (1981) 98; Yoran Dinstein, 'Collective Human Rights of Peoples and Minorities' (1976) 25 *The International and Comparative Law Quarterly* 102; Felix Ermacora, 'The Protection of Minorities before the United Nations' (1982) 4 *Recueil des Cours de l'Académie de droit international* 247; Jochen Abr. Frowein, Rainer Hofmann, and Stefan Oeter (eds), *Das Minderheitenrecht europäischer Staaten* (1993); Konrad Ginther, 'Intermediary Groups and Parallel Structures: International Legal Aspects of Developing Constitutional Orders in Sub-Saharan Africa' [1989] *Third World Legal Studies* 85; Hurst Hannum, *Autonomy, Sovereignty, and Self-Determination - The Accomodation of Conflicting Rights* (1990); Christoph Gusy, 'Von der Selbstbestimmung durch den Staat zur Selbstbestimmung im Staat' (1992) 30 *Archiv des Völkerrechts* 385; Rainer Hofmann, 'Minderheitenschutz in Europa – Überblick über die völker- und

Efforts to work out further standards have ultimately led to some notable developments. In December 1992 the General Assembly of the United Nations adopted the Declaration on the Rights of Persons Belonging to National or Ethnic, Religious and Linguistic Minorities.[9] This document embraces in a somewhat loose and vague form the idea that national minorities should be given a right to effective participation in State decision-making, but on the whole it does not carry the concept of minority protection much further than is already provided for in Article 27 of the ICCPR.[10] It should be added that, on the global plane, the International Labour Organisation (ILO) Convention 169 concerning Indigenous and Tribal Peoples in Independent Countries contains provisions clearly pointing in the direction of special protections for (minority) groups.[11]

---

staatsrechtliche Lage' (1992) 52 *Zeitschrift für ausländisches öffentliches Recht und Völkerrecht* 1; Otto Kimminich, 'Aufsätze für ein europäisches Volksgruppenrecht' (1991) 28 *Archiv des Völkerrechts* 1; Peter Kustor, 'Die Neuordnung Europas und das Selbstbestimmungsrecht der Völker' (1997) *Humanitäres Völkerrecht* 27; Nathan Lerner, *Group Rights and Discrimination in International Law* (1991); Joseph Marko, *Minderheitenschutz im östlichen Europa* (1996); Peter Pernthaler, *Allgemeine Staatslehre und Verfassungslehre* (2nd ed, 1996); Peter Pernthaler and Sergio Ortino, *Europaregion Tirol – Euregio Tirolo* (1997); Juha Räikkä (ed), *Do We Need Minority Rights? Conceptual Issues* (1996); Wolfgang Seifert, *Selbstbestimmungsrecht und deutsche Vereinigung* (1992); Louis Sohn, 'The Rights of Minorities' in Louis Henkin (ed), *The International Bill of Rights* (1981) 270; Henry Steiner, 'Ideals and Counter-Ideals in the Struggle over Autonomy Regimes for Minorities' (1991) 66 *Notre Dame Law Review* 153; Patrich Thornberry, *International Law and the Rights of Minorities* (1991); Daniel Thürer, 'Das Selbstbestimmungsrecht der Völker und die Anerkennung neuer Staaten' in Hanspeter Neuhold and Bruno Simma (eds), *Neues Europäisches Völkerrecht nach dem Ende des Ost-West-Konflikts?* (1996) 13; Daniel Thürer, 'Entwicklung, Inhalt und Träger des Selbstbestimmungsrecht', in Erich Reiter (ed), *Grenzen des Selbstbestimmungsrechts: die Neuordnung Europas und das Selbstbestimmungsrecht der Völker* (1996) 34; Daniel Thürer, 'Region und Minderheitenschutz – Aufbauelemente einer europäischen Architektur', in Ulrich Beyerlin, Rainer Hofmann and Ernst Ulrich Petersmann (ed), *Festschrift für Rudolf Bernhardt* (1995) 1337; Daniel Thürer, 'The Right of Self-determination of Peoples', in (1987) 35 *Law and State* 22; Christain Tomuschat (ed), *Modern Law of Self-Determination* (1993); Christian Tomuschat, 'Protection of Minorities under Article 27 of the International Covenant on Civil and Political Rights' in Rudolf Bernhardt et al, *Völkerrecht als Rechtsordnung, internationale Gerichtsbarkeit, Menschen: Festschrift für Hermann Mosler* (1983) 949; Christian Tomuschat, 'Menschenrechte und Minderheitenschutz' in Hanspeter Neuhold and Bruno Simma (eds), *Neues Europäisches Völkerrecht nach dem Ende des Ost-West-Konflikts?* (1996) 89; Vernon van Dyke, *Human Rights, Ethnicity and Discrimination* (1985); Ben Whitaker (ed), *Minorities – A Question of Human Rights?* (1984).

[9] GA Res 47/135, 18 December 1992, 47 UN GAOR Supp (N0 49) 210, UN Doc A/Res/47/135(1993).

[10] See, Christian Tomuschat, 'Self-Determination in a Post-Colonial World' in Christian Tomuschat (ed), *Modern Law of Self-Determination* (1993) 11.

[11] *Convention Concerning Indigenous and Tribal Peoples in Independent Countries*, opened for signature 27 June 1989, 28 ILM 1382, (entered into force 5 September 1991). See also Gudmundur Alfredsson, 'The Right to Self-Determination and Indigenous Peoples' in Christian Tomuschat (ed), *Modern Law of Self-Determination* (1993) 41.

Within the European framework, the Conference on Security and Co-operation in Europe (CSCE) has on several occasions dealt with the issue of minorities. The document adopted by the Conference on the Human Dimension in Copenhagen in 1990 is especially relevant in that weight is given to the concept of autonomy.[12] The CSCE (now the OSCE) also created the office of a High Commissioner on National Minorities at the Helsinki Summit in 1992. On 10 November 1994 the Committee of Minis-ters of the Council of Europe adopted a Framework Convention for the Protection of National Minorities, which came into effect on 1 February 1998.[13]

Globally, the regime provided for in public international law concerning the protection of minorities remains based on the two basic elements just mentioned:

1. the individual rights of persons belonging to minorities as defined in the Covenant; and
2. the principle of non-discrimination.

It is important to add that the principle of non-discrimination – so at least it seems to the present author[14] – is a concept broad enough to also embrace affirmative measures: that is, special actions taken to advance the rights of a category of persons disadvantaged or repressed in order to ensure equal treatment or to redress imbalances caused by past practices.[15]

2.2 Institutions in Need of Evolution: Designs for New Concepts

Existing general international law is – as we have stated – in its essence 'minority blind'. But does the concept of individual-based liberalism satisfy the needs and aspirations of modern international society as we see it and experience it in today's political reality? Should not, under certain specific conditions and in special contexts, minority group rights be recog-nized and worked out in detail?

As far as the realities of modern societies are concerned, since the end of the Cold War we have again become more aware of the fact that the popu-lations of most countries in Europe, Asia and Africa, but also in other parts of the world have no homogeneous ethnic structures, but are composed of

---

[12] For the texts of all CSCE documents see Arie Bloed (ed) *The Conference on Security and Co-operation in Europe: Analysis and Basic Documents, 1972-1993* (1993).

[13] *Framework Convention for the Protection of National Minorities*, opened for signature 1 February 1995 (entered into force 1 February 1998). As at 28 October 1998, there were 37 States Parties. See also Giorgio Malinverni, 'La Convention-cadre du Conseil de l'Europe pour la protection des minorités nationales' (1995) 5 *Revue suisse de droit international et de droit européen* 521.

[14] See Daniel Thürer, 'National Minorities: A Global, European and Swiss Perspective' (1995) 19 *The Fletcher Forum of World Affairs* 13.

[15] See, on the whole topic, Manfred Novak, *UN Covenant on Civil and Political Rights – CCPR Commentary* (1993) Article 27.

many diverse groups and peoples with their own character and self-consciousness and their own specific, often conflicting goals, aims and projects, i.e. collectives which have – to quote Jean-Jacques Rousseau – their own *sentiment de l'existence*.

In the sense of a *déjà vu* the world of Versailles and the following inter-war period seem somehow to be re-emerging on the global level.[16] Domestic law systems and international law should not ignore this newly visible reality, if justice and peace in our highly pluralistic global society are to be preserved and safeguarded in the long term.

On the internal plane, notice should be taken of the fact that the old-established 'Westminster model' of constitutional law and the radical democratic concept of 'winner-takes-all-majoritarianism' are not necessarily the ideal system for all countries. More participative 'federalistic' and consensus-oriented models of constitutional structure seem better suited to do justice to the legitimate desires of special groups and peoples to preserve their existence and to maintain, develop and enrich their identity. The principles of human dignity which should be considered the source of legitimacy for all law seem to demand, for many societies, more flexible constitutional structures.

On the level of international law, although the principle of sovereignty of States as well as, to a certain extent, human rights and the principle of non-discrimination are cornerstones of the system, I think that the development of the concept of autonomy and participation for groups and peoples within States should be pursued by the international community in the future.[17] First steps might be undertaken on a bilateral or multilateral basis, further steps within a regional framework such as the Organization of Security and Cooperation in Europe and final steps worldwide.

The concept of autonomy and participation understood in a very broad and flexible way should be taken seriously as emanating from the principle of internal self-determination as well as of human dignity. It might help to prevent secession and thus be a factor of stability and peace in international relations. Of course, human rights in their classical sense should remain the ultimate yardstick by which to judge minority claims. In no case should self-determination serve as a pretext for ethno-nationalism in its exclusive sense (arbitrary restrictions on citizenship, deportations, etc.) or in its inclusive sense (forced assimilation). Only the ideals of 'citizen-nationalism' as opposed to 'ethno-nationalism' are able to safeguard sta-

---

[16] See Koskenniemi, above n 3, 243, 257; Nathaniel Berman, ' "But the Alternative is Despair": European Nationalism and the Modernist Renewal of International Law' (1993) 106 *Harvard Law Review* 1793.

[17] See Antonio Cassese, *Self-Determination of Peoples* (1995) 348; Hurst Hannum, above n 8; Yoram Dinstein (ed), *Models of Autonomy* (1981); Daniel Thürer, 'Self-determination' in Rudolf Bernhardt (ed), *Encyclopedia of Public International Law* (2nd ed, 1998).

bility and to turn cultural and ethnic diversity into a rich political and cultural dialogue.[18]

3. STATUS OF MINORITIES IN INTERNATIONAL HUMANITARIAN LAW

3.1 *The Law as it Stands*

3.1.1 *Factual Situation*

We know that nowadays most armed conflicts take place within States and are due to tensions arising from minority problems and ethnic or nationalistic claims.[19] Their aim is often to displace or even exterminate sections of the population. Even if the problems faced by minorities are not a new phenomenon, they are particularly striking in today's world.

Increasingly, minorities come under pressure and lose protection in situations where State structures have broken down in chaos and anarchy. Conflicts of this type result in large-scale civilian deaths and injuries, extensive damage to healthcare and education systems and substantial movements of refugees and displaced persons. Minority groups are particularly vulnerable in such situations, where even the usual levels of tolerance or specific supportive or protective measures are under strain, abandoned or even turned against particular groups. In addition, forced population movements may generate new minorities and yet new conflicts. Tensions between different groups may escalate into armed conflicts and armed conflicts may, in turn, have direct consequences for a minority. Sri

---

[18] See Asbjørn Eide, 'Ethno-Nationalism and Minority Protection: For Institutional Reforms' in Jean Marie Becet and Karel Vask (eds), *The Reform of International Institutions for the Protection of Human Rights* (1993) 130.

[19] See Keynote Address by Mr Cornelio Sommaruga, President of the ICRC, at the XXI International Conference of the Red Cross and Red Crescent, 'Humanitarian Challenges on the Threshold of the Twenty First Century: Keynote Address' (1996) 310 *International Review of the Red Cross* 20, 23–4:

> in many of the new conflicts that have broken out since the end of the Cold War there has been an upsurge in predatory and lawless behaviour, and *war and banditry have become inextricably linked*. Until recently, in situations where a government was pitted against a rebel movement, both sides usually had structured and organised armed forces pursuing identifiable ideologies and goals and more or less coherent military objectives. Today we are faced with quite different situations, in which the '*belligerents*' are often very young and poorly organized. While the ideologies and objectives involved in many conflicts are generally difficult to define, at first glance it would seem that the chief aim is to *destroy the other side*, whether for racial, religious, nationalistic or economic reasons. Front lines no longer exist, and the *traditional and vital distinction between combatants and non-combatants*, which is the very cornerstone of humanitarian law, is *all too seldom recognized*.

Lanka, Bosnia-Herzegovina,[20] Burundi and Rwanda, Afghanistan, the Kurds and other cases of acute or 'frozen' conflicts could be quoted as examples.

How does international humanitarian law deal with this type of situation? It is, after all, fundamentally challenged as its aim is to prevent and mitigate suffering in armed conflict.

3.1.2 *The Applicable Principles and Rules*

International humanitarian law contains two sets of rules, the first being applicable in international armed conflicts[21] and the second in non-international armed conflicts.[22] As a matter of fact, the legal regime concerning internal armed conflict[23] stands at the forefront. It is laid down in Article 3 common to the four Geneva Conventions of 1949 and, with an elevated threshold of application and a more detailed set of rules, in Additional Protocol II. Common Article 3 of the four Geneva Conventions constitutes, according to the decision of the International Court of Justice in the *Nicaragua Case*,[24] the 'minimum yardstick' that is applicable in all armed conflicts. It embraces, so to speak, in a compressed and crystallized form the essence of the rules of international humanitarian law that had originally been elaborated not for civil wars, but for international wars in the classical sense. Common Article 3 reads as follows:

> Persons taking no active part in the hostilities, including members of armed forces who have laid down their arms and those placed *hors de combat* by sickness, wounds, detention, or any other cause, shall in all circumstances be treated humanely, without any adverse distinction

---

[20] See Yves Sandoz, 'Réflexions sur la mise en oeuvre du droit international humanitaire et sur le rôle du Comité international de la Croix-Rouge en ex-Yugoslavie' (1993) 3 *Revue suisse de droit international et de droit européen* 461.

[21] See *Geneva Convention for the Amelioration of the Condition of the Wounded and the Sick in Armed Forces in the Field*, 75 UNTS 31 (*'First Geneva Convention'*); *Geneva Convention for the Amelioration of the Condition of Wounded, Sick and Shipwrecked Members of Armed Forces at Sea*, 75 UNTS 85 (*'Second Geneva Convention'*); *Geneva Convention Relative to the Treatment of Prisoners of War*, 75 UNTS 135 (*'Third Geneva Convention'*); *Geneva Convention Relative to the Protection of Civilian Persons in Time of War*, 75 UNTS 287 (*'Fourth Geneva Convention'*). All these Conventions entered into force on 21 October 1950, and as at 17 March 1999, there were 188 States Parties.

[22] See *Protocol Additional to the Geneva Convention of 12 August 1949, and Relating to the Protection of Victims of International Armed Conflict*, 1125 UNTS 3; 16 ILM 1391 (entered into force 7 December 1978) (*'Additional Protocol I'*). As at 17 March 1999, there were 153 States Parties. See also *Protocol Additional to the Geneva Convention of 12 August 1949, and Relating to the Protection of Victims of Non-International Armed Conflicts*, 1125 UNTS 609; 16 ILM 1442 (entered into force on 7 December 1978) (*'Additional Protocol II'*). As at 17 March 1999, there were 145 State Parties.

[23] On this topic, see Hans-Peter Gasser, 'International Humanitarian Law – An Introduction', in Haug, above n 1, 66.

[24] *Military and Paramilitary Activities in and against Nicaragua (Nicaragua v US) (Merits)* [1986] ICJ Rep 14, [218] (*'Nicaragua Case'*).

founded on race, colour, religion or faith, sex, birth or wealth, or any other similar criteria.

International humanitarian law is, as indicated in Common Article 3 and elaborated in detail in a corpus of principles and rules applicable in international armed conflict, made up of two main normative elements: (1) specific obligations to protect and assist certain categories of victims of war as well as, in a more limited sense, the corresponding rights of those victims; and (2) a general principle of non-discrimination.[25] Both types of material rules are ultimately entrenched in the basic ideal and legal recognition of human dignity inherent in the concept of the rule of law as such. With these basic values proclaimed and elaborated on by the Red Cross Movement from its inception in 1864,[26] international humanitarian law anticipated the structural framework of human rights which, in its essence, has only taken shape on the international plane since the Second World War.[27]

The picture of humanitarian law which I am trying to sketch would not be complete and its specific way of functioning could not be adequately understood, if the institutional mechanisms and procedures were not mentioned which – as the reverse side of the material rules and principles – are designed to implement them. A key element, which is thereby provided for in international humanitarian law, is the principle of impartiality. The attitude of impartiality is considered constitutive for any truly humanitarian actor and action. Accordingly, reference is made in various provisions of the Conventions and Protocols to an 'impartial humanitarian body', such as the International Committee of the Red Cross.[28] In addition, several formal rules, which embody the institutional or procedural setting of humanitarian

---

[25] See, eg, First and Second Geneva Conventions, art 12, Third Geneva Convention, art 16 or Additional Protocol I, art 10 paragraph 2 and art 75 paragraph 1.

[26] The First Geneva Convention of 1864, *Convention for the Amelioration of the Condition of the Wounded in Armies in the Field,* opened for signature 22 August 1864, 55 BSFP 43; (1907) 1 *American Journal of International Law (Supp)* 90 (entered into force 22 June 1865): this Convention laid down that 'wounded or sick combatants, to whatever nation they may belong, shall be collected and cared for.' On the origins and developments of the Red Cross see François Bugnion, *Le Comité International de la Croix-Rouge et la Protection des Victimes de la guerre* (1994) 31; Pierre Boissier, *History of the International Committee of the Red Cross* (1985).

[27] Authors dealing with non-discrimination on a general basis mistakenly fail to refer to this early origin of the principle. See, eg, Wilhelm Kewenig, *Der Grundsatz der Nichtdiskriminierung im Völkerrecht der internationalen Handelsbeziehungen: Band 1, Der Begriff der Diskriminierung* (1972). On the whole topic see also, Günther Jaenicke, 'Diskriminierung' in Hans-Jürgen Schlochauer (ed), *Wörterbuch des Völkerrechts* (1960) 387.

[28] Such a reference can be found in the Common arts 9 of the first three Geneva Conventions and art 10 of the Fourth Geneva Convention, which deal with the activities of the ICRC in situations of international armed conflicts, and in Common art 3 of the four Geneva Conventions for non-international armed conflicts.

action, are laid down in the Seven Fundamental Principles of 1965/86 of the International Red Cross and Red Crescent Movement, of which the most important are independence, neutrality and impartiality.[29] They constitute the essential, inherent preconditions of humanitarian action. Impartiality is at the heart of the problem we are dealing with. This criterion has been underlined by the International Court of Justice as an essential component of any truly humanitarian action.[30] Jean Pictet illustrates its content in the following anecdote:

> At the end of the Second World War, a column of soldiers reconquering their own country came to a small town. The commander of the unit approached the woman in charge of the hospital and told her that he had a number of wounded men to leave at the hospital. She told him that the hospital was already full of enemy wounded. 'Put them out then and make room for our own men', the officer said. 'Over my dead body' she replied, and he realized that she really meant it as she stood barring the doorway. For a moment, the officer was nonplussed, and then he realized the truth – that enemies who had been wounded were no longer enemies – and ordered his unit to move on.[31]

A warning is appropriate in this context. Quite often, the principle of proportionality[32] is, explicitly or implicitly, invoked as forming a component element of the concept of impartiality. Assistance should be given, so it is said, according to the degree and urgency of need. However, this element seems to be inherent already in the principle of non-discrimination (or, expressed positively, in the principle of equality)[33] which does not claim *idem cuique* but *suum cuique*.[34] The same applies for the principle of impartiality. Certainly, we read in the ICRC-Commentary:

> It should be noted that the new Geneva Conventions only prohibit adverse distinctions: this is reasonable, since there are legitimate distinctions, even distinctions which must be made, such as those, in fact,

---

[29] See Haug, above n 1, 443; Dietrich Schindler, 'Die Neutralität des Roten Kreuzes' in Jürgen Jekewitz, *Des Menschen Recht zwischen Freiheit und Verantwortung: Festschrift für Karl Joseph Partsch zum 75. Geburtstag* (1989) 141; Marion Harroff-Tavel, 'Neutrality and Impartiality' (1989) 71 *Revue Internationale de la Croix-Rouge* 563; Frits Kalshoven, 'Impartiality and Neutrality in Humanitarian Law and Practice' (1989) 71 *Revue Internationale de la Croix-Rouge* 541.

[30] Nicaragua Case, above n 24, [243].

[31] Jean Pictet, *The Fundamental Principles of the Red Cross Proclaimed by the Twentieth International Conference on the Red Cross, Vienna, 1965 - Commentary by Jean Pictet* (1979) 37–8.

[32] On this topic see Jost Delbrück, 'Proportionality' in Rudolf Bernhardt (ed), vol 7 *Encyclopedia of Public International Law* (1984), 396; Peter Lerche, *Übermass und Verfassungsrecht* (1961).

[33] See Dietrich Schindler, *Gleichberechtigung von Individuen als Problem des Völkerrechts* (1957).

[34] Kewenig, above n 27, 43.

which are based on suffering, distress, or the weakness of the protected person. It is in this sphere that the Red Cross tries to assist suffering man in his distress. The Conference did not therefore prohibit distinctions in treatment, intended to take into account, for example, a person's age, state of health or sex. It is normal and natural to favour children, old people and women; the Geneva Conventions expressly stipulate that women are to be treated with all respect due to their sex.[35]

However, privileging those in need which is called for in international humanitarian law and Red Cross doctrine does not mean stating exceptions or modifications of the principle of non-discrimination. What is at stake is rather an emanation and an application of this principle. It would, so it seems to me, be dangerous to introduce the principle of proportionality into international humanitarian law, at least in the form adopted within the system of limitations set in the concept of human rights. This would suggest a meaning which might considerably water down core elements of international humanitarian law, unduly restrict their application and render them unclear or even inoperative.

3.1.3 *Relevance and Application Toward Minorities*

International humanitarian law does not offer specific protection to minorities as such though it does apply in conflict situations when minorities are under particular pressure. This set of rules does not refer to minorities as a group but to persons protected because of their status as victims of a conflict. It only deals implicitly with minorities insofar as they fall into this last category. The term minority is excluded from the language of international humanitarian law. Minority problems do not constitute a relevant phenomenon for international humanitarian law, except in situations of specific victimization.

In any case, given that the field of application of international humanitarian law is in essence related to situations of armed conflict and hence limited in time and scope (thresholds of applicability as well as geographical scope), this part of international law does not appear to be the most appropriate channel to deal with minority questions because, taken as a whole, they usually cover extremely long periods of time and stretch over entire regions. However, international humanitarian law still has a role to play and not only by the mere fact that it aims to channel and restrain violence in times of armed conflict. As we have already stressed, the fact that a minority group can be rendered particularly vulnerable and thus constitutes a victimized group, means that its members might thereby fall under the protection afforded by international humanitarian law.

---

[35] Jean Pictet (ed), *The Geneva Conventions of 12 August 1949 – Commentary on the IV Geneva Convention Relative to the Protection of Civilian Persons in Times of War* (Ronald Griffin and C W Dumbleton trans, 1958) 119, art 13.

Non-discrimination and impartiality are the guiding principles for humanitarian action, which – by way of indirection – may be a valuable means for the protection of minorities. Thus, when the ICRC visits detainees in a prison it does not distinguish between the detainees of one ethnic group or another in its approaches to the authorities. Its concern has, as such, nothing to do with their membership of a specific ethnic group but only with their sufferings as human beings. Furthermore, the ICRC has a duty to oppose discrimination in connection with its prison visits. It will request access to all detainees and call on the detaining authorities to give humane treatment to all. None of them should suffer additional hardship or be placed at any kind of disadvantage for reasons of nationality, cultural or ethnic identity or religious or political convictions.[36]

The realities of contemporary conflicts, however, where the victims are so very numerous, sometimes make it impossible to maintain this individual approach. Membership of a minority can then be a criterion for determining the population group that is especially vulnerable in any given place. To put the impartiality principle into practice in situations of armed conflict might thus, in practice, be a very difficult task. It is sometimes nearly impossible to assess objectively the relative needs of the different victims. The task to truly apply the principle of impartiality is also complicated by the fact that in several cases of civil war one party to the conflict (ie the incumbent government) objects to assistance being given to its 'enemy' (eg the rebels), or aid is earmarked or directed by donors to favor one party only.

As far as the International Red Cross and Red Crescent Movement are concerned, they are acting in both conflict and peace situations. In both areas its actions are to be guided, *inter alia*, by the principle of impartiality which means providing assistance on the basis of need without discrimination on religious, ethnic, political or similar grounds. However, needs of minority groups may not be the same as those of other groups and impartiality may dictate that greater help is given to those whose vulnerability is greater. Specific programs may thus need to be carried out in favor of certain groups so that humanitarian action complies with the principle of impartiality. A minority will thereby – to be sure – be favored only insofar as it is more vulnerable, which is not always the case.

---

[36] On this topic see Jacques Moreillon, *Le Comité International de la Croix-Rouge et la protection des détenus politiques* (1973); Christian Dominicé, 'La personnalité juridique internationale du CICR' in Christophe Swinarski (ed), *Studies and Essays on International Humanitarian Law and Red Cross Principles in Honour of Jean Pictet* (1984) 663; Paul Reuter, 'La personnalité juridique internationale du Comité international de la Croix-Rouge' in Christophe Swinarski (ed), *Studies and Essays on International Humanitarian Law and Red Cross Principles in Honour of Jean Pictet* (1984) 783; John Barberis, 'El Comité Internacional de la Cruz Roja como sujeto del Derecho de gentes' in Christophe Swinarski (ed), *Studies and Essays on International Humanitarian Law and Red Cross Principles in Honour of Jean Pictet* (1984) 635.

Having said that, if a minority is subjected to discrimination, it is normal for the Red Cross or Red Crescent to give that community extra support. Such preferential treatment is not considered discriminatory any more, for example, than an aid program for female refugees would be once they had been identified as a particularly vulnerable group in a given situation. It should finally be mentioned that in some cases identifying someone as a member of a minority group might create prejudice for him or her. A minority will therefore be identified as such by the Red Cross or Red Crescent only if to do so is in that minority's interests or necessary for practical reasons and will entail no negative consequences.

3.2 *A Continuum with Elements in Need of Preservation and Adaptation*

What are the conclusions to be drawn for the further development of international humanitarian law?

I think that international humanitarian law will and should only be marginally touched by the course of (institutional) development as is, in this article, considered desirable for the protection of minorities in general international law. To be more exact, a general distinction should be made between crisis or emergency situations in the traditional sense on the one hand, and conflict evolution, as it might be observed from a longer term perspective, in a grey zone between war and peace in the present-day context on the other hand. As far as the rules applicable in crisis situations in armed conflicts are concerned, the principles of independence, neutrality and impartiality prohibit the consideration of minorities or the fact that a person belongs to a minority being used as a category or as a criterion in its own right. Crisis rules are supposed to be clear-cut and practicable. Whereas ambiguity and richness of meaning may be helpful as a potential in developing social structures, only simple, workable rules are capable of guiding and directing actors under the pressure of taking operative decisions. In this sense, individual victims and their special needs is the primary point of reference for humanitarian action. However, the identification of categories of persons, including the fact that they belong to a particular group may – as a *prima facie* consideration – in practice help to target humanitarian action and to make it more effective.

The other broader perspective is that it seems, at present, to be more and more appropriate to conceive of international humanitarian law and the principles of humanitarian action as a system of norms to be applied along the lines of a long-term continuum. The traditional types of conflicts such as international or civil wars or other major disasters are now, in modern reality, preceded by a multitude of ubiquitous, spontaneous, unpredictable and discontinuous eruptions of violence which seem to dictate a broader approach in theory and doctrine as well as in practice. Various phases of conflict evolution may be distinguished along the axis of time: (1) situations of unstable peace; (2) internal tensions characterized by systematic and serious violations of human rights, but lacking widespread acts of violence; (3) crisis and armed violence as well as unresolved (frozen) conflicts; and (4) post-conflict rehabilitation. The further we move – so it seems – from the actual crisis and the urgency of action, the more admissible or even desirable it seems to refer to and to take into consideration peace law concepts such as human rights and principles of minority protection. At the pre-conflict and post-conflict 'fringe' of the 'continuum', humanitarian and human rights law seem to come together.

To be sure, it cannot be the purpose of humanitarian law or be part of the mandate of humanitarian actors to contribute to the development of concepts of group protection and integration. However, a special consideration of minority concerns might be legitimate in so far as it contributes to maintaining or reestablishing stability and peace in the long run. With this goal in mind it may well be legitimate, in a future-oriented strategy, to give special attention to, and to develop special programs for the assistance, education and protection of certain groups.[37] It will thereby not be the task of humanitarian actors to design institutional structures for the harmonious cohabitation of groups in a pluralistic society or to elaborate programs and schemes of affirmative action. But the principle of impartiality can, so it seems to me, be applied in a more relaxed, flexible and pragmatic way inasmuch as humanitarian action is removed from the scene of crisis and the imperatives of urgent decision-making.[38]

Seen from this perspective, it seems natural that National Red Cross or Red Crescent Societies take preventive action regarding minorities if they constitute potentially vulnerable groups in a specific context. Peacetime educational programs that seek to promote values such as tolerance among cultural, social or political groups might well benefit minorities. National Societies contribute to this process by actively encouraging participation from all groups in the population and by promoting intercultural exchange. In this sense the problems concerning minorities are a matter of concern for the International Red Cross and Red Crescent Movement as a whole.

Thus, wherever and whenever international humanitarian law and humanitarian action reach out into the field of conflict prevention, the protection of minorities may evolve as a valuable concept full of potential. On

---

[37] Examples may be found in programs developed in South Africa in the 1980s to overcome racial discrimination or, at present, in Central Europe in order to promote mutual understanding among ethnic groups.

[38] An example might be found in the activities the Movement has developed for the prevention of ethnic conflicts by addressing issues relating to the identity and security of members of minority groups. The Movement tries to work against threats to the cultural or physical existence of an ethnic or other minority group (such as forced assimilation, discrimination, repression or isolation) before communication breaks down. Special (community) programs by national societies at government level to promote minorities and foster tolerance among groups should also be mentioned. They should not be considered contradictory to the principle of impartiality.

the horizon, to use a metaphor of the German philosopher Gadamer, we may observe two worlds coming together and being fused into one.

4. CONCLUSION: THE TWO WORLDS RECONSIDERED

Two basic questions may be raised in concluding this essay. First: What observations might be made concerning the relationship between human rights law and humanitarian law as the basic concepts of international law underlying our analysis? And second: Might any conclusion be drawn from the above concerning the capacity of international law to contain and to channel the eruptive forces of nationalism as well as to design and develop workable, sustainable solutions? Our focus on the protection of minorities might well serve as a catalyst revealing answers to both these questions.

4.1 *Human Rights Law and Humanitarian Law*

As we know, there are three possible ways of conceiving the relationship between human rights law and humanitarian law. Human rights may be considered, as once suggested by Jean Pictet,[39] as a branch of humanitarian law understood in the sense of a broad, overarching normative concept; or international humanitarian law might, according to an opposite view widely shared within the United Nations, be described as human rights law applicable in armed conflict; finally, an intermediary and – so it seems – dominant view holds that human rights and humanitarian law represent separate, but largely overlapping systems of regulation.[40] Our analysis seems to confirm the correctness of the third model of perception. Despite the growing measure of interrelationship between both spheres of law there are important divergences. Not only does international humanitarian law possess a much longer tradition comprising, from its very inception, the concepts of human dignity and nondiscrimination (equality) which only many decades later emerged as the basic, constitutive elements of human rights. More importantly, as is made clear by the challenges implied by the

---

[39] Jean Pictet, asserts thus: 'International Humanitarian Law, in the broadest sense, is constituted by all the international legal provisions, whether of statute or common law, ensuring respect for the individual and promoting his development': *Humanitarian Law and the Protection of Victims of War* (1975) 13.

[40] See Theodor Meron, *Human Rights and Humanitarian Norms as Customary Law* (1989); Jean Pictet, *Development and Principles of Humanitarian International Law* (1985) 89ff; Cornelio Sommaruga, *Menschenrechte in bewaffneten Konflikten* (1995); Frits Kalshoven, *Constraints on the Waging of War* (1987) 77ff; Dietrich Schindler, 'Kriegsrecht und Menschenrechte', in Ulrich Häfelin, Walter Haller, and Dietrich Schindler, *Menschenrechte, Föderalismus, Demokratie: Festschrift zum 70. Geburtstag von Werner Kägi* (1979) 327; Louise Doswald-Beck and Silvain Vité, 'Le droit international humanitaire et le droit des droits de l'homme' (1993) 293 *Revue Internationale de la Croix-Rouge* 97.

problems of minorities protection, both branches of international law are certainly directed, in the final analysis, towards the same goals, but still serve inherently different functions. Both legal regimes are, as far as the protection of minorities is concerned, supposed to take on a different shape and to develop at varying speeds so as, in combination, to best serve stability and justice as the ultimate goals of the international legal order.

4.2 *Guiding Capacity of International Law?*

This last point is only phrased as a question. It is concerned with the basic phenomenon encountered in many minority conflicts such as evidenced in former Yugoslavia: that human nature seems to be psychologically structured so as to make possible almost instantaneous changes of vision, outlook, lifestyle, loyalties and alliances among individuals and groups.[41] The good neighbor of today may become, overnight, the enemy of tomorrow. Ambiguity, divergence or clashing identities within individuals might, set off by spectacular outside events and re-enforced by propaganda, contain the seeds for unexpected divisions of societies and eruptions of violence. Does law – this is our question – have the capacity to contain or to channel such events? Does the idea or concept of law as such have the potential to shape the collective imagination and aspirations of a community whilst maintaining its pursuit of order and justice? Are, and to what extent are, stable institutions and expectations of certainty which are inherent in the concept of rule of law capable of directing deep-rooted patterns of human behavior? To what extent can (international) law contribute to find, experiment with and implement workable solutions to resolve challenges of passion and identity as discussed in this article?[42]

It would be presumptuous to try to give an answer. But one fact seems to be, after all, quite remarkable: In the midst of conflict, and just because of the basic and simple values flowing from the ideals of human dignity and equality, international humanitarian law is proving itself to be a positive and motivating force. And: humanitarian institutions such as the ICRC are effective only because, in their essence and as their *raison d'être*, they are devoted exclusively to safeguarding a minimum of humanity and justice in situations where these values are most endangered. To be sure, there are other factors such as operational efficiency and effectiveness which are indispensable elements of humanitarian action and which are perhaps the

---

[41] Nathaniel Berman, 'A Perilous Ambivalence: Nationalist Desire, Legal Autonomy, and the Limits of the Interwar Framework' (1992) 33 *Harvard International Law Journal* 352, 378.

[42] On this whole subject, see Antonio Cassese, *International Law in a Divided World* (1986) 393ff.

main reason for their success.[43] There are, of course, other roads, too, by which justice or at least fragments of this ideal can be realised – for example by international criminal law.[44] However, it is interesting to observe how, in extreme situations such as civil war, where the spirals of hatred, violence and revenge escalate and the climate is emotionally charged with a destructive impulse, the idea of justice nevertheless seems essential as a minimum element and goal of order in a double sense:

1. as a 'substantive' principle of respect for human dignity and equality of human beings;
2. as embodied in the 'formal' principles of independence, neutrality and impartiality which together constitute a 'humanitarian space' and of which impartiality, as a fundamental attitude of humanitarian institutions and the *état d'esprit* of its agents, is of predominant importance.

It seems to be this basic sense of justice fixed in the conscience of human beings and linking them together to which the teaching and promotion of humanitarian law should be directed. The power of values and normative principles of justice should not be underestimated as a directive force of action even though we seem to witness, in our daily observations, more cases of defeat than of success. In any event, these norms are the constitutive factors *par excellence* which render humanitarian law and action as well as their underlying ideas more plausible and understandable and humanitarian institutions more credible and effective.

---

[43] See Jacques Freymond, *Guerres, Révolutions, Croix-Rouge* (1976) 4:

> c'est dans son action sur le terrain que le CICR puise sa légitimité. C'est en fonction du terrain que ses structures, ses méchanismes internes doivent être analysés. Le CICR est né, à Solferino, de la guerre. Il vit dans les guerres et dans les troubles, au milieu des victimes. Il est ce qu'on appelle une institution opérationnelle, et non pas seulement, comme certains le conçoivent, un centre de réflexion.

[44] See Theodor Meron, 'International Criminalization of Internal Atrocities' (1995) 89 *American Journal of International Law* 554; Theodor Meron, 'War Crimes in Yugoslavia and the development of International Law' (1994) 88 *American Journal of International Law* 74. For further sources and references see also Daniel Thürer, 'Vom Nürnberger Tribunal zum Jugoslawien-Tribunal und weiter zu einem Weltstrafgerichtshof?' (1993) 3 *Revue suisse de droit international et de droit européen* 491.

PART III

Controlling the Weapons of War

4. The Relationship Between International Humanitarian Law and Arms Control

1. INTRODUCTION

The notion of legal constraint upon the waging of war is as old as the earliest extant history of the conduct of war. From Sun Tzu's *The Art of War*, written in 5th Century BC (China), throughout every subsequent stage of human history and in every major human civilisation, warriors were subject to specified limitations on the means and methods of warfare and, in many cases, were subject to legal sanction for violations of those limitations.[1] Restrictions on the means and methods of warfare have consistently included prohibitions on, or regulation of, the use of particular weapons. For example, the use of poison and poisoned weapons was prohibited in ancient Hindu law and by the Greeks and Romans,[2] and the use of the arbalest (crossbow) was prohibited by the Lateran Council in the Middle Ages.[3] It is hardly surprising then, that from the early development of the international law of war in the mid-Nineteenth Century, efforts to reach multilateral agreement to regulate the conduct of war would include attempts to prohibit or restrict the use of particular weapons. To this extent, there is a clear correlation between international humanitarian law and arms control.

International humanitarian law is concerned with the legal regulation of the conduct of armed conflict and is limited in its application to the existence of an armed conflict. Consequently, the primary focus in relation to weapons of war has been on their *use* in armed conflict and the regulation

---

[1] See, eg, Geoffrey Best, *Humanity in Warfare* (1980); Christopher Greenwood, 'Historical Development and Legal Basis' in D Fleck (ed), *The Handbook of Humanitarian Law in Armed Conflicts* (1995); Timothy L H McCormack, 'From Sun Tzu to the Sixth Committee: The Evolution of an International Criminal Law Regime' in Timothy LH McCormack and Gerry J Simpson (eds) *The Law of War Crimes: National and International Approaches* (1997) 31.

[2] Joseph Kelly, 'Gas Warfare in International Law' (1960) 9 *Military Law Review* 1, 3-5.

[3] Captain Paul A Roblee, 'The Legitimacy of Modern Conventional Weaponry' (1976) 71 *Military Law Review* 95, 99.

Helen Durham and Timothy L.H. McCormack (eds.), The Changing Face of Conflict and the Efficacy of International Humanitarian Law, 65–98.

has not extended to the use of weapons in circumstances short of armed conflict let alone to their development, possession or transfer in circumstances other than armed conflict. Humanitarian concerns for victims of armed conflict in relation to the deployment of weapons has either involved prohibitions on the use of certain specific weapons or restrictions upon the manner of deployment of other weapons types.[4]

By contrast, the negotiation of arms control and disarmament treaty regimes have been motivated primarily by national and international security concerns and not necessarily by humanitarian concerns. The focus of arms control regimes has ranged from: limiting the stockpiles of a certain weapon type; through reductions in stockpiles to the comprehensive prohibition of weapons types, including prohibitions on the development, production, stockpiling, testing and transfer, as well as the destruction of existing stockpiles, of weapons. Often arms control regimes also include one or more of a range of associated verification or compliance monitoring activities. The scope of application of arms control regimes is, thus, much broader than that for international humanitarian law.

The purpose of this chapter is to examine the relationship between international humanitarian law and the international law of arms control to explore the areas of interaction, to understand the influence of humanitarian principles on the negotiation of arms control regimes and to expose the possible weaknesses inherent in a naïve and exclusive humanitarian approach to the topic of arms control.

2. INTERNATIONAL HUMANITARIAN LAW
AND THE REGULATION OF WEAPONS

International humanitarian law purports to regulate the conduct of armed conflict in two key respects: (1) by imposing minimum standards of protection for victims of armed conflict, whether they be injured combatants, prisoners of war, or civilians who happen to be caught up in the conduct of armed hostility;[5] and (2) by restricting the permissible means and methods

---

[4] These two aspects of the approach of international humanitarian law to specific categories of weapons is captured in the title of the 1980 *Convention on Prohibitions or Restrictions on the Use of Certain Conventional Weapons Which May be Deemed to be Excessively Injurious or to Have Indiscriminate Effects and Protocols I-III,* opened for signature 10 October 1980, 1342 UNTS 137; 19 ILM 1523 (entered into force 2 December 1983) (*'1980 Certain Conventional Weapons Convention'*). As at 17 March 1999, there were 73 States Parties.

[5] So-called 'Geneva Law' because the principal instruments dealing with this aspect of international humanitarian law were negotiated and adopted in Geneva. Most notably, these instruments include the Four Geneva Conventions of 1949: *Geneva Convention for the Amelioration of the Condition of the Wounded and the Sick in Armed Forces in the Field,* 75 UNTS 31 (*'First Geneva Convention'*); *Geneva Convention for the Amelioration of the Condition of Wounded, Sick and Shipwrecked Members of Armed Forces at Sea,* 75 UNTS

of warfare, including the types of weapons that can be deployed, targets that they can be deployed against and limitations on the amount of force used proportionate to the legitimate military necessity.[6] While the popular nomenclature for distinguishing these two aspects of international humanitarian law ('Geneva Law' and 'Hague Law'), on the basis of the city in which the negotiations for the principal relevant instruments took place, is overly simplistic,[7] the distinction itself is valid. In this chapter we are concerned with the second of these two aspects of international humanitarian law – particularly with the regulation of specific weapons types.

---

85 ('*Second Geneva Convention*'); *Geneva Convention Relative to the Treatment of Prisoners of War*, 75 UNTS 135 ('*Third Geneva Convention*'); *Geneva Convention Relative to the Protection of Civilian Persons in Time of War*, 75 UNTS 287 ('*Fourth Geneva Convention*'). All these Conventions entered into force on 21 October 1950, and as at 17 March 1999, there were 188 States Parties. See also the two Additional Protocols of 1977; *Protocol Additional to the Geneva Convention of 12 August 1949, and Relating to the Protection of Victims of International Armed Conflict*, 1125 UNTS 3; 16 ILM 1391 (entered into force 7 December 1978) ('*Additional Protocol I*'), as at 17 March 1999, there were 153 States Parties; and *Protocol Additional to the Geneva Convention of 12 August 1949, and Relating to the Protection of Victims of Non-International Armed Conflicts*, 1125 UNTS 609; 16 ILM 1442 (entered into force on 7 December 1978) ('*Additional Protocal II*'), as at 22 October 1998, there were 145 States Parties. However, these principal instruments were preceded by a succession of other conventions dealing with protection for victims of armed conflict including: the 1864 *Convention for the Amelioration of the Condition of the Wounded in Armies in the Field*, opened for signature 22 August 1864, 55 BSFP 43; (1907) 1 *American Journal of International Law* (*Supp*) 90 (entered into force 22 June 1865); the 1906 *Convention for the Amelioration of the Condition of the Wounded in Armies in the Field*, opened for signature 6 July 1906, GBTS 15 (1907), Cd 3502; (1907) 1 *American Journal of International Law* (*Supp*) 201 (entered into force 9 August 1907) ('*1906 Hague Convention*'); the 1929 *Convention for the Amelioration of the Condition of the Wounded and Sick in Armies in the Field*, opened for signature 27 July 1929, 118 LNTS 303; (1933) 27 *American Journal of International Law* (*Supp*) 43 (entered into force 19 June 1931) ('*1929 Hague Convention*'); and, the 1929 *Convention Relative to the Treatment of Prisoners of War*, opened for signature 27 July 1929, 118 LNTS 343; (1933) 27 *American Journal of International Law* (*Supp* 59)) (entered into force 19 June 1931) ('*1929 POW Convention*').

  [6] So-called 'Hague Law' because the principal instruments regulating the means and methods of warfare are the Declarations and Conventions from the two Hague Peace Conferences of 1899 and 1907: see *Final Act of the International Peace Conference*, opened for signature 29 July 1899, 91 BFSP 963; (1898-1899) 1 *American Journal of International Law* (*Supp*) 103 ('*1899 Final Act*'); *Convention Concerning the Laws and Customs of War on Land*, opened for signature 18 October 1907, 205 CTS 277; (1908) 2 *American Journal of International Law* (*Supp* 90) (entered into force 26 January 1910) ('*1907 Hague Convention IV*'). The Regulations are Annexed to the Convention.

  [7] Louise Doswald-Beck, 'International Humanitarian Law and the Advisory Opinion of the International Court of Justice on the Legality of the Threat or Use of Nuclear Weapons' (1997) 316 *International Review of the Red Cross* 35, 36.

2.1 *Early Development of International Humanitarian Law Principles*

The origins of contemporary international humanitarian law are often traced to 1859 and Henri Dunant's experiences in the aftermath of the Battle of Solferino. Dunant successfully used his observations, recorded in his book *Souvenir de Solferino*,[8] to push for the establishment of voluntary 'relief societies for the purpose of having care given to the wounded in wartime by zealous, devoted and thoroughly qualified volunteers'[9] (which became known as the International Committee of the Red Cross) for the relief of victims of war and for the adoption of a binding legal instrument enumerating minimum standards of protection for victims of war.[10] Although the thrust of Dunant's energy was in the area of protection and relief for the victims of war, he was also well aware of the importance of controlling the deployment of specific weapons. Dunant's concluding paragraph to *Souvenir de Solferino* shows great prescience on his part:

> If the new and frightful weapons of destruction which are now at the disposal of the nations, seem destined to have bridged the duration of future wars, it appears likely, on the other hand, that future battles will only become more and more murderous. Moreover, in this age when surprise plays so important a part, is it not possible that wars may arise, from one quarter or another, in the most sudden and unexpected fashion? And do not these considerations alone constitute more than adequate reason for taking precautions against surprise?

As early as 1868, just a few years after the creation of the International Committee of the Red Cross, following Henri Dunant's successful endeavours in Europe, the international community agreed to the Declaration of St. Petersburg.[11] The Declaration was adopted as a result of an initiative of the Russian Czar, Alexander II, who was concerned about the development of an anti-personnel explosive bullet. The Declaration of St. Petersburg is important for two reasons. First, it incorporates a prohibition of a specific type of weapon – in this particular case a projectile of weight below 400 grams, which is either explosive or charged with fulminating or inflammable substances. That in itself represents a significant achievement of the late Nineteenth Century. But the Declaration does more than simply attempt to impose a restriction on a specific weapon type.

---

[8] Henri Dunant, *Un Souvenir de Solferino* (1862). All references in the present work are to the translation *A Memory of Solferino* (1986), the original of which was published by the American National Red Cross in 1939.

[9] Ibid 115.

[10] Ibid 128.

[11] *Declaration Renouncing the Use, in Time of War, of Explosive Projectiles Under 400 Grammes Weight*, opened for signature 29 November 1868, 138 CTS 297; (1907) 1 *American Journal of International Law (Supp)* 95 (entered into force 11 December 1868) ('*Declaration of St Petersburg*').

Second, and perhaps more importantly, the Declaration offers a principled rationale for the specific prohibition. The Preamble to the Declaration, which may well be better known than the operative text itself, states that:

> [The] Commission having by common agreement fixed the technical limits at which the necessities of war ought to yield to the requirements of humanity ... declare as follows:
> Considering that the progress of civilization should have the effect of alleviating as much as possible the calamities of war;
> That the only legitimate object which States should endeavour to accomplish during war is to weaken the military forces of the enemy;
> That for this purpose it is sufficient to disable the greatest possible number of men;
> That this object would be exceeded by the employment of arms which uselessly aggravate the sufferings of disabled men, or render their death inevitable;
> That the employment of such arms would, therefore, be contrary to the laws of humanity.

The significance of the Preamble is its reaffirmation of the existence of binding limitations to the means and methods of warfare – that on the basis of a commitment to apply the "Laws of Humanity" the international community, as it existed in 1868, considered itself obligated to prohibit a specific type of weapon.

While these two positive aspects of the Declaration deserve emphasis, some additional comments are also valid. At least one of the parties to the negotiations for the Declaration, Prussia, argued for a more general enquiry into 'the application of scientific discoveries to armed conflict' with a view to agreement on a broader prohibition than the one originally envisaged. That suggestion was vigorously and successfully opposed. All that the negotiating parties were prepared to accept was a paragraph which stated that:

> The Contracting or Acceding Parties reserve to themselves to come hereafter to an understanding whenever a precise proposition shall be drawn up in view of future improvements which science may effect in the armament of troops, in order to maintain the principles which they have established, and to conciliate the necessities of war with the laws of humanity.

Furthermore, the wording of the prohibition itself is narrow and limited – the prohibition only extends to the use of the projectiles in war between contracting parties and is, therefore, waived in a war involving a non-party or a war involving parties where a non-party joins one of the belligerents.

The tensions inherent in the text of the Declaration of St. Petersburg are as evident now as they were in 1868. The international community willingly concedes that the deployment of military force is subject to restriction and to limitation, but jealously guards the right to determine exactly what the limitations are in respect of specific categories of weapon. While States have found it relatively easy to declare their acceptance of the binding nature of general principles, there has always been a gap between the articulation of commitment to the general principles and the effective application of those general principles to specific weapons categories.

The preambular formulation in the St. Petersburg Declaration declaring illegal 'the employment of arms which uselessly aggravate the sufferings of disabled men, or render their death inevitable' was affirmed and applied to additional categories of weapons with the adoption of subsequent instruments. In 1899, for example, Czar Nicholas II initiated a gathering of international political leaders, this time at the First Hague Peace Conference, with the objective of a general limitation on armaments.[12] The Czar was concerned about technological advances in weaponry and saw an international peace conference as a way of facilitating implementation of the general principles articulated in the St. Petersburg Declaration 30 years before. The States participating at the 1899 Conference refused to commit to a general limitation of armaments but did agree to several specific instruments prohibiting the use of, for example, projectiles for the diffusion of asphyxiating or deleterious gases and expanding, or "dum-dum" bullets. It is interesting to note that in the particular instruments dealing with each of these two specific weapons types, the preambles explicitly refer to the inspiration for agreement from the 'sentiments which found expression in the Declaration of St. Petersburg'. Again, though, the prohibitions are narrowed to apply to the use of the weapons in conflicts between States Parties only.

The Final Act of the 1899 Hague Peace Conference proposed a follow-up conference to consider matters on which there had been no agreement.[13] States were invited to a second Hague Peace Conference in 1907 and again failed to reach agreement on a general limitation on armaments. However, there were other significant achievements at the 1907 Conference – most notably Convention IV Respecting the Laws and Customs of War on Land.[14] This convention represented the most comprehensive attempt to codify the international law regulating the means and methods of warfare to date[15] and contained a number of key provisions to regulate the use of weapons. Articles 22-28 dealt with the means and methods of warfare and

---

[12] Joseph H Choate, *The Two Hague Conferences* (1969); Frederick W Holls, *The Peace Conference at the Hague* (1900).

[13] 1899 Final Act, above n 6.

[14] 1907 Hague Convention IV, above n 6.

[15] Convention IV of 1907 was not the first multilateral treaty regulating the means and methods of warfare. However, earlier treaties including the *Declaration of St Petersburg* of 1868 and the various instruments emerging from the 1899 Hague Conference were focussed on specific weapons types or specific methods of warfare. Convention IV of 1907 represented a broader codification than earlier instruments.

Article 23(a) prohibited the use of poison and poisoned weapons while Article 23(e) prohibited the use of 'arms, projectiles, or material calculated to cause unnecessary suffering'. In addition, the preamble to the Convention incorporated the celebrated Martens Clause to the effect that:

> Until a more complete code of the laws of war has been issued, the high contracting parties deem it expedient to declare that, in cases not included in the Regulations adopted by them, the inhabitants and the belligerents remain under the protection and the rule of the principles of the law of nations, as they result from the usages established among civilized peoples, from the laws of humanity, and the dictates of the public conscience.

The Martens Clause was considered a particularly significant development because it purported to extend the key principles of the international law of armed conflict to situations not covered by the existing instruments – including, therefore, those conflicts involving non-States-Parties to the various instruments.

2.2 *Contemporary General Principles of International Humanitarian Law*

In addition to the Martens Clause of 1907, there are two key general principles of customary international humanitarian law which limit the deployment of weapons, both of which are now codified in Protocol I Additional to the Geneva Conventions of 1949. The first of these two principles is a reiteration of the general prohibition first referred to in the Declaration of St. Petersburg: the prohibition on the deployment of weapons which 'cause superfluous injury or unnecessary suffering'.[16] This is a problematic formulation because the legal prohibition on the causing of 'superfluous injury or unnecessary suffering' has never been defined. The international community has simply characterised some weapons as "abhorrent" without ever articulating criteria for that determination.[17] International humanitarian law accepts the general proposition that force can be deployed for legitimate military objectives determined on the basis of the notion of *military necessity*. The deployment of military force, including the choice of particular weapons, must be limited to causing no more suffering than is necessary to achieve the legitimate military objective.

As we have seen, at various stages since 1868, the international community has been able to agree that certain weapons types fall within this general prohibition against weapons which cause superfluous injury and unnecessary suffering. However, despite virtually universal agreement on

---

[16] Additional Protocol I, art 35(2).

[17] Robin M Coupland (ed), *The SIrUS Project: Towards a Determination of Which Weapons Cause 'Superfluous Injury or Unnecessary Suffering'* (1997), reproduced in this volume as Chapter 5.

the relevance and application of the principle that weapons which cause superfluous injury and unnecessary suffering are prohibited, the only weapons types which have actually been prohibited are those which have been subjected to specifically agreed prohibitions. In other words, the existence of the general prohibition itself has never resulted in the prohibition of a specific weapons type.[18] The inconsistency of approach by the international community to the negotiation of treaty prohibitions of certain weapons but not others leads to the conclusion that humanitarian principles, while somewhat influential, are rarely, if ever, determinative of outcomes in arms control negotiations.

All developments in the international legal regulation of weapons prior to World War II focused exclusively on consequences for combatants. In World War II, with new technological developments in weapons, the international community witnessed the relative proportions of military to civilian casualties in armed conflict beginning to change with a much greater incidence of civilian casualties. Consequently, it became imperative to further develop the general principles of international humanitarian law regulating the deployment of weapons. The second of the general principles referred to above is the so-called principle of "distinction": that civilians and non-combatants must be protected from the conflict and are not to be the specific target of the deployment of weapons.[19] Weapons which are incapable of discriminating between military and civilian targets are prohibited, and weapons can only be deployed in a discriminatory manner. This general principle has led to the somewhat euphemistic phrase 'collateral damage' to describe the use or deployment of weapons against a military target which happen to have incidental effects on the civilian population. The international community accepts the general proposition that civilians are not to be the targets of the deployment of weapons, but it is clear from the proportion of civilian casualties in armed conflict that this is often the effect of the deployment of the modern weapons of war. While it may be true that this general principle has had some influence on limiting the number of civilian casualties from armed conflict, the challenge for international humanitarian law clearly is to translate the broad acceptance

---

[18] It will be shown that at the Rome Diplomatic Conference to Establish an International Criminal Court the international community agreed to an unprecedented nexus between this general principle and a negotiated multilateral treaty prohibition of a specific category of weapons as a precondition for the exercise of the subject matter jurisdiction of the International Criminal Court. The negotiation of this new position supports the view that the international community is unwilling to accept the general prohibition as a 'stand alone' principle in the absence of a negotiated treaty prohibition on a specific category of weapons. See, *Rome Statute of the International Criminal Court*, adopted by the United Nations Diplomatic Conference of Plenipotentiaries on the Establishment of an International Criminal Court on 17 July 1998; 37 ILM 1002. The text of the Statute is located at <http://www.un.org/icc/> (Website of the ICC).

[19] See Additional Protocol I, arts 51(4) and (5).

of a principle in peacetime into one that is fully respected during armed conflict.

Despite the relatively recent development of the principle of distinction, it has readily been accepted by the international community as a "stand alone" principle – including as a general principle the violation of which carries individual criminal culpability.[20] Perhaps the reason for the contrast between attitudes toward the principle of distinction and the prohibition on weapons which cause superfluous injury or unnecessary suffering has to do with the relative certainties in the application of the principle of distinction. There is a well established definition of "civilian" and there are clear instances where civilians or civilian objects are deliberately targeted as the object of attack. These measurables are in stark contrast to the uncertainties in an undefined phrase such as 'superfluous injury or unnecessary suffering'. However, it is also true that the principle of distinction is more often applied to the manner of deployment of particular weapons rather than to the weapons themselves. While the principle can also operate to prohibit weapons which are "inherently indiscriminate", it must be recognised that weapons are inanimate objects and so must be targeted and deployed.[21] To the extent that any particular weapon type can be deployed in a discriminatory manner, it ought not be illegal by reason solely of the application of this general principle. Weapons types can be, and often are, regulated on the basis of specific treaty regimes and it is to arms control regimes we now turn.

3. THE REGULATION OF WEAPONS THROUGH ARMS CONTROL REGIMES

As discussed above, international humanitarian law – the law of armed conflict – includes principles of a humanitarian nature intended to restrict or prohibit the *use* of specific weapons. The weapon types include those that are deemed to exert their effects indiscriminately or cause superfluous injury or unnecessary suffering. Unfortunately, these laws of war have had very limited success in reducing the extent of superfluous injury or unnecessary suffering. As noted by the arms control specialist Jozef Goldblat:

> All laws of war suffer from one common weakness: the rules of conduct established for belligerents in time of peace may not resist the pressure of military expedience generated in the course of hostilities, and the attempts to "humanise" war may sometimes prove futile. The danger that the weapons prohibited may, under certain circumstances, be resorted to

---

[20] In the Rome Statute for the ICC, for example, any violation of the principle of distinction constitutes a war crime whether committed in an international or non-international armed conflict. Articles 8(2)(b)(i) and (ii) and 8(2)(e)(i) of the Court's Statute now reflect the principle earlier enshrined in art 85(3)(a) of Additional Protocol I.

[21] See Doswald-Beck, above n 7, 39.

– as has occurred on several occasions – will not disappear as long as these weapons remain in the arsenals of states. Hence the intrinsic link between the development of the humanitarian laws of war and progress in the field of disarmament.[22]

Indeed, one could argue that if the principle of distinction or the prohibition on use of weapons which cause superfluous injury or unnecessary suffering had been respected by all belligerents, disarmament and arms control treaties would be less necessary.

Disarmament is the traditional term for the elimination, as well as the limitation or reduction, through negotiation of an international agreement, of the means by which nations wage war. The goal of eliminating war goes far back in history, but in modern times disarmament came into focus with the Hague Conferences in 1899 and 1907. The term "arms control" was coined in the 1950's to denote an international agreement to limit the arms race, in particular, at that time, the nuclear arms race between the USA and the Former Soviet Union (FSU), following recognition that general and complete nuclear disarmament would not be readily achieved.[23] The term "arms control" originally was meant to denote internationally agreed rules limiting the arms competition rather than reversing it; it had a connotation distinct from the reduction of armaments (ie disarmament). Indeed, the term "arms control" was not popular with a number of supporters of disarmament.[24] Subsequently, however, the meaning of the term "arms control" has become significantly broadened,[25] and is now commonly used to denote international agreements which are intended to:

- freeze, limit or abolish specific categories of weapons;
- prevent certain military activities;
- regulate the deployment of forces;
- proscribe the transfers of militarily important items;
- reduce the risk of an accidental war;
- constrain or prohibit the use of certain arms in war; or
- build up confidence among states through greater openness in the military field, and thereby produce an international climate conducive to disarmament.

It is in this broad sense that the term "arms control" will be used throughout this chapter. It should be noted that, with this definition, "arms control" includes the complete prohibition of possession of a category of weapons (that is, disarmament has become regarded as a subset of arms

---

[22] Jozef Goldblat, *Agreements for Arms Control: A Critical Survey*, Stockholm International Peace Research Institute (1982) 89.

[23] In fact, in 1973, a Scientific American journal dedicated to Arms Control devoted 376 of its 416 pages to Nuclear Weapons related issues. See Herbert F York, 'Arms Control', (Readings from *Scientific American*) January 1973.

[24] Alva Myrdal, *The Game of Disarmament* (1977).

[25] Jozef Goldblat, above n 22, xv.

control). Likewise, various international agreements (for example, the 1925 Geneva Protocol[26]) which were originally regarded as being international humanitarian law agreements, also fall within the "arms control" rubric. As far as its basic purpose is concerned, arms control serves four objectives:[27]

- reducing the likelihood of war, especially by trying to impose limits on the evolution and proliferation of weapons that may destabilise strategic relationships and thus create incentives for preventive attacks;
- reducing the suffering and damage in the event of war;
- reducing the expenditure on armaments and saving resources; and
- contributing to conflict management by providing a framework for negotiation between opposing sides, by reducing suspicion and by generally contributing to an atmosphere conducive to relaxation of tensions.

The weapons that arms control negotiators have attempted to either prohibit or restrict include certain types of weapons that are deemed to exert their effects indiscriminately or cause superfluous injury or unnecessary suffering. Traditional arms control and disarmament has for the most part concentrated on containing the threat caused by the existence of nuclear, chemical and biological weapons. However, within the broad definition already referred to, arms control includes the 1980 Convention on Prohibitions or Restrictions on the Use of Certain Conventional Weapons Which May be Deemed to be Excessively Injurious or to Have Indiscriminate Effects[28] which covers a number of specific conventional weapons, as well as the recently concluded 1997 Convention on the Prohibition of the Use, Stockpiling, Production and Transfer of Anti-Personnel Mines and on Their Destruction.[29] More recently, international attention has been drawn to the dangers of unregulated trade in conventional weapons, although current responses to these dangers are limited to a voluntary register of the transfer of certain conventional weapons.

In the past, international humanitarian law treaties have been relatively easy to negotiate (because of the limited, if any, implications for national security) compared with arms control treaties. Arms control treaties have generally been more difficult to negotiate because of the need for balanced reductions, verification of compliance (and the associated concerns about loss of national security or other sensitive information). While arms control efforts have met with limited success (seldom meeting the goals set by

---

[26] *Protocol for the Prohibition of the Use in War of Asphyxiating, Poisonous, or other Gases and Bacteriological Methods of Warfare*, (opened for signature 17 June 1925), 94 LNTS 65; 26 UST 571) (entered into force 8 February 1928) ('*Geneva Protocol*').

[27] Daniel Frei, 'International Humanitarian Law and Arms Control' (1988) 267 *International Review of the Red Cross* 491.

[28] See above n 4.

[29] *Convention on the Prohibition of the Use, Stockpiling, Production and Transfer of and on Their Destruction*, opened for signature 18 September 1997, 36 ILM 1507 (entered into force on 1 March 1999) ('*The Ottawa Land Mines Convention*'). As at 17 March 1999, there were 67 States Parties.

their more ambitious proponents), recent political events including the collapse of the Soviet Union and the end of the 'Cold War' have provided new opportunities for substantial developments in arms control, including significant reductions in the nuclear and conventional weapons arsenals of the major powers.

In the remainder of this chapter, we present a series of case studies on specific weapons categories and attempt to analyse the relationship between international humanitarian law principles and other arms control considerations in the negotiations for the specific multilateral treaty regimes which seek to regulate those particular weapons categories. Some attempt is also made to evaluate the effectiveness of various arms control treaties and to consider the proposals for strengthening those regimes.

4. CASE STUDIES ON SPECIFIC WEAPONS

4.1 Chemical Weapons

As discussed above, the use of poisons and diseases in war, which has been practised since ancient times, was condemned and prohibited in a number of international declarations and treaties, including in the Hague Conventions of 1899 and 1907.[30] However, these humanitarian advances in the development of legal principles regulating the means and methods of warfare failed to prevent the extensive use of some weapons already the subject of specific prohibition in World War I. The use of chemical weapons in World War I was particularly severe with the deployment of approximately 125,000 tonnes of toxic chemicals resulting in 1,300,000 casualties, more than 100,000 of which were fatal.[31] In an appeal to the belligerents of 6 February 1918, the International Committee of the Red Cross stated that:

> We wish to-day to take a stand against a barbaric innovation ... This innovation is the use of asphyxiating and poisonous gas, which will it seems increase to an extent so far undreamed of ... We protest with all the force at our command against such warfare which can only be called criminal.[32]

Articles in various peace treaties at the conclusion of the War reiterated, and in some cases extended, the prohibition incorporated in the 1899

---

[30] For a brief history of the use of poisons and diseases as methods of warfare prior to World War I see Joseph Kelly, above n 2.

[31] United Nations, (1986) 11 *Disarmament Yearbook* 241.

[32] Stockholm International Peace Research Institute, *The Problem of Chemical and Biological Warfare*, Vol IV, 'CB Disarmament Negotiations, 1920-1970' (1974) 41.

Hague Declaration Concerning Asphyxiating Gases.[33] In the immediate aftermath of World War I, chemical weapons were described as 'a fundamentally cruel method of carrying on war' and 'criminal' and their deployment against non-combatants was described as 'barbarous and inexcusable'.[34]

In 1920 there were preliminary discussions within the League of Nations on the feasibility of developing a chemical disarmament treaty. However, on the issue of verification of 'non-production' of chemical weapons by chemical industry, it was concluded that 'it would be useless to seek to restrict the use of gases in wartime by prohibiting or limiting their manufacture in peacetime'.[35] So diplomats settled for an easier option based on the principles of international humanitarian law. The International Conference on the Control of the International Trade in Arms, Munitions, and Implements of War, convened in Geneva in 1925 under the auspices of the Council of the League of Nations, adopted the text of the Protocol for the Prohibition of the Use in War of Asphyxiating, Poisonous or Other Gases, and of Bacteriological Methods of Warfare.[36] Under the terms of the Protocol, the States Parties 'so far as they are not already Parties to Treaties prohibiting such use' were prohibited from the use in war of 'asphyxiating, poisonous or other gases, all analogous liquids, materials or devices ... [and] bacteriological [weapons]'.

The 1925 Geneva Protocol, like most of its contemporary multilateral instruments, represented a mixed achievement. On one hand, the instrument did represent a collective response to the horrors of the use of chemical weapons in World War I and was intended to achieve more than its predecessors in relation to that particular category of weapons. However, the Protocol also suffered from some major limitations. Firstly, it represented a compromise – several States were keen to see agreement on a comprehensive prohibition of chemical weapons but the resultant prohibition only on *use* was the best that could be achieved. Secondly, the Protocol only prohibited use in warfare and not in conflict situations where war had not formally been declared. Thirdly, many States Parties entered reservations on reciprocal use of chemical weapons so that the Protocol ended up constituting a *de facto* prohibition on first use in warfare rather than a comprehensive prohibition on any use in warfare. Fourthly, the Protocol contained the common exclusion clause limiting the prohibition to war between States Parties only. As a result of these limitations, the Proto-

---

[33] *Declaration Prohibiting the Use of Asphyxiating Gases ('Hague Declaration II')*, opened for signature 29 July 1899, 187 CTS 456; (1907) 1 *American Journal of International Law (Supp)* 155 (entered into force 4 September 1900).

[34] Stockholm International Peace Research Institute, above n 32, 44.

[35] Ibid.

[36] Opened for signature 17 June 1925, 94 LNTS 65; 14 ILM 49 (entered into force 8 February 1928) ('*1925 Geneva Protocol*').

col did not prevent future first use of chemical weapons by States Parties –
even in wars against only other States Parties.[37]

Even at the time of agreement, there was a view that the 1925 Geneva
Protocol was inadequate, that a mere declaration of determination not to
have recourse to the prohibited means of warfare might not stand the strain
of actual hostilities, and that the envisaged convention on the reduction and
limitation of armaments should include more stringent measures. In 1926, a
Disarmament Conference (DC) was established by the League of Nations
and held several sessions between 1926 and 1930. The expert bodies
associated with the DC expressed the view that it would not be practical to
verify 'non-production' of chemical weapons by chemical industry because
'preparations for chemical war could not be detected and prevented:
chemical factories could be quickly adapted to manufacturing poison
gases; and some of these types of gases are current commercial products of
industry'[38]. By 1932, it was accepted, in the light of the technical assessment made for the DC, that no reliable system of verification was possible.
Following the withdrawal of Germany from the DC, a decision was taken
in early 1936 to postpone further meetings of the DC – it never recon-
vened.

As already mentioned, chemical weapons have been used at various
times since World War I despite the existence of the 1925 Geneva Protocol. The most blatant recent example of this was in the 1980s by Iraq
against Iranian soldiers and against Kurds in northern Iraqi villages. In the
years since World War I, the military utility of chemical weapons has
diminished. States have developed effective protective equipment against
chemical weapon attack and other weapons have been developed which are
less dependent upon favourable climatic conditions such as wind speed and
direction, and the absence of rain. Most States had reached the conclusion
that chemical weapons were not indispensable to their strategic military
capabilities. Additionally, the Iraqi use of chemical weapons against un-
protected civilians demonstrated the dangers of increasing proliferation of
chemical weapons. This combination of diminished strategic value and
potential proliferation threat facilitated a greater level of multilateral
agreement than had been possible hitherto.

An additional factor complemented the congruence of circumstances
facilitating the conclusion of a comprehensive treaty ban on chemical
weapons. In 1987, the Former Soviet Union (FSU) (following on from the
advent of *glasnost* and *perestroika*) accepted the concept of challenge
inspection for verification of compliance with a chemical weapons convention, admitted possession of chemical weapons, and hosted an interna-

---

[37] For a more detailed discussion about the limitations of the 1925 Geneva Protocol see
Timothy L H McCormack, 'International Law and the Use of Chemical Weapons in the
Gulf War' (1990-1) 21 *California Western International Law Journal* 1, 5-10.
[38] Stockholm International Peace Research Institute, above n 32, 105.

tional meeting of arms control negotiators at one of its chemical weapons facilities. All of these developments would have been inconceivable prior to the improvement in East-West relations in the mid-1980s.

Negotiation of the Chemical Weapons Convention (CWC)[39] commenced in 1969 in Geneva and was not concluded until 1992. Although this 23 year process was a very slow and tortuous one, it was ultimately rewarding. Unlike the 1925 Geneva Protocol, the CWC requires the complete elimination of chemical weapons (within 10 years of entry into force) and will introduce a verification regime which will provide assurance of compliance by States Parties, but which will not hinder the development of peaceful chemical industry. Verification under the CWC includes compulsory national declarations about relevant industrial and military activities, and a regime of routine inspections of declared industrial and military facilities. An additional feature is the provision of a "challenge inspection" whereby a State Party can request an inspection of any site in another State Party at short notice. While there is a filtering process to dismiss spurious requests for challenge inspections, the underlying principle is that such inspections can occur literally anywhere in a State Party.[40]

The CWC is justifiably heralded as a major breakthrough in multilateral arms control. It was the first comprehensively verifiable multilateral treaty that completely banned an entire class of weapons, and firmly limited activities that may contribute to the production of those weapons. Thus, it went further than any other treaty in terms of the scope of prohibition, and the depth, extent and intrusiveness of verification provisions.

The CWC entered into force on 29 April 1997 and there are currently 121 States Parties. Perhaps most importantly, States Parties include: both the USA and the Russian Federation (RF), which are the two largest possessors of chemical weapons; the major chemical producing and exporting States of Western Europe; and some of the major developing States with chemical production capability. Several key Middle Eastern States have still refused to participate in the Convention but an increasing number of States are choosing to participate. The Organisation for the Prohibition of Chemical Weapons (OPCW), which has been established in The Hague to administer the CWC, is responsible for the verification regime.[41] There are

---

[39] *Convention on the Prohibition of the Development, Production, Stockpiling and Use of Chemical Weapons and on their Destruction*, opened for signature 13 January 1993; 32 ILM 800 (entered into force 29 April 1997) ('*CWC*'). As at 31 December 1998, there were 121 States Parties and an additional 48 State Signatories.

[40] It is interesting to note that the CWC will attempt to achieve adequate monitoring of chemical industry which was deemed not possible in 1926 - partly a consequence of the major developments in chemical analysis instrumentation which allow effective verification.

[41] For details of the Verification measures of the CWC, see Robert J Mathews, 'Verification of Chemical Industry Under the Chemical Weapons Convention' in John B Poole and Richard Guthrie (eds), *Verification 1993: Arms Control, Peacekeeping and The Environment* (1993) 41.

now more than 200 inspectors employed by the OPCW and inspection teams from the Organisation have already undertaken many of the inspection tasks outlined in the verification regimes to provide assurance of States Parties' compliance with CWC obligations.[42]

At the time the Convention was opened for signature and again, at the First Conference of States Parties after the Convention had entered into force, many representatives of States and of international organisations acknowledged the significance of the multilateral achievement to ban these weapons with such terrible consequences – which cause superfluous injury and unnecessary suffering to those unfortunate enough to be exposed to them.[43] While many of these sentiments were undoubtedly genuine, the

---

[42] Robert J Mathews, 'Entry into force of the Chemical Weapons Convention', *SIPRI Yearbook 1998: Armaments, Disarmament and International Security* (1998) 490-500.

[43] See, eg, the statement by Boutros Boutros-Ghali:

je veux ouvrir le volumineux dossier qui nous réunit ici sur sa pièce essentielle: l'angoisse d'hommes, de femmes, d'enfants devant des armes imparables; des armes qui détruisent et tuent sans qu'il soit possible ni de combattre, ni de fuire, ni même de se défendre. Leurs effets fulgurants sur les soldats qui y étaient exposés, les séquelles irrémédiables qu'elles laissent aux combattants qui avaient la chance d'en réchapper, les souffrances et la terreur que leur emploi engendraient chez les hommes des tranchées, disent l'horreur de cette arme. Nous sommes rassemblés ici pour dire que nous ne l'acceptons plus.

Discours de M. Boutros Boutros-Ghali, Secrétaire général des Nations Unies, prononcé lors de la cérémonie d'ouverture à la signature de la Convention sur les armes chimiques, Paris, 13 January 1993 (copy on file with authors); and the statement by François Mitterrand:

Il a fallu l'émotion suscitée par les massacres de Halabja en mars 1988, évoqués par Ronald Reagan et par moi-même à la tribune des Nations-Unies ... pour que le débat fût relancé et qu'à l'initiative des Etats-Unies et de la France ... fussent réaffirmés l'autorité du Protocole de 1925 et le caractère insupportable des armes chimiques. Un élan décisif avait été donné.

Discours de Monsieur François Mitterrand, Président de la République à l'Occasion de la Signature de la Convention d'Interdiction des armes Chimiques, Maison de l'UNESCO, 13 January 1993 (copy on file with authors). See also the statement by Kofi Annan:

What you have done of your own free will is to announce to this and all succeeding generations that chemical weapons are instruments that no state with any respect for itself and no people with any sense of dignity would use in conflicts whether domestic or international. You have been summoned by history and you have answered its call. One of the most monstrous tools of warfare has been ruled intolerable by all States Parties

Kofi A Annan, *Opening Remarks at the First Conference of the States Parties to the Chemical Weapons Convention,* The Hague, 6 May 1997 (copy on file with authors); and the statement by Tony Lloyd:

The images of blinded men at the battle of Ypres in 1915, pathetically struggling to walk, a hand on the shoulder of the man in front are imprinted on all our minds. Other images are sadly more recent but equally horrifying. Which of us can forget the traumatic pictures of Iraqi Kurdish women and children brutally gassed to death by their own government at Halabja?

Statement by Mr Tony Lloyd MP, Minister of State, Foreign and Commonwealth Office of Great Britain and Northern Ireland to the First Session of the Conference of the States Parties to the Chemical Weapons Convention, The Hague, 8 May 1997 (copy on file with authors).

principal motivation for the conclusion of the Convention had less to do with deleterious humanitarian consequences of the weapons and more to do with other strategic security factors – most importantly, the growing concerns of horizontal proliferation of chemical weapons and the recognition by both the USA and the RF that they did not need to retain their chemical weapons stockpiles post Cold War. This much is clear in the contrast between the willingness of the international community to agree to the comprehensive prohibition of chemical weapons while demonstrating reluctance to commit to similar prohibitions in relation to other specific categories of weapons.

4.2 *Biological Weapons*

As already mentioned, the 1925 Geneva Protocol, *inter alia*, prohibited the use of 'bacteriological methods of warfare'. However, as with asphyxiating, poisonous or other gases, the Geneva Protocol prohibited neither the production nor the stockpiling of biological weapons. Again, the limitations of the Geneva Protocol resulted in extensive use of biological weapons by Japan against China in the early 1940s in clear violation of international legal norms. Apparently the biological agents deployed by Japanese forces included cholera, anthrax and plague. Estimates of the number of biological weapons-related deaths in China range from several thousand[44] to 'hundreds of thousands'.[45]

The Convention on the Prohibition of the Development, Production and Stockpiling of Bacteriological (Biological) and Toxin Weapons and on Their Destruction[46] (BWC) was negotiated between 1969 and 1971, opened for signature in 1972 and entered into force in 1975. It now has 141 States Parties. The BWC was the first true multilateral disarmament treaty, being the first Convention to ban an entire class of weapons. States Parties to the BWC undertook never to develop, produce, stockpile or otherwise acquire or retain biological agents or toxins, or their delivery systems. Furthermore, the BWC obligated each State Party to destroy, or to divert to peaceful purposes, all agents, toxins, weapons, equipment and means of delivery not later than 9 months after the Treaty entered into force for it.

The BWC has now been in force for over 20 years. Though it constitutes an important landmark in arms control, a number of developments since 1975 have resulted in assessments that the BWC is seriously weak and

---

[44] See Stockholm International Peace Research Institute, *Yearbook on World Armaments and Disarmament* (1996) 687.

[45] News Chronology, *Chemical Weapons Bulletin* (31 July 1995).

[46] *Convention on the Prohibition of the Development, Production and Stockpiling of Bacteriological (Biological) and Toxin Weapons and on Their Destruction*, opened for signature 10 April 1972; 11 ILM 3320; 1971 *UN Juridical Year Book* 118) (entered into force 26 March 1975) ('*BWC*') As at 17 March 1999, there were 141 States Parties.

lacks credibility because it contains no effective verification provisions.[47] For example, the advances in biotechnology since the mid-1970s have increased the capability to manufacture a number of highly useful biological products (including agricultural and pharmaceutical products) on an industrial scale. Unfortunately, the same technology can also be used to produce biological agents for weapons purposes.[48]

Unresolved allegations of clandestine production or use of biological weapons since 1975 have caused a serious loss of credibility in the BWC. In 1980, the USA claimed that an outbreak of anthrax at Sverdlovsk, in the Former Soviet Union (FSU), raised questions concerning compliance by the FSU with its BWC obligations. In 1992, President Yeltsin admitted that there had been an offensive biological weapons program in the FSU during the previous 20 years, and acknowledged that the Sverdlovsk anthrax outbreak was the result of military research to make biological weapons.[49]

The recent revelations from the UN Special Commission for Iraq[50] (UNSCOM) concerning an offensive biological weapons program in Iraq, in which Iraq had spent several years developing, producing, weaponising and testing a number of biological agents, provides further evidence of the need to strengthen the provisions of the BWC.[51] In addition, intelligence assessments from the USA[52] and the RF[53] have concluded that about 8

---

[47] For a critique of the BWC see Jozef Goldblat, 'The Biological Weapons Convention: An Overview' (1997) 318 *International Review of the Red Cross* 251.

[48] For example, using recombinant techniques, toxin producing genes could be spliced to a common host organism, enabling large scale production (within a short time) of toxic agents which have previously only existed in nature in small quantities. See Malcolm Dando, *Biological Warfare in the 21st Century: Biotechnology and the Proliferation of Biological Weapons* (1994).

[49] Stockholm International Peace Research Institute, *Yearbook on World Armaments and Disarmament* (1993) 287-288.

[50] The UN Special Commission for Iraq was established pursuant to UN Security Council Resolution 687, 46 UN SCOR, UN Doc. S/RES/687 (3 April 1991) with the responsibility to identify the full scope of Iraq's capabilities in relation to nuclear, biological and chemical weapons and long-range missile delivery systems, to oversee the destruction of each of those programs and to monitor Iraq's compliance with its obligations not to rebuild those programs.

[51] Iraq's BW program embraced a comprehensive range of agents and munitions. Agents included lethal agents (eg. anthrax, botulinum toxin and ricin), incapacitating agents (eg. aflatoxins, mycotoxins and rotavirus) and "economic" agents (eg. wheat cover smut). The BW delivery systems ranged from tactical weapons (eg. artillery shells) through to strategic weapons (eg. aerial bombs and missile warheads filled with anthrax). See UN Security Council Doc. S/1995/864, dated 11 October 1995. At the time when Iraq was developing its BW program, it was a Signatory but not a State Party to the BWC. Iraq ratified the BWC in 1991 at the direction of the UN Security Council under the provisions of UN Security Council Resolution 687.

[52] USA Congress, Office of Technology Assessment (OTA), 'Proliferation of Weapons of Mass Destruction: Assessing the Risks', OTA-ISC-559 (1993) 65.

countries either have, or are seeking, an offensive biological weapons capability. Most States Parties to the BWC now accept that the Convention does require additional strengthening through the development of verification or compliance monitoring procedures.[54] Progress towards that goal is well under way.[55]

The analysis of the influence of humanitarian concerns in the negotiations for the BWC is similar to that for the CWC. No one doubts the potentially diabolical effects of germ warfare, hence, expressions of the significance of concluding multilateral agreement to prohibit any effort to attain an offensive biological weapons capability, let alone use biological weapons, are entirely justified. The argument here, however, is that the BWC was not concluded primarily because of the deleterious humanitarian consequences of biological weapons but because of concerns about horizontal proliferation of these weapons and of the difficulties of effective defence against biological weapon attack.

4.3 *Nuclear Weapons*

Following various unsuccessful attempts in the early post World War II years to negotiate a treaty to eliminate nuclear weapons, negotiations focussing on the less ambitious objective of non-proliferation of nuclear weapons were commenced by the Eighteen Nation Disarmament Committee in 1962. The negotiation of the Nuclear Non Proliferation Treaty[56] was concluded in 1968 and the treaty entered into force in 1970. It now has 187 States Parties and can claim broad and diverse membership. It is unique among key global multilateral treaties in that it establishes a discriminatory regime among States Parties. The NPT distinguishes between nuclear weapon States Parties and non-nuclear weapon States Parties based on those States (coincidentally the permanent five (P5) members of the UN Security Council) which had 'manufactured and exploded a nuclear weapon or other nuclear explosive device prior to 1 January 1967'.[57] Under the provisions of the NPT, the former are entitled to retain their existing nuclear weapons stockpiles and are not prohibited from developing new

---

[53] Yevgeny Primakov, 'New Challenge after the Cold War: The Proliferation of Weapons of Mass Destruction', Report by the Foreign Intelligence Service of the Russian Federation (1993).

[54] Based on the decisions taken at the 1994 Special Conference of States Parties to the BWC.

[55] Annabelle Duncan and Robert J Mathews, 'Development of a Verification Protocol for the Biological Weapons Convention' in Richard Guthrie (ed), *Verification 1996: The VERTIC Yearbook* (1997) 151-70.

[56] *Treaty on the Non-Proliferation of Nuclear Weapons*, opened for signature 1 July 1968, 729 UNTS 161; 7 ILM 809 (entered into force 5 March 1970) ('*NPT*'). As of 17 March 1999, there were 187 States Parties.

[57] NPT, art IX(3).

weapons systems or from testing and stockpiling any such weapons. The only NPT obligation purporting to limit the right of nuclear weapon possessor States Parties to continue an indefinite nuclear arms build-up is the obligation to undertake negotiations for an agreement for nuclear disarmament.[58]

By contrast, non-nuclear weapon States Parties undertake not to acquire nuclear weapons and to open any peaceful nuclear facilities to inspection by the International Atomic Energy Agency (IAEA) – the body responsible to administer the NPT and to monitor compliance by States Parties with their treaty obligations. IAEA inspection teams inspect nuclear facilities on a routine basis to confirm that declared fissionable material can be accounted for, and has not been diverted to non-peaceful purposes.

The NPT has proved largely successful as an effective regime in controlling horizontal proliferation of nuclear weapons. A former Australian Foreign Minister, Gareth Evans, has described the NPT as 'the single most effective and widely supported arms control agreement in existence: without it we would by now be facing a world with perhaps twenty or thirty nuclear weapons states'.[59] It should be noted, though, that the NPT has clearly not prevented horizontal proliferation altogether. A number of key States have been able to produce nuclear weapons or have at least reached a 'threshold nuclear weapons capability' outside the NPT regime and continue to refuse to renounce nuclear weapons and to join the NPT as non-nuclear weapon States.[60] Furthermore, two NPT States Parties (Iraq and the Democratic People's Republic of Korea) managed to avoid their NPT obligations in spite of IAEA inspections.[61]

Subsequently, many have called for a strengthening of the NPT/IAEA safeguards regime. For example, in 1993 the Board of Governors of the IAEA requested the IAEA's Standing Advisory Group on Safeguards Implementation to make proposals for tightening the NPT Safeguards

---

[58] Article VI of the NPT requires States Parties to the NPT to 'pursue negotiations in good faith on effective measures relating to the cessation of the nuclear arms race at an early date and to nuclear disarmament' leading to the negotiation of a treaty banning nuclear weapons. It should be noted, however, that the USA and the RF have agreed to substantial reductions to their nuclear arsenals in bilateral treaty arrangements - particularly the Treaties on the Reduction and Limitation of Strategic Offensive Arms (START I and II).

[59] Gareth Evans and Bruce Grant, *Australia's Foreign Relations in the World of the 1990s* (2nd ed, 1995) 84.

[60] The principal examples are India, Pakistan and Israel. South Africa also developed a nuclear weapons capability outside the NPT regime but, after the end of apartheid, unilaterally destroyed its nuclear weapons capability and joined the NPT as a non-nuclear weapon State Party.

[61] In both cases, the UN Security Council became actively involved, condemning these particular violations and reiterating the general principle that the proliferation of nuclear weapons, particularly in violation of NPT obligations, poses a threat to international peace and security. See, in particular, UN Security Council Resolutions 687 and 825 - 46 UN SCOR, UN Doc. S/RES/687 (3 April 1991) and 48 UN SCOR, UN Doc. S/RES/825 (11 May 1993) respectively.

Regime and making it more efficient.[62] Measures which have been developed under the subsequent "Programme 93+2" have included: expanded declarations of nuclear activities by States Parties; "no notice" (unannounced) inspections which would include access to non-declared parts of nuclear sites and non-declared sites where nuclear facilities are located (similar to the "Challenge Inspections" provisions under the CWC); and improved monitoring of import and export data.[63] The agreement to the indefinite extension of the NPT at the Review Conference in April-May 1995[64] was an important event for the future of the NPT.

The conclusion of the negotiation of the Comprehensive Test Ban Treaty[65] (CTBT) in 1996 was seen as a positive development in promoting the non-proliferation of nuclear weapons. There have also been recent attempts to encourage the nuclear weapons States to reduce their nuclear weapons stockpiles (eg The Canberra Commission[66]) which may well assist in working towards the ultimate objective of elimination of nuclear weapons.

In contrast to the situation with chemical and biological weapons, there has still been no agreement on a general prohibition on nuclear weapons. By participating in the Nuclear Non-Proliferation Treaty, 178 States, the overwhelming majority of the international community, have agreed to a prohibition on the acquisition, production, stockpiling, development and use of nuclear weapons. Only the five permanent members of the Security Council, as the privileged nuclear-weapon States Parties to the NPT, and the so called 'nuclear threshold states' – particularly Israel, India and

---

[62] 'Strengthening of the Safeguards System', Report by the Director-General to the IAEA General Conference, IAEA Doc. GC(XXXVI)/1017 (15 September 1992). See also Hans Blix, 'IAEA Safeguards: New Challenges' (1992) XV *Disarmament: A Periodic Review by the United Nations* 40-6.

[63] Suzanna van Moyland, 'Programme 93+2: Evolution of IAEA Safeguards' in Richard Guthrie (ed), *Verification 1996: The VERTIC Yearbook* (1997) 151-70.

[64] Report of the Australian Delegation, *1995 Review and Extension Conference of the Parties to the Treaty on the Non-Proliferation of Nuclear Weapons*, Department of Foreign Affairs and Trade (1995).

[65] Opened for signature 24 September 1996, UN Doc A/50/1027/Annex (1996), adopted by GA Res 50/245, 50 UN GAOR (125th mtg), UN Doc A/50/L.78 (1996); (1996) 35 ILM 1439 (not yet in force) ('*CTBT*'). As at 17 March 1999, there were 29 States Parties.

[66] In November 1995, the Australian government convened an international commission (composed of seventeen distinguished, internationally diverse members) with the specific mandate 'to propose practical steps towards a nuclear-free world'. In August 1996, the Commission issued a consensus report that rejected the utility of nuclear weapons and recommended a series of steps to bring about the verifiable elimination of nuclear weapons, commencing with all nuclear powers taking nuclear forces off alert and, ultimately, the elimination of nuclear weapons and a ban on the production of fissile materials for nuclear explosive purposes. See Canberra Commission, *Report of the Canberra Commission on the Elimination of Nuclear Weapons* (1996).

Pakistan[67] – which have all refused to become parties to the Nuclear Non-Proliferation Treaty and to relinquish the right to develop nuclear weapons, are not bound by the conventional obligation prohibiting possession of nuclear weapons.[68]

Many of the non-nuclear States Parties to the NPT, particularly many "Non-Aligned" States, had become frustrated with the lack of progress by the P5 in fulfilling their obligations under Article VI of the NPT towards a comprehensive treaty ban on nuclear weapons.[69] The UN General Assembly Resolution requesting an Advisory Opinion from the International Court of Justice[70] on the Legality of the Threat or Use of Nuclear Weapons was adopted by a substantial majority.[71] The request for an advisory opinion was a controversial strategy but one clearly designed to advance the cause of nuclear disarmament.

In July 1996, the International Court of Justice handed down the long awaited Advisory Opinion on the Legality of the Threat or Use of Nuclear Weapons.[72] The Advisory Opinion was a somewhat disappointing, if not entirely unsurprising, decision for advocates of nuclear disarmament. Some aspects of the Opinion were approved unanimously – in particular, the reaffirmation that any use of nuclear weapons is subject to the customary international law principles governing the conduct of armed conflict, and the reminder to Nuclear Weapons States of the obligation to negotiate and to conclude agreement on a comprehensive ban on nuclear weapons. These two unanimous findings produced some positive outcomes from the Opin-

---

[67] The term 'nuclear threshold State' is arguably no longer apt to describe India and Pakistan after the dramatic shift in position with reciprocal, multiple nuclear weapons testing by both States in May 1998.

[68] These few, but influential, States have successfully determined that the general principles prohibiting weapons which cause superfluous injury or unnecessary suffering or which are inherently indiscriminate have no effect on the legality of the possession of nuclear weapons in the absence of a comprehensive, multilateral treaty prohibition.

[69] This sense of frustration was heightened following the Non-Aligned States' perception that this issue was not adequately addressed at the 1995 NPT Review Conference.

[70] The competence of the Court to provide an Advisory Opinion is outlined in Article 65(1) of the Court's Statute: 'The Court may give an advisory opinion on any legal question at the request of whatever body may be authorised by or in accordance with the Charter of the United Nations to make such a request.'

[71] UN General Assembly Resolution 49/75K was adopted by 78 votes to 43 (France, the Russian Federation, the United Kingdom and the United States voting against) with 38 abstentions. China was absent from the voting. See: *Request for an Advisory Opinion from the International Court of Justice on the Legality of the Threat or Use of Nuclear Weapons*, GA Res 49/75K, UN GAOR, 49th Sess, Supp No 49 at 71, UN Doc A/49/49 (1995).

[72] *Advisory Opinion on the Legality of the Threat or Use of Nuclear Weapons* ('*Joint Opinion*'), 8 July 1996, reprinted in (1996) 4 ILM 809. For a detailed analysis of the international humanitarian law implications of the Opinion see the articles by Yves Sandoz, Luigi Condorelli, Eric David, Louise Doswald-Beck, Hisakazu Fujita, Christopher Greenwood, Timothy L H McCormack, Manfred Mohr and John H McNeill in the symposium issue dedicated to analysis of the Opinion in (1997) 316 *International Review of the Red Cross* 3-118.

ion. However, on the crucial issue of the legality of the threat or use of nuclear weapons, only seven judges could endorse the finding of the court. The other seven judges dissented from the decision for different reasons.[73]

The Court determined that, despite the lack of a specific prohibition on the threat or use of nuclear weapons in conventional or in customary international law, the general principles of customary international law, particularly the principles of international humanitarian law, would apply to any use or threat of use of nuclear weapons. Although the Court was able to conclude that the use of nuclear weapons 'seems scarcely reconcilable with respect for such requirements', the judges felt compelled to reach a qualified conclusion because of their perceived lack of 'sufficient elements to enable [the Court] to conclude with certainty that the use of nuclear weapons would necessarily be at variance with the principles and rules of law applicable in any circumstance'.[74] Implicit in the reasoning of the Court in the Advisory Opinion on the Legality of the Threat or Use of Nuclear Weapons is the conclusion that, in the absence of a specific agreement by the international community to prohibit a particular weapons category, the general principle of prohibition of weapons which cause superfluous injury and unnecessary suffering has limited practical effect.

The limited application of the general prohibition on weapons which cause superfluous injury or unnecessary suffering, implicit in the reasoning of the Court, has been made explicit in the final text of the Rome Statute for the International Criminal Court. In the negotiations in Rome, a number of States called for an explicit reference to the use of nuclear weapons as one of the possible acts constituting a war crime. Not surprisingly, such a reference was unacceptable to a number of delegations including the P5. However, other delegations had anticipated broad acceptance to include the general prohibition on the use of weapons which cause superfluous injury or unnecessary suffering in the definition of a war crime, particularly because of the established customary law status of this prohibition. Again, several delegations refused to countenance any such general principle which might be capable of being interpreted to extend to the use of a nuclear weapon.

---

[73] According to art 55 of the Statute of the Court, the President has a casting vote in the event of a split decision. In this Opinion, President Bedjaoui voted for the finding in the Joint Opinion and, as a consequence, the position enunciated in the *dispositif* was the prevailing one.

[74] International law has traditionally distinguished between the law regulating the legitimate resort to force (the *jus ad bellum*), and the law regulating the actual deployment of force (the *jus in bello*). Any legitimate exercise of force must be consistent with both sets of principles. The Joint Opinion, however, confused the *jus ad bellum* with the *jus in bello*, because the majority of the Court declared a non-finding (*non liquet*) - a determination that it was not possible to rule out the possibility of a legitimate use of nuclear weapons in an 'extreme circumstance of self-defence, in which the very survival of a State would be at stake'.

We are not suggesting here that the *effects* of the use of nuclear, or any other, weapons are not covered by other aspects of the definition of a war crime. Article 8(b)(i)-(v) and 8(e)(i)-(iv), for example, prohibit intentional attacks against the civilian population, civilian objects or other protected targets. Additionally, it is possible that in certain circumstances the effects of the use of particular weapons will be covered by the definition of crimes against humanity in Article 7 of the Court's Statute and, in exceptional circumstances, by the definition of genocide in Article 6 of the Statute. Clearly, it is essential that the Rome Statute cover the illegal consequences of the effects of weapons. Had the Statute focused exclusively upon the *effects* of weapons rather than on their *use*, there would be less reason for concern here. However, the Statute establishes an inconsistent regime to cover the *use* of particular weapons.

Article 8(b)(xvii)-(xix) incorporates customary law prohibitions against the use of poison or poisonous weapons; asphyxiating, poisonous or other gases; and, dum dum bullets. The list of weapons the use of which explicitly falls within the subject matter jurisdiction of the Court is limited to these three categories. The use of any other weapons not covered in the list will only fall within the subject matter jurisdiction of the Court if the criteria in Article 8(2)(b)(xx) are satisfied:

> Employing weapons, projectiles and material and methods of warfare which are of a nature to cause superfluous injury or unnecessary suffering or which are inherently indiscriminate in violation of the international law of armed conflict, *provided that such weapons, projectiles and material and methods of warfare are the subject of a comprehensive prohibition* and are included in an annex to this Statute, by an amendment in accordance with the relevant provisions set forth in articles 121 and 123.[75]

This formulation in Article 8(2)(b)(xx) introduces an unprecedented nexus between the prohibition on 'superfluous injury or unnecessary suffering' and the conclusion of multilateral negotiations for a comprehensive ban on a weapons type. Apart from the three categories of weapons specifically referred to in Article 8(2)(b)(vii)-(xix), the use of any other weapons can only constitute a war crime if the weapon is already the subject matter of a 'comprehensive prohibition' and is also added to an annex to the Statute added by amendment at some stage in the future and pursuant to the amendment procedure stipulated in Articles 121 and 123. One implication from this formulation is that while chemical weapons, biological weapons, laser blinding weapons and anti-personnel landmines, all the subject of comprehensive treaty prohibitions, may possibly be included in an Annex to the Statute at some future stage, nuclear weapons

---

[75] Emphasis added.

cannot be included until a comprehensive treaty prohibition on nuclear weapons has been concluded.

The possibility that the decision to deploy dum dum bullets, for example, can constitute a war crime but that any decision to deploy nuclear weapons cannot *per se* constitute a war crime will always raise some questions of consistency of approach in the subject matter jurisdiction of the Court. It is for this reason that it may have been preferable to have deleted any reference in the subject matter jurisdiction of the Court to the *use* of specific weapons.

4.4 *Anti-Personnel Land Mines*

The International Committee of the Red Cross (ICRC) estimates that as many as 27,000 people are either killed or severely injured by anti-personnel land mines every year. The overwhelming majority of these victims are civilians because most land mines remain active in the ground long after the cessation of armed conflict – in some cases for up to sixty years or longer. It has also been estimated that there are up to 120 million sown land mines in 64 countries around the world. While these land mines are being cleared at a rate of 100,000 per year, millions of new land mines are being sown every year. Even if from today no new land mines were sown, at current rates of clearance it would still take at least 1,000 years to clear the land mines currently in the ground at a cost of approximately US$33 billion.[76] Most anti-personnel land mines detonate on the exertion of a minimum amount of pressure[77] but, whatever the triggering mechanism, no land mine distinguishes between soldiers and civilians as the victims of the explosion.

Concerns were expressed during the 1970s about the problem posed by anti-personnel land mines and there were calls to negotiate a treaty to prohibit anti-personnel land mines and other "inhumane weapons". In 1980, a UN sponsored conference adopted the text of the Convention on Prohibitions or Restrictions on the Use of Certain Conventional Weapons Which may be Deemed to be Excessively Injurious or to have Indiscriminate Effects.[78] This Convention, often referred to as the 'Certain Conventional Weapons Convention' (CCWC) was opened for signature in New

---

[76] These UN-based figures are cited in International Committee of the Red Cross, *Special Brochure: Landmines Must be Stopped* (1995) 4. More recently, some sources have claimed that the total number of landmines deployed world-wide is closer to half of the estimated 110 million or more. See Zdzislaw Lachowski, 'The Ban on Anti-Personnel Mines', *SIPRI Yearbook 1998: Armaments, Disarmament and International Security*, 545-58.

[77] There are types of anti-personnel land mines which are detonated by trip wires or by remote control but these types are not as prevalent as those which explode under the pressure of body weight.

[78] Above n 4.

York on 10 April 1981, and entered into force on 2 December 1983 (ie. 6 months after 20 ratifications).[79]

Protocol II of the CCWC placed restrictions on the use of anti-personnel land mines, booby traps and similar devices.[80] The Protocol also prohibited, in all circumstances, the deployment of anti-personnel land mines against the civilian population; prohibited the indiscriminate use of mines; specified that all feasible precautions must be taken to protect civilians from the effects of mines; restricted the use of mines (other than remotely delivered mines) in populated areas; prohibited the use of remotely delivered mines unless their locations can be accurately recorded or an effective neutralising mechanism is used; specified that effective early warning shall be given of any delivery or dropping of remotely delivered mines which may effect the civilian population, unless circumstances do not permit; specified that the Parties to a conflict shall record the location of all pre-planned minefields laid by them and endeavour to ensure the recording of the location of all other minefields.

However, there were serious limitations in the CCWC. For example, there was lack of clarity of some provisions and obligations, including the responsibility of removal of minefields after the conclusion of hostilities. There were no provisions for "undetectable" plastic mines, no procedures for verifying a party's compliance, no procedures for investigating alleged non-compliance and no provisions on production of, or trade, in land mines. In addition, Protocol II did not apply to internal armed conflict (for example, insurgents, rebels, civil wars).

The CCWC may, arguably, have raised international norms against the inhumane use of certain types of weapons. However, based on the relatively low rate of participation in the CCWC, this is less than certain.[81] Furthermore, based on the amount of terrible suffering and devastation currently being caused by anti-personnel land mines, the CCWC has clearly been ineffective in reducing the inhumane deployment of anti-personnel land mines. Unfortunately, the attempts to strengthen Protocol II to the CCWC with the Revised Protocol II negotiated through the 1995/1996 CCWC Review Conference[82] (eg. application of Revised Protocol II to non-international armed conflicts; prohibition on the use of non-

---

[79] For a detailed discussion of the negotiating history of the Convention, see Captain J Ashley Roach, 'Certain Conventional Weapons Convention: Arms Control or Humanitarian Law?' (1984) 105 *Military Law Review* 3.

[80] For a detailed discussion of the negotiating history of Protocol II see Lieutenant Colonel Burris M Carnahan, 'The Law of Land Mine Warfare: Protocol II to the United Nations Convention on Certain Conventional Weapons' (1984) 105 *Military Law Review* 73.

[81] For example, there were only 31 States Parties to the CCWC at the beginning of 1992. This number rose to 57 in the lead up to the CCWC Review Conference in 1995.

[82] *Protocol on Prohibitions or Restrictions on the Use of Mines, Booby-Traps and Other Devices* as Amended on 3 May 1996, (1996) 35 *ILM* 1209 (*'Revised Protocol II to the UN Convention on Conventional Weapons'*).

detectable, non-self destructive or non-deactivating mines) are unlikely to significantly reduce the anti-personnel land mines problem.[83]

Until recently, many defence ministries have argued that anti-personnel land mines are essential to their strategic security interests despite the terrible humanitarian consequences of the illegitimate use of these weapons. In the context of intergovernmental negotiations on attempts to regulate the deployment of land mines, the deleterious humanitarian consequences of the use of land mines have often been overlooked. The intergovernmental negotiation process, dominated by representatives from foreign ministries and defence establishments, has laboured over wording for limitations on the use of anti-personnel land mines – for example, how many grams of detectable material need to be included in each mine, what weight of pressure is required to trigger a mine, what number of mines in a sample of 1,000 which fail in the detectable or self destructing processes is adequate? While this process has dragged on, tens of thousands of civilians have died or lost limbs as a result of contact with land mines, and millions more land mines have been manufactured, sold and sown.

The anti-personnel land mine problem again exposes the gap between general principles and their application to specific weapons. It is self-evident that, like all weapons, land mines are inanimate objects and, therefore, incapable of independently distinguishing between soldiers and civilians. The legal prohibition of weapons which do not discriminate applies to the *use* or *deployment* of weapons more often than to their *design*. Defence lawyers have argued that, in the absence of a specific conventional prohibition, the legitimate deployment of land mines in accordance with Protocol II to the Certain Conventional Weapons Convention (in marked fields which are mapped and cleared after the cessation of armed conflict) renders the weapon discriminate and therefore not inconsistent with the general prohibition on weapons which fail to discriminate between military and civilian targets. This argument continues that the weapon itself cannot be illegal if the possibility of legitimate deployment exists.

For many States, the conclusion of the Ottawa Convention on the Prohibition of the Use, Stockpiling, Production and Transfer of Anti-Personnel Land Mines and on Their Destruction[84] removes much of the uncertainty raised by the two versions of Protocol II to the 1980 Convention. For States Parties to the Ottawa Convention, not only are anti-personnel land mines

---

[83] If anything, the regulation of anti-personnel land mines has only become more complicated because some States are party to neither Protocol II nor Revised Protocol II, some States are party to both Protocol II and Revised Protocol II and still other States are party to one version of the Protocol or the other but not both instruments. This establishes a confusing and complex web of international legal obligations between various States in their relations with each other.

[84] See above n 29.

prohibited but all stockpiles must be destroyed within specific time periods after entry into force of the Convention.

Many see the conclusion of the Ottawa Convention as a major victory for arms control, particularly for a weapon which causes incredible suffering primarily to innocent civilians. The Convention was negotiated in record time and demonstrates what can be achieved when the requisite political will exists. Others are more circumspect. The Ottawa Convention may be a step in the right direction but it has two major limitations: (1) it will not change the reality of the devastation caused by the anti-personnel land mines still in the ground and waiting to explode; (2) several significant producers, users and exporters of anti-personnel land mines did not participate in the negotiations and have stated that they will not become parties to the convention.[85]

In recognition of these limitations, some States, including Australia which has recently ratified the Ottawa treaty,[86] have suggested that other supplementary measures are required. It has been argued that the conclusion of the Ottawa treaty cannot be allowed to turn attention away from the enormous challenge of anti-personnel land mine clearance, and that increased global resources for mine clearance and rehabilitation for victims is essential. Additionally, it has been suggested that the UN Conference on Disarmament negotiate a ban on *transfer* of anti-personnel land mines that might include some States which have refused to participate in the Ottawa process.[87] One thing is certain. Future developments in arms control and disarmament which will increase protection for the victims of armed conflict will not happen overnight. There is a role for 'creeping incrementalism' (characterised by negotiations in the Conference on Disarmament) as there also is for 'dramatic progress' (characterised by the negotiations for the Ottawa Convention) and one should not be seen as mutually exclusive from the other.

Perhaps the most significant aspect of the Ottawa Convention for the relationship between international humanitarian law and arms control is that the conclusion of this treaty is the first occasion on which an arms control agreement banning an entire category of weapons has been motivated primarily by humanitarian concerns. The international humanitarian law instruments purporting to regulate the use of anti-personnel land mines were demonstrably ineffective in alleviating the suffering of huge numbers

---

[85] See Zdzislaw Lachowski, 'The Ban on Anti-personnel Mines', *SIPRI Yearbook 1998: Armaments, Disarmament and International Security*, 545-58.

[86] Minister for Foreign Affairs, The Hon. Alexander Downer MP, *Australia Ratifies Landmines Ban Convention*, Media Release (15 January 1999), text available online at: <http://www.dfat.gov.au/media/releases/downer/fa003_99.html>.

[87] 'Address by the Hon Alexander Downer MP, Minister for Foreign Affairs, to the Conference on Disarmament in Geneva on 3 February 1998: Two Swords for the Beating', (March 1998) *Peace and Disarmament News* 10, 12-13.

of civilian casualties.[88] However, the fascinating reality has been that complete disarmament has been widely acknowledged as a fundamental step in the process of improving protection for victims of armed conflict. The Ottawa Convention thus represents an unprecedented level of relationship between the negotiation of arms control regimes as a means of improving respect for fundamental principles of international humanitarian law.

4.5 *Other Conventional Weapons*

One of the most encouraging recent developments in the whole area of controlling the weapons of war was the agreement in 1995 to prohibit laser and blinding weapons in a new Protocol IV to the CCWC.[89] This agreement was unique in arms control history because the prohibition was negotiated before the weapons were actually deployed in battle. A number of countries had been developing the technology to inflict blindness on victims of laser weapons and in some circumstances these weapons had gone into production. However, the weapons have not been deployed in battle situations and to have reached agreement in the international community for their prohibition before that has happened is a landmark development.

By contrast, achievements in the regulation of the use of other conventional weapons have been much more modest.[90] The UN Register of Conventional Arms is currently the only global co-operative security regime dealing with the transfer and accumulation of major conventional weapons. The idea of an international register may be traced at least as far back as the aftermath of World War I, and such a register was operated for a number of years by the League of Nations. More recently, there have been repeated proposals in the UN to establish a register of arms transfers, but it was only in 1991 that the idea gained wide international support. In December 1991, the UN General Assembly agreed to establish the Register.[91]

---

[88] For example, as discussed above, the imperatives of intense human suffering forced the traditionally apolitical ICRC to adopt anything but a neutral position in the campaign to ban anti-personnel land mines. Of course, neutrality was not jeopardised in the sense that the ICRC was not critical of specific States in this campaign.

[89] *Additional Protocol to the Convention on Prohibitions or Restrictions on the Use of Certain Conventional Weapons which may be Deemed to be Excessively Injurious or to have Indiscriminate Effects* (*Protocol on Blinding Laser Weapons*), opened for signature 13 October 1995; 35 ILM 1218 (entered into force 30 July 1998) ('*Protocol IV to the 1980 Weapons Convention*') As at 28 October 1998, there were 30 States Parties.

[90] On the increasingly deleterious consequences, particularly for civilians, of the unrestrained transfer of conventional weapons, see International Committee of the Red Cross, *Arms Availability, Violations of International Humanitarian Law and the Deterioration of the Situation of Civilians in Armed Conflict* (1998).

[91] UNGA Resolution 46/36 L, 46 UN GAOR, UN Doc. A/RES/46/36 L (6 December 1991).

In December 1992, the details of its initial design were agreed. It first came into operation in April 1993, which was the date by which States were requested to supply data on their arms transfers in 1992.

The UN Register is a transparency measure. Participation is voluntary, includes both suppliers and recipients and does not involve any controls on arms transfers. The Register aims to improve transparency relating to conventional arms transfers and holdings in the hope that this may: contribute to the timely identification and prevention of excessive and destabilising accumulations of arms; promote confidence and restraint; and provide a basis for regional or global confidence and security building measures.

The participation rate in the Register has been encouraging – since April 1993, over 130 States have provided information. Some of these States have only submitted information intermittently so that each annual report has only contained information from approximately 90 States.[92] Most major importing and exporting States now provide data. It has been concluded that the Register already has the potential to contribute to regional and international security and domestic accountability, and may have already done so on a modest scale. However, it is far from achieving its full potential.

States have also been invited to provide "background information" on their total holdings of these weapons and their annual procurement of arms from national production. There have been suggestions from some States that the Register should be expanded to cover holdings and national procurement on the same basis as transfers. However, this expansion has been postponed owing to objections from a number of other States including China, India and Israel. For the time being, the Register remains primarily a register of arms transfers.[93]

However, with respect to comprehensive multilateral treaty prohibitions on other conventional weapons there is little cause for any optimism, at least in the immediate future. This point was succinctly made by former Australian Foreign Minister Gareth Evans in 1991:

> It has to be acknowledged that the international community has yet to come to grips with the problem posed by the huge volumes of conventional arms transfers. While agreements are in place or under negotiation to control or eliminate weapons of mass destruction, there is as yet no remotely comparable process for conventional weapons. We need to acknowledge openly the difficulties which stand in the way of conventional arms control: compared with weapons of mass destruction, they are relatively readily available; trade is well established and lucrative;

---

[92] The region with the poorest response rate is the Middle East.

[93] Malcolm Chalmers and Owen Greene, 'The UN Register of Conventional Arms: the Third Year of Operation', in John B Poole and Richard Guthrie (eds), *Verification 1996: Arms Control, Peacekeeping and The Environment* (1996) 249-80.

and considerations of national sovereignty, and the legitimate responsibility of any government to ensure national security, mean that countries are reluctant to forgo the right to acquire conventional arms.[94]

Unfortunately, little has happened since 1991 which could warrant a more promising prognosis.

Thus, with respect to conventional weapons, other than those specifically covered by the 1980 CCWC, international humanitarian law instruments are all that is currently available to minimise the risk of these types of weapons causing superfluous injury or unnecessary suffering. The ongoing lack of a definition for superfluous injury or unnecessary suffering makes the ICRC's current project to define the concept all the more significant. At present the ICRC surgeon, Dr. Robin Coupland, is developing a study which attempts to provide precise medical formulae to define the phrase 'superfluous injury or unnecessary suffering'.[95] Coupland's study relies on data from ICRC field hospitals to monitor the injuries caused by specific weapons types and the intention is to develop medical criteria for evaluating particular weapons. If the study can influence the international debate, it will be a major step forward for international humanitarian law.

However, it is also clear that the best guarantee of effective implementation of international humanitarian law principles will be through negotiated comprehensive multilateral prohibitions – not just on *use* but also on *possession, production, stockpiling, testing and transfer.* As the ICRC itself has discovered, sometimes arms control regimes which result in comprehensive prohibitions on specific weapons types are an imperative step in the process of improving respect for the international humanitarian law principles.

5. CONCLUSIONS

General principles of international humanitarian law have been developed to alleviate the suffering of combatants and civilians during armed conflict; while efforts to develop arms control treaties to limit, reduce or eliminate stockpiles of particular types of weapons have primarily been motivated by national security concerns. Despite these different motivations, the development of effective arms control treaties can play a major role in supporting the objectives of international humanitarian law, particularly for the control of weapons types that are deemed to cause superfluous injury and unnecessary suffering. Clearly, there is considerable overlap between certain areas of international humanitarian law and arms control (in par-

---

[94] 'Seize the Moment', speech by Senator Gareth Evans to the UN Conference on Disarmament Issues, Kyoto, Japan, 27 May 1991 and extracted in Stockholm International Peace Research Institute, *Yearbook on World Armaments and Disarmament* (1992) 291.

[95] Coupland (ed), above n 17.

ticular, the prohibition or restriction on the use of specific categories of weapons) and other specific areas of arms control should be regarded as complementary to international humanitarian law objectives (for example, the prohibition of the development, production and stockpiling of specific categories of weapons). Indeed, as discussed in the case studies in this chapter, there have been interesting interactions between the efforts of international humanitarian practitioners and arms control negotiators in the efforts to control weapons that are deemed to cause superfluous injury and unnecessary suffering. For example, the failed attempt to effectively prohibit chemical weapons through international humanitarian law principles (1899 Hague Convention) led to the unsuccessful attempts to in the 1920s to negotiate a disarmament treaty, followed by acceptance that the international humanitarian law-based 1925 Geneva Protocol was the only achievable outcome at that time. Following the very limited success of the 1925 Geneva Protocol, a comprehensive disarmament treaty (the CWC) was negotiated between 1969 and 1992.

With biological weapons, the limited success of the international humanitarian law based 1925 Geneva Protocol led to the negotiation of an arms control treaty (the BWC) in 1972, which prohibited, *inter alia*, possession of biological weapons and required all States Parties to destroy any existing stockpiles. The limited success of the BWC, at least in part because of its lack of effective verification provisions, is currently being addressed through efforts to negotiate a Verification Protocol, based in substantial part on the verification provisions developed for the CWC.

The situation has been somewhat different again with nuclear weapons. The unsuccessful attempts in the 1950s at the objective of complete nuclear disarmament, which was driven partly by humanitarian concerns, led to the acceptance of the less ambitious objective of an arms control treaty which was designed to stop horizontal proliferation (NPT, 1969). By the mid-1990s, the lack of progress by the Nuclear Weapons States in efforts towards nuclear disarmament led a number of other States to seek to have the use of nuclear weapons declared illegal on the basis of general principles of international humanitarian law (ICJ Advisory Opinion, Rome Statute of the International Criminal Court).

The efforts to control anti-personnel land mines in the 1970s, which were driven by humanitarian concerns, resulted in the 1980 CCWC, which contained a combination of international humanitarian law-based principles and arms control measures. The failure of the CCWC to significantly reduce the extent of superfluous injury and unnecessary suffering caused by antipersonnel land mines led to very strong humanitarian quest which resulted in the negotiation of a disarmament treaty (the 1997 "Ottawa Treaty"), in record time, externally to the UN-based arms control negotiation machinery.

Clearly, in the past, for both political and technical reasons, treaty negotiators had to be satisfied with restrictions on the use of weapons, rather than total prohibition/elimination of weapons, and minimal (if any) compliance monitoring machinery. As discussed above, more recently the international community has been confronted with, and has been prepared to respond to, the reality that perhaps the only way to effectively deal with the adverse humanitarian consequences of certain specific weapons categories is a comprehensive prohibition of that weapon type (not simply a prohibition on use) which extends to the destruction of stockpiles.[96] So, for example, the international community of States was subjected to an unprecedented level of influence from humanitarian concerns in the negotiation of an anti-personnel land mines disarmament regime.

The end of the Cold War has opened up unprecedented possibilities in arms control. The more constructive relationship between the USA and the RF, which has emerged post Cold War, may well facilitate the negotiation of future global multilateral arms control agreements. Likewise, scientific research has enabled the development of rapid, cost-effective verification tools which can be designed to make on-site verification more efficient as well as less burdensome to the State being inspected.

The CWC is already being touted as an important precedent for other arms control instruments. The CWC has also set a new standard for future negotiations and it is now difficult to imagine discussions about a new treaty without effective verification measures as an integral part of the instrument. Its verification regime has important implications for the current proposals to strengthen the existing inspection regime under the NPT and for the establishment of a verification regime for the BWC. It should be less difficult to negotiate similar verification provisions for other treaties after the CWC has demonstrated its effectiveness and acceptability to States Parties.

That said, negotiation of arms control treaties is likely to remain a slow tortuous process through the "conventional" forum of the Conference on Disarmament (or similar fora such as the BWC *Ad Hoc* Group). A so-called "fast-track" process, such as that which resulted in the Ottawa Treaty, presents a different, potentially complementary, approach. The Ottawa process demonstrated the emergence of a global 'civil society' willing and able to effectively communicate its own expectations of substantive outcomes from inter-governmental negotiation processes and is an encouraging indication of future possibilities.

With the exception of nuclear, chemical and biological weapons, and those categories of weapons covered specifically by the CCWC and Ottawa Treaty, international humanitarian law treaties are likely to remain the major instruments in reducing the risk of specific types of weapons causing

---

[96] See Christopher Greenwood, *International Humanitarian Law and the Laws of War, Preliminary Report for the Centennial Commemoration of the First Hague Peace Conference 1899* (1998) [93], [41]. Text available online at: <http://www.minbuza.nl/english/f_sum conferences14.html>.

superfluous injury or unnecessary suffering. To date, international humanitarian law instruments have had very limited success in reducing the extent of superfluous injury or unnecessary suffering caused by various weapons types. To be effective, the international humanitarian law instruments need to be strengthened by effective compliance monitoring mechanisms, with appropriate penalties for non-compliance, along the lines of recently negotiated arms control treaties. In this context, the recent negotiation of the ICC is a promising development.

5. The SIrUS Project: Towards a Determination of which weapons cause 'Superfluous Injury or Unnecessary Suffering'

1. WEAPONS, LAW, INJURY AND SUFFERING

1.1 *Weapons: A Health Issue?*

Weapons are, by their design, a health issue.[1] This was recognised at the Montreux Symposium in March 1996[2] and by the General Assembly of the World Medical Association in October 1996. The fact that the medical profession has responsibilities in relation to this health issue was also recognised at both these meetings. These responsibilities range from the gathering of data about the effects of weapons on health, thus making the subject objective and understandable, to advocating limits on means of warfare by invoking international humanitarian law and to educating governments, the public and the military about the effects of weapons.

Examination of the effects of weapons on health clarifies legal considerations relating to technology and use of weapons. To limit more effectively the human suffering caused by weapons both current and future, the nature of that human suffering must be understood and quantified. It has been pointed out that objective criteria for measuring suffering would provide a useful tool for lawyers.[3] It has also been noted that, in relation to chemical and biological weapons, there is no objective definition of what makes any particular weapon 'abhorrent',[4] although this has not prevented the signing of treaties prohibiting the production and use of these weapons.

---

[1] Robin M Coupland, 'The Effects of Weapons on Health' (1996) 347 *Lancet* 450-1; V W Sidel, 'The International Arms Trade and its Impact on Health' (1995) 311 *British Medical Journal* 1677; Don G Bates, 'The Medical and Ecological Effects of Nuclear War' (1983) 28 *McGill Law Journal* 717.

[2] The International Committee of the Red Cross, 'The Medical Profession and the Effects of Weapons: The Symposium, Geneva' (1996) ('*ICRC Symposium*').

[3] Ibid. See also Robin M Coupland (ed), *The SIrUS Project: Towards a Determination of Which Weapons Cause 'Superfluous Injury or Unnecessary Suffering'* (1997).

[4] The ICRC Symposium, above n 2, 28.

Helen Durham and Timothy L.H. McCormack (eds.), The Changing Face of Conflict and the Efficacy of International Humanitarian Law, 99–118.

1.2 *An Important Distinction: Design and Use of Weapons*

When a weapon is used against human beings the factors that determine its effects on health relate to both the design of the weapon and the way it is used. The nature of the injury caused is closely related to the design of the weapon. How many people are injured and who is injured are determined largely by the use of the weapon. Which part of the body is injured may relate to either the design of the weapon or its use. A modern rifle may be used to inflict bullet wounds, each wound representing the deposit of energy of up to 2,500 joules to the human body;[5] this wounding capacity is the foreseeable effect resulting from the design of the weapon. When such bullets are fired indiscriminately into a crowd or aimed by a sniper at the head of specific individuals, factors relating to use come into play which determine who is injured, their mortality and, for example, the proportion of wounded with limb injuries. By contrast, a 'point-detonating' (buried) anti-personnel mine, when triggered by foot pressure, causes traumatic amputation of the foot or leg – a foreseeable effect resulting from the design; user-dependent factors determine, for example, the number and category of people injured. Retinal haemorrhage from a blinding laser weapon is obviously a design-dependent effect. The distinction between design-dependent effects and user-dependent effects is central to this document, which focuses exclusively on the design-dependent, foreseeable effects of weapons.

An examination of the design-dependent, foreseeable effects of weapons must include the question as to whether a weapon can be inherently indiscriminate in its effects. A weapon which injures combatants and non-combatants alike usually does so as a result of user-dependent factors. However, indiscriminate effect may be design-dependent;[6] a topical example being anti-personnel mines.[7] This aspect of the design of weapons is not examined further here. There are legal instruments to limit the indiscriminate use of weapons; the same instruments also cover weapons, which as a function of their design, are indiscriminate in their effects.

---

[5] Karl G Sellier and Beat P Kneubuehl, *Wound Ballistics and the Scientific Background* (1994) 341-5.

[6] A weapon which is inherently indiscriminate in its effects is one which affects combatants and non-combatants without distinction, ie even when aimed at or used for a military objective, it will affect civilians in a way that the aimer or user cannot control.

[7] See Robin M Coupland and A M Korver, 'Injuries From Antipersonnel Mines: The Experience of the International Committee of the Red Cross' (1991) 303 *British Medical Journal* 1509; A Ascherio et al, 'Deaths and Injuries Caused by Landmines in Mozambique' (1995) 346 *Lancet* 721; N Andersson, C Palha da Sousa and S Paredes, 'Social Cost of Landmines in Four Countries: Afghanistan, Bosnia, Cambodia and Mozambique' (1995) 311 *British Medical Journal* 718; S Jeffrey, 'Anti-Personnel Mines: Who Are The Victims?' (1996) 13 *Journal of Acccident Emergency Medicine* 343.

1.3 Weapon Design and International Law

The concept that States' right to choose methods and means of warfare is not unlimited has been generally recognized in treaties and custom for centuries. The most important treaty reaffirming the concept is the Hague Regulations of 1907;[8] this rule was recognised as reflecting customary international law by the Nuremberg Tribunal;[9] more recently, the International Court of Justice recognized its customary international law nature.[10] The most recent treaty to recognise this principle is Additional Protocol I[11] to the Geneva Conventions of 1949.[12]

These treaties and others enshrine the concept that any weapon system should not be of a nature to inflict 'superfluous injury or unnecessary suffering'[13] beyond the military purposes of the user and should not render

---

[8] *Convention Concerning The Laws and Customs of War on Land (Hague Convention IV)*, signed at The Hague, 18 October 1907, 205 CTS 277. The Regulations are Annexed to the Convention (*'The Hague Convention'*).

[9] The International Military Tribunal for the Prosecution and Punishment of Major War Criminals of the European Axis, established pursuant to the *Agreement for the Prosecution and Punishment of Major War Criminals of the European Axis, (London Agreement)*, 8 August 1945, 82 UNTS 279. The Charter of the International Military Tribunal is appended to the Agreement (*'The Charter of the IMT'*).

[10] *The Legality of the Threat or Use of Nuclear Weapons, Advisory Opinion of 8 July 1996*, [1996] ICJ Rep 226, 35 ILM 809 (*'The Advisory Opinion of the ICJ'*). For an analysis of this case, see Louise Doswald-Beck, 'International Humanitarian Law and the Advisory Opinion of the International Court of Justice on the Threat or Use of Nuclear Weapons' (1997) 316 *International Review of the Red Cross* 35; Eric David, 'The Opinion of the International Court of Justice on the Legality of the Use of Nuclear Weapons' (1997) 316 *International Review of the Red Cross* 21.

[11] *Protocol Additional to the Geneva Convention of 12 August 1949, and Relating to the Protection of Victims of International Armed Conflicts*, 1125 UNTS 609; 16 ILM 1442 (entered into force on 7 December 1978) (*'Additional Protocol I'*). As of 17 March 1999, there were 153 States Parties.

[12] *Geneva Convention for the Amelioration of the Condition of the Wounded and the Sick in Armed Forces in the Field*, 75 UNTS 31 (*'First Geneva Convention'*); *Geneva Convention for the Amelioration of the Condition of Wounded, Sick and Shipwrecked Members of Armed Forces at Sea*, 75 UNTS 85 (*'Second Geneva Convention'*); *Geneva Convention Relative to the Treatment of Prisoners of War*, 75 UNTS 135 (*'Third Geneva Convention'*); *Geneva Convention Relative to the Protection of Civilian Persons in Time of War*, 75 UNTS 287 (*'Fourth Geneva Convention'*) All these conventions entered into force 21 October 1950, and as at 17 March 1999, there were 188 States Parties.

[13] This concept is to be found in the preamble to the *Declaration Renouncing the Use, in Time of War, of Explosive Projectiles Under 400 Grammes Weight*, opened for signature 29 November/11 December 1868, 138 CTS 297; (1907) 1 *American Journal of International Law (Supp)* 95 (entered into force 29 November/11 December 1868) (*'St Petersburg Declaration'*), but was not formulated until 1899 in the *Regulations Respecting the Laws and Customs of War on Land*, annexed to the *Hague Convention II of 1899, Declaration Concerning the Prohibition of the Use of Projectiles Diffusing Asphyxiating Gases* (signed at The Hague, 29 July 1899), 26 Martens (2d) 998 (*'First Hague, IV, 2'*); *Declaration Concerning the Prohibition of the Use of Expanding Bullets,* (signed at The Hague, 29 July 1899), 26 Martens (2d) 1002. In the English translation of these Regulations, the expression

death inevitable. Whether the effects of a weapon might constitute 'super-fluous injury or unnecessary suffering' on the part of the victim have, up to now, remained within the realm of emotional reaction or philosophical argument.

The first international treaty relating to the design of weapons was the St Petersburg Declaration of 1868, which on a proposal made by the Russian Tsar, banned bullets which explode on impact with the human body. Simi-lar treaties were the Hague Declaration of 1899, which banned the use of dum-dum bullets, the Geneva Protocol of 1925,[14] which banned the use of chemical and biological weapons, the Biological Weapons Convention of 1972[15] and the Chemical Weapons Convention of 1993.[16] (The use of poison or poisoned weapons has been banned by customary law for centu-ries.) Adoption of these treaties was not based on an objective analysis of the suffering caused by the weapons concerned; such means of warfare were simply deemed 'abhorrent' or 'inhuman'. It is important to note that these notions originated with and were promoted by politicians and senior military figures out of concern for the effects that such weapons might have on their troops.

Applying the principles of these treaties to existing weapons is difficult; applying them to weapons under development is even more difficult. As weapon systems being developed for potential military use have differing effects on the human body and may not inflict injury by physical means (transfer of kinetic energy), it is essential that some yardstick of injury and suffering be created against which the effect of any weapon can be meas-ured.

Another pertinent element of existing law is the Martens clause.[17] This originated in the first Hague Peace Conference in 1899, was repeated at the second Peace Conference in 1907 and has been carried forward into Addi-tional Protocol I. It states that civilians and combatants 'remain under the

---

'*maux superflus*' was translated by '*superfluous* injury'; in the 1907 revised version this was replaced by the term 'unnecessary suffering'. Since 1977 'superfluous injury or unnecessary suffering' has been generally adopted as a more appropriate translation. For an in-depth study into the concept of superflous injury, see Henri Meyrowitz, 'The Principle of Unnec-essary Suffering' (1994) 299 *International Review of the Red Cross* 98.

[14] *Protocol for the Prohibition of the Use in War of Asphyxiating, Poisonous, or other Gases and Bacteriological Methods of Warfare*, (opened for signature 17 June 1925), 94 LNTS 65; 26 UST 571 (entered into force 8 February 1928) ('*Geneva Gas Protocol*').

[15] *Convention on the Prohibition of the Development, Production and Stockpiling of Bacteriological (Biological) and Toxin Weapons and on their Destruction*, (signed on 10 April 1972), as at 17 March 1999, there were 141 States Parties; 11 ILM 320; 1971 *UN Juridical Yearbook* 118 ('*BWC*').

[16] *United Nations Convention on the Prohibition of the Development, Production, Stock-piling and Use of Chemical Weapons and on their Destruction*, opened for signature 13 January 1993; 32 ILM 800 (entered into force 29 April 1997) ('*CWC*'). As at 31 December 1998, there were 121 States Parties.

[17] Hague Convention IV, Preamble [6]-[8].

protection and the rule of the principles of the law of nations, as they result from the usages established among civilized peoples, from the laws of humanity and the dictates of the public conscience.'[18]

That the Martens clause now constitutes an element of customary international humanitarian law has been recognised in the Advisory Opinion of the ICJ on 8 July 1996.[19] In addition, the extent to which policy-makers are influenced by strong public opinion on any issue is now fully recognized. The effect on governments of the publicity campaigns securing a ban on anti-personnel mines is evidence of this.

2. HEALTH PROFESSIONALS, WEAPONS AND THE LAW

Legislation on many health-related issues originates with the collection of data that make the relevant concerns understandable and objective; controls on cigarette advertising and the compulsory wearing of seat belts are examples. In the same way, determination of which effects of weapons constitute 'superfluous injury or unnecessary suffering' requires input of health-related data. Injury and suffering are health issues and so health professionals are in a position to help lawyers, governments and the public to decide, on the basis of objective criteria, what is superfluous or unnecessary. Using medical data and arguments to support existing law is a responsibility of the medical profession; this has been recognized by the World Medical Association. Another responsibility of the medical profession is to educate the public about health issues.

The effects of weapons on health should be the basis for legal, ethical, technical and political decisions with respect to weapons; in other words, what weapons really do to human beings should be the lowest common denominator for different professional concerns. This can be demonstrated by examining the focus on bullet construction as a means of limiting human damage in warfare. Dum-dum bullets, which have an exposed lead tip and so splay open on impact with the body, were prohibited in 1899 on moral grounds because of the large wounds they caused. However, technology can circumvent the law by, for example, giving 'legal' bullets a higher velocity and thus the potential to produce the same large wounds. This century, many wound ballistic studies have been performed which have fuelled legal debate about bullet construction. If the effects on health of small arms, which are measurable by a clinical wound classification,[20]

---

[18] Hague Convention IV, Preamble [8].

[19] Advisory Opinion of the ICJ, [78].

[20] See Robin M Coupland, *The Red Cross Wound Classification* (1991); Robin M Coupland, 'The Red Cross Classification of War Wounds: The EXCFM Scoring System' (1992) 16 *World Journal of Surgery* 910.

or can be modelled in a laboratory,[21] were used as the basis for considering bodily harm, the international law governing means and methods of warfare would not get bogged down in technical specifications for bullet construction; scientist, designer, lawyer, soldier and surgeon would have a common point of understanding. A recent and significant legal development is the 1995 Protocol to the Convention on Certain Conventional Weapons, which prohibits the use of laser weapons designed specifically to cause blindness.[22] This is important because it applies to a weapon before that weapon's effects have been observed on the battlefield. However, other 'optical munitions' have been developed which could be used specifically to blind people in war.[23] Although these examples show how politicians agree that there should be a limit to the means and methods of warfare, the prohibition of dum-dum bullets and blinding laser weapons exposes a fundamental defect in this part of international law. In both cases, it is the technology of a weapon that has been prohibited and not its foreseeable effect on human beings. Bullets causing large wounds should have been prohibited in 1899; intentional blinding as a method of warfare should have been prohibited in 1995. In brief, the objective of international law in relation to the design of weapons is to prevent certain adverse or excessive effects on health; prohibition of the use of certain technologies may not suffice.

3. THE SIrUS PROJECT

The principal element of the SIrUS Project is the idea that the effect of a weapon should be considered before its nature, type or technology; this is a reversal of current thinking. The project has involved a group of experts in the areas of weapons, medicine, law and communications, whose work proceeded in three stages. First, they collated data relating to the effects of conventional weapons;[24] second, they used this data as a baseline for the

---

[21] Beat P Kneubuehl, 'Small Calibre Weapon Systems' *in Expert Meeting on Certain Weapon Systems and on Implementing Mechanisms in International Law* (1994) 26-39.

[22] *Additional Protocol to the Convention on Prohibitions or Restrictions on the Use of Certain Conventional Weapons which may be Deemed to be Excessively Injurious or to have Indiscriminate Effects (Protocol on Blinding Laser Weapons),* opened for signature 13 October 1995; 35 ILM 1218 (entered into force 30 July 1998) ('*Protocol IV to the 1980 Weapons Convention*'). As at 28 October 1998, there were 30 States Parties. See also Louise Doswald-Beck (ed), *Blinding Weapons* (1993); 'Weapons Intended to Blind' (Editorial) (1994) *Lancet* 1649-50.

[23] Anonymous author, 'Non-Lethal Weapons: Emerging Requirements for Security Strategy' in *The Institute for Foreign Policy Analysis* (1996) 27; N Lewer and S Schofield, *Non-Lethal Weapons: A Fatal Attraction?* (1997) 10-11.

[24] There is no formal definition of 'conventional weapons'; in this chapter, the term refers to weapons which are currently in use by armies and which utilize projectiles or (non-nuclear) explosions.

consideration of the effects of all weapons; third, they defined four criteria which make an objective distinction between what constitutes and what does not constitute the effects of conventional weapons.[25] They now propose these criteria as a basis for determining which effects of weapons constitute 'superfluous injury or unnecessary suffering' and request endorsement of this proposal by professional and academic bodies.

States have an obligation to determine the legality of any new means and method of warfare they are procuring or developing. The objective of the SIrUS Project is to facilitate such determination without legal wrangling about certain technologies.

4. THE EFFECTS OF CONVENTIONAL WEAPONS: A STUDY

4.1 Introduction

The effects of projectiles and explosions on individuals can be documented by using the Red Cross wound classification.[26] In a clinical setting, this classification has been used to document the incidence of bullet disruption in armed conflict[27] and the categories of wounds caused in civilians by hand grenades,[28] and to refine the wounds of people injured by fragments or bullets according to structures injured and extent of tissue damage.[29] From the score given to any wound its grade, which denotes its size and so reflects energy deposit, can be computed: Grade 1 denotes skin wounds of less than 10 cm without a cavity; Grade 2 denotes skin wounds of less than 10 cm but with a cavity; Grade 3 denotes skin wounds of 10 cm or more with a cavity. It is not possible to establish a precise correlation between grade and energy deposit nor between grade and type of weapon. However, handgun bullets usually inflict Grade 1 wounds and deposit up to 500 joules of energy.[30] A close-range shotgun wound or a wound from a dum-

---

[25] In this document, the term 'effects of conventional weapons' does not include those of 'point-detonating' anti-personnel mines.

[26] See Coupland, above n 20.

[27] Robin M Coupland et al 'Assessment of Bullet Disruption in Armed Conflict' (1992) 339 Lancet 35.

[28] Robin M Coupland, 'Hand Grenade Injuries Among Civilians' (1993) 270 Journal of the American Medical Association 624-6.

[29] Ibid; G W Bowyer, M P M Stewart, J M Ryan, 'Gulf War Wounds: Application of the Red Cross Wound Classification' (1993) 24 Injury 597; G W Bowyer 'Afghan War Wounded: Application of the Red Cross Wound Classification' (1995) 38 Journal of Trauma 64; M P M Stewart and A Kinninmouth, 'Shotgun Wound of the Limbs' (1993) 24 Injury 667; Robin M Coupland, 'Classification and Management of War Wounds' in C D Johnson and I Taylor (eds), Recent Advances in Surgery 17 (1994) 121-34; J Savic et al 'Glucose as an Adjunct Triage Tool to the Red Cross Wound Classification' (1996) 40 Journal of Trauma 144.

[30] See Sellier and Kneubuehl, above n 5 341-5.

dum bullet will invariably be of Grade 3 and is associated with deposit of more than 1,500 joules of energy.[31] Modern assault rifles can inflict all grades of wound, depending on range, bullet construction and length of the wound track in the body. Fragments of shells, bombs, grenades and mortars are capable of inflicting all three grades of wounds, depending on their mass and velocity.

It is also possible to measure the collective effects of weapons by determining, for example, the mortality caused by a weapon system in the field (in military terms: 'killed in action'), the proportion of casualties who die after reaching a medical facility ('died of wounds'), hospital mortality, the number of days the survivors stay in hospital, the number of operations they require, the number of units of blood they need during treatment, or the proportion of survivors with a particular residual disability.

The ICRC's wound database grew out of a simple system of data collection which was originally designed to give an indication of the activities of independent ICRC hospitals. Included in the information recorded for each patient is the cause of injury, the time lapse between injury and admission, the wound classification, the region or regions injured, whether the patient has died in hospital, the number of operations, the number of units of blood required, the number of days spent in hospital, and whether the patient was discharged with amputation of one or both lower limbs. This method of data collection was introduced in January 1991. Since then, all war-wounded patients who have been admitted to the ICRC hospitals in Peshawar and Quetta (Pakistan/Afghan border), Kabul (Afghanistan), Khao-I-Dang (Thai/Cambodian border), Butare (Rwanda) and Lokichokio (Kenyan/Sudanese border) have had a data form filled out on their death or discharge from surgical wards as part of the hospital routine. The database currently contains data relating to 26,636 patients, of whom 8,805 (33.1%) were females, males less than 16 years old or males of 50 years or more and hence were unlikely to have been combatants.

There is inevitably an unknown proportion of forms that are not filled out correctly; an enormous effort has been made to reduce this proportion to a minimum. The readiness of surgeons to score wounds according to the Red Cross wound classification is variable. Some patients lie about the cause of their injuries to gain admission to hospital or may not know exactly what injured them. Because of the constraints imposed on the collection of these data under field conditions, their 'validity' and 'reliability' have not been ascertained by formal independent means.

4.2 *Method*

The patients' data were analysed by cause of injury. 'Fragment' indicates injury from shell, bomb, grenade or mortar. 'Bullet' indicates any gunshot

---

[31] Ibid.

wound. 'Mine injury' refers to any person admitted as a result of a mine explosion, whether anti-tank or anti-personnel mine. 'Burn' indicates burn injury from any cause. 'Mine causing amputation' is a subgroup of all the mine-injured but is taken to correspond broadly to those who have stepped on a 'point-detonating' anti-personnel mine.[32]

For patients with fragment and bullet wounds and for whom a wound score according to the Red Cross wound classification was recorded, the grades of the first or only wound scored were computed. Site or sites of injury (head/neck, chest, abdomen, back, pelvis/buttocks, right upper limb, left upper limb, right lower limb and left lower limb) for those admitted to hospital within 24 hours were analysed according to cause of injury.

For those injured by fragments, bullets, burn or mines and who were admitted to hospital within 24 hours, hospital mortality was computed. For the surviving patients of the same group the following were computed: average number of days spent in hospital (this is the number of days to surgical discharge, excluding the portion of stay of those who had to wait in hospital for political or geographical reasons); average number of operations required; proportion of patients transfused, average number of units of blood transfused; total number of lower limbs amputated (this is not given as a proportion of all patients because of the small number who had bilateral lower limb amputation). Those injured by mines and who arrived with traumatic amputation or who subsequently underwent surgical amputation were analysed as a subgroup of all mine injuries. In this part of the study only data from patients who were admitted within 24 hours of injury were analysed, so those who had delayed access to medical care did not influence the results.

4.3 Results

Table 1 shows the proportion of the grades of the first wound scored on the records of 8,295 patients injured by fragments or bullets.

Table 1

	Grade 1	Grade 2	Grade 3
Fragments (shell, bomb, grenade, etc.) (3,157 patients)	1841 (58.3%)	1054 (33.4%)	263 (8.3%)
Bullets (5,138 patients)	2333 (45.4%)	2296 (44.7%)	509 (9.9%)

The proportion of grades of the first wound scored by the Red Cross wound classification in 8, 295 patients injured by fragments and by bullets. The classification and the significance of the grade of the wound is explained in the text. The 95% Confidence Interval (CI) on the presence of Grade 3 wounds resulting from fragments is 7.3; that for wounds from bullets is 9.1% to 10.7%.

---

[32] Coupland and Korver, above n 7.

Table 2 shows hospital mortality according to cause of injury in 8,762 patients who were admitted within 24 hours of injury.

Table 2

Cause of Injury	Number of patients	Number dies (mortality %)
Fragments	2926	118 (4.0%)
Bullet	2706	124 (4.6%)
Burn	102	19 (18.6%)
Mine	3028	121 (4.0%)
Mine causing amputation	890	55 (6.2%))

Mortality in 8, 762 patients admitted to independent ICRC hospitals within 24 hours of injury according to cause of injury. "Mine" = all mine-injured patients. "Mine causing amputation" = patients who arrived with a traumatic amputation or who underwent surgical amputation; it is a subgroup of all the mine-injured.

The percentages dying by cause of injury are different (χ^2=51.83 on 3 d.f., p<0.001). The percentages dying from fragments, bullets and mines are not significantly different from each other as shown by partitioning of the chi-square statistics (χ^2=1.50 on 2 d.f., p>0.05), confirming that the overall significance is due to the high proportion dying from burns.

Table 3 shows the regions injured according to wounding agent in 8,660 non-burn patients admitted within 24 hours of injury.

Table 3

	Number of Patients	Number of regions injured	Regions injured per patient	Central injuries (% all injuries)	Upper limb injuries (% all injuries)	Lower limb injuries (% all injuries)
Fragments	2,926	5,531	1.9	43.5	23.8	32.6
Bullet	2,706	3,491	1.3	45.2	20.2	34.5
Mine	3,028	7,282	2.4	27.8	27.2	44.9

The number and distribution of wounds in 8,660 patients admitted to independent ICRC hospitals within 24 hours of injury according to cause of injury. "Central injuries" = wounds of the head/neck, chest, abdomen, back, buttocks/pelvis.

The distribution of the sites of injury is very different for the different types of weapons. (patients frequently had multiple injuries, so the standard chi-square test is not computed due to non-independence of data.) Inspection shows that the proportion of lower limb injuries due to mines was much higher than for the other two types of weapon.

Table 4 shows, for the 8,380 patients surviving to discharge and according to cause of injury: average number of days spent in hospital; average number of operations; proportion of patients transfused; average volume of blood transfused in units; number of lower limbs amputated.

Table 4

	Total Survived	Mean days in hospital	Mean number of operations	Proportion transfused (%)	Mean units of blood given	Number of lower limbs amputated
Fragments	2,808	14.3	1.9	14.1	0.4	63
Bullet	2.582	19.1	2.1	15.9	0.5	20
Burn	83	18.8	1.7	8.4	0.3	1
Mine	2,907	22.3	2.8	33.6	1.3	915
Mine causing amputation	835	32.9	4.0	74.9	3.1	915

Data from 8,380 war-wounded patients who survived, showing days in hospital, operations per patient, blood transfusion and lower limb amputation. All patients were admitted to independent ICRC hospitals within 24 hours of injury. The number of lower limb amputations is not given as a percentage of all patients because of the few requiring bilateral amputation. "Mines" = all mine-injured patients who survived; "Mine causing amputation" = those mine-injured who survived with either a below-knee amputation, an above-knee amputation or bilateral lower limb amputation. The percentage of patients receiving transfusion were significantly different across the different causes of injury (χ^2=401.3 on 3 d.f., p<0.001). By far the highest proportion was in the mine-injured, the excess being almost wholly due to amputation.

4.4 *Discussion*

When patients are admitted to an ICRC hospital, their military status is neither ascertained nor recorded. The fact that at least 33% of the patients could be presumed to be 'non-combatants' reflects the reality of modern conflicts. There are no means of establishing how many die before reaching hospital.

Table 1 shows that for those patients injured by either fragments or bullets, the proportion with Grade 1 wounds and Grade 2 wounds differs. However, the corresponding proportion with Grade 3 wounds is similar in both cases and is less than 10%. This establishes a baseline for the proportion of large wounds in those who survived to hospital. The majority of bullet wounds seen in ICRC hospitals are caused by the Kalashnikov AK-47.

A review of data from military medical sources, who know the number of fatalities in the field, shows how little mortality has changed since World War II.[33] The proportion of wounded who die in the field varies between 18% and 22%. Likewise, the proportion of all casualties who die

---

[33] See M A Melsom, M D Farrar and R C Volkers, 'Battle Casualties' (1975) 56 *Annals of the Royal College of Surgeons, England* 287; R F Bellamy, 'The Medical Effects of Conventional Weapons' (1992) 16 *World Journal of Surgery* 888 ('*Bellamy 1992*'); R F Bellamy, 'Combat Trauma Overview' in R Zaitchuk and C M Grande (eds), *Anaesthesia and Preoperative Care of the Combat Casualty* (1996) ('*Bellamy 1996*').

after reaching a medical facility varies between about 2.5% and 4.5%.[34] This gives a baseline proportion of deaths among casualties which has been accepted by military and political leaders and lawyers as a consequence of war waged in this period of history. The figures for hospital mortality by cause of injury given in Table 2 are comparable, except for those who suffer burns. As the plight of burn patients in hospital is particularly miserable, this high hospital mortality in ICRC facilities represents a lingering death.

Table 3 shows that the distribution of regions wounded by fragments and by bullets are similar. The higher proportion of lower limb injuries and the lower proportion of central injuries in mine-injured patients reflects the foreseeable effects resulting from the design of these weapons; 'point-detonating' anti-personnel mines cause traumatic amputation of the contact foot or leg and fragmentation mines tend to damage the lower limbs.[35] Table 3 also indicates that, in addition to their predilection for lower limbs, mines injure more regions per wounded person than fragmentation weapons.

'Point-detonating' anti-personnel mines are designed to be triggered by foot pressure and thus cause traumatic amputation of a lower limb (a Grade 3 wound). Table 4 shows that mines are a much greater drain on hospital resources as compared with other conventional weapons, and inflict permanent and severe disability on anyone who survives injury. Days spent in hospital, the number of operations and the requirement for blood transfusion are all greater in this group – a reflection of the volume of severe tissue damage which the surgeon must treat.[36] Combining these foreseeable and measurable effects with the fact that ejected fragmentation mines cause 100% mortality among those that trigger them[37] not only raises the question of 'superfluous injury or unnecessary suffering' in relation to the design of anti-personnel mines,[38] but could also support the argument that 'point-detonating' anti-personnel mines should be put in a separate category from other conventional weapons because of their foreseeable effects on health.

The surgical facilities of the ICRC, as a matter of policy, work with a basic level of technology, non-specialist surgery, and no onward evacuation to other facilities; emphasis is placed on certain basic principles of

---

[34] Ibid. See also Robin M Coupland, 'Epidemiological Approach to the Surgical Management of the Casualties of War' (1994) 308 *British Medical Journal* 1693.

[35] See Coupland and Korver, above n 7.

[36] Ibid. See also B Eshaya-Chauvin and Robin M Coupland, 'Transfusion Requirements for the Management of War Wounded: The Experience of the International Committee of the Red Cross' (1993) 71 *British Journal of Anaesthesia* 172.

[37] D B Adams and C W Schwab, 'Twenty One Year Experience With Land-Mine Injuries' (1988) 28 *Journal of Trauma* 159.

[38] Cornelio Sommargua, 'Does the Nature of Mine Injuries Also Justify a Total Ban?', *Landmines: Demining News From the United Nations* (1996) 11.

surgical management.[39] These facilities often give a better standard of care than is available in the countries where war is being fought and may even represent a 'best-case'scenario. Hospital mortality differs little from that reported in military publications.[40] In terms of meeting medical and surgical needs for treating explosive and missile wounds these hospitals provide a baseline standard of care. However, the medical facilities required to improve survival in cases of burn injury simply cannot be made accessible to victims of modern wars without enormous input in terms of funds and specialized personnel.

4.5 *Conclusions*

The study shows some of the foreseeable and measurable effects of conventional weapons on human beings. These effects stem from two important features which distinguish conventional weapons (except 'point-detonating' anti-personnel mines) from all others: first, they exert their effects by physical injury to the tissues of the human body; second, excluding user-dependent factors, there is a randomness as to which part of the body is injured. A series of baselines relating to injury and suffering resulting from the effects of conventional weapons, including a baseline of treatment requirements, is established.

The data pertaining to the effects of 'point-detonating' anti-personnel mines show how their foreseeable effects differ measurably from those of other conventional weapons and that these different effects can only be design-dependent.

5. A PROPOSAL FOR DETERMINATION OF WHICH WEAPONS CAUSE 'SUPERFLUOUS INJURY OR UNNECESSARY SUFFERING'

5.1 *A Combination of Concepts*

The proposal for determination of which design-dependent, foreseeable effects of weapons constitute 'superfluous injury or unnecessary suffering' assumes that:
- the effect of a weapon resulting from its design rather than the weapon's nature, type or technology is the primary consideration;
- the effects of all weapons both on individuals and on groups of people are measurable;
- the effects of conventional weapons on health which are well-documented, provide a reference baseline or yardstick for deter-

---

[39] Robin M Coupland, *War Wounds of Limbs: Surgical Management* (1993) 12-35; see also R C Gray, *War Wounds: Basic Surgical Management* (1994).

[40] See Melsom, Farrar and Volkers, above n 33; Bellamy 1992, above n 33.

mining the foreseeable effects of all weapons when used against human beings;

- the degree of suffering caused by a weapon is increased if there is no treatment available.

The effect of a weapon on any individual may be described and certain parameters of injury measured; however, these may not reflect the effect on all individuals. The collective effects measured in groups of people wounded by the weapon in question has significance:[41] it reflects more accurately the foreseeable effect of the weapon resulting from its design when in normal use. The study described above demonstrates some of the foreseeable and measurable effects of conventional weapons on both individuals and groups. This is the best index of injury and suffering available and, up to now, neither law nor public opinion in general have wanted to prohibit these weapons because of their design-dependent effects. The basis of the SIrUS Project is the use of data relating to the effects of conventional weapons to determine what is not 'superfluous injury or unnecessary suffering'. Any other foreseeable effects of weapons would therefore constitute 'superfluous injury or unnecessary suffering'.

5.2 *The Proposal of the SIrUS Project*

The proposal is that what constitutes 'superfluous injury and unnecessary suffering' be determined by design-dependent, foreseeable effects of weapons when they are used against human beings and cause:

- specific disease, specific abnormal physiological state, specific abnormal psychological state, specific and permanent disability or specific disfigurement (Criterion 1); or
- field mortality of more than 25% or a hospital mortality of more than 5% (Criterion 2); or
- Grade 3 wounds as measured by the Red Cross wound classification (Criterion 3); or
- effects for which there is no well recognized and proven treatment (Criterion 4).

The criteria thus combine to form a clear picture of injury and suffering that is not the equivalent of the effects of conventional weapons. This is the nucleus of the SIrUS Project.

---

[41] See, Coupland and Korver, above n 7; Coupland, above n 28; Bellamy 1992, above n 33; Coupland, above n 34; R M Garfield and A I Neugut, 'Epidemiological Analysis of Warfare: A Historical Analysis' (1991) 226 *Journal of the American Medical Association* 688.

5.3 An Examination of the Criteria

Criterion 1 – specific disease, specific abnormal physiological state, specific abnormal psychological state, specific and permanent disability or specific disfigurement
Criterion 1 draws an important distinction between the effects of all other weapons and the effects of conventional weapons (except 'point-detonating' anti-personnel mines).

The foreseeable psychological effects of weapons have been stressed.[42] Whilst all weapons produce fear and stress, these reactions are neither specific nor abnormal. Criterion 1 would apply to a weapon designed to disorientate, confuse, induce calm or precipitate seizures or psychosis. In the same context, the known neuroendocrine response to physical trauma from conventional weapons is part of their effects.[43] The same neuroendocrine response produced by an agent or energy form without physical injury would represent a specific and abnormal physiological response.

Conventional weapons do not generate an absolute necessity for blood transfusion, as shown in the study. Criterion 1 would apply to any weapon which, for example, foreseeably causes gastrointestinal haemorrhage for which a blood transfusion would be needed. The implications of the need for blood transfusion are particularly important; without a reliable and safe blood bank, which is difficult to establish in a war zone, there is a risk of transfusing blood that has not been cross-matched or tested for communicable diseases such as syphilis, hepatitis B and HIV (the virus causing AIDS).[44]

The need for multiple operations compounds the suffering from the effects of weapons; patients wounded by conventional weapons do not require, on average, more than three operations in a non-specialized surgical facility. Thus a weapon which, for example, causes facial disfigurement as a foreseeable effect would give rise to the need for multiple reconstructive operations in a specialized facility. Criterion 1 would apply, possibly in combination with Criterion 4.

Criterion 2 – field mortality of more than 25% or hospital mortality of more than 5%
The use of weapons whose design renders death inevitable is already prohibited as part of the same legal concept that prohibit those causing 'superfluous injury or unnecessary suffering' (Appendix 3). The study shows, for different categories of conventional weapons, how constant the

---

[42] ICRC Symposium, above n 2, 36-7; Doswald-Beck, above n 22, 258-313.

[43] Savic, above n 29; I Cernak, J Savic and A Lazarov, 'Relations Among Plasma Prolactin, Testosterone and Injury in War Casualties' (1997) 8 *World Journal of Surgery* 240, 240-6.

[44] Eshaya-Chauvin and Coupland, above n 36.

figures are both for field mortality and for later mortality after the wounded person reaches a medical facility.[45] The figures for field mortality and hospital mortality must be considered separately because death from a weapon may occur days or weeks after injury, as is the case with burns and as shown in Table 2 of the study. The figures of 25% and 5% for field and hospital mortality respectively are proposed as limits which are on the conservative side of the established baseline.

Criterion 3 – Grade 3 wounds as measured by the Red Cross wound classification

This criterion is needed to apply to weapons which, without targeting a particular part of the body, simply inflict large wounds. This would be the case for exploding bullets and dum-dum bullets. Table 1 of the study shows that conventional weapons produce less than 10% Grade 3 wounds. This figure would be exceeded by any missile or wave form which carried much more energy and which foreseeably deposited this energy in the human body over a short track.

In an attempt to move law away from an approach focusing on technology – as exemplified by the prohibitions on exploding and dum-dum bullets – towards an approach focusing on effect, the Swiss government has proposed to States a means of testing munitions for their potential to produce large wounds; the application of Criterion 3 to a weapon could be tested in a laboratory.[46]

Criterion 4 – exerts effects for which there is no well recognized and proven treatment

Criterion 4 is closely linked to Criterion 1. For the laser-damaged retina there is no known successful treatment even in the best facilities. The effects of other new weapons are not fully known and so treatment is unlikely to be successful.[47] This criterion also highlights the imbalance between the finance and technology that goes into the development of weapons on the one hand and, on the other, the comparatively scanty resources that are made available to treat the wounded and record the true effects of weapons on health.

5.4 *Applying the Criteria to Different Weapons*

One or more of the four criteria apply to weapons which are already prohibited: Criterion 1 and possibly Criteria 2 and 4 apply to chemical and

---

[45] See Melsom, Farrar and Volkers, above n 33; Bellamy 1992, above n 33; Coupland, above n 34; Garfield and Neugent, above n 41.

[46] Kneubuehl, above n 21.

[47] Robin M Coupland, '"Non-Lethal Weapons": Precipating a New Arms Race' (1997) 315 *British Medical Journal* 72

biological weapons; Criteria 2 and 3 apply to exploding bullets; Criterion 3 and possibly Criterion 2 apply to dum-dum bullets; Criteria 1 and 4 apply to blinding laser weapons. These criteria also apply to weapons which are subject to either a review of the law pertaining to them or widespread stigmatization: Criteria 1, 2 and 3 apply to 'point-detonating' anti-personnel mines; Criterion 2 and possibly Criterion 1 apply to burning weapons.

Conventional weapons are not necessarily 'lethal'; this is an important point to make when new weapons are considered in the context of the SIrUS Project. The term 'non-lethal' has been applied to a new generation of weapons, implying that technological advances have provided the means to achieve military objectives whilst minimizing deaths and injuries. A variety of energy forms, physical agents and chemicals have been developed along these lines.[48] This concept must be examined carefully from the point of view of the effects of such weapons. The purpose is to "disable" – to inflict disability – but the difficult question of how long the disability will last is not considered. If it is established what energy output, concentration or dose is 'non-lethal' or temporary, one has also discovered what is lethal or permanent. Thus for new weapons the dividing line between 'non-lethal' and 'lethal' may be fine or non-existent. In tactical terms, new weapons will always be backed up by or used in conjunction with conventional weapons;[49] 'softening the target' may increase the 'lethality' of conventional weapons. In addition, a doctor treating the wounded may have to treat people suffering from the effects of both conventional and 'non-lethal' weapons. All new weapons can and should be considered in terms of their effects and therefore in relation to the four criteria.

With regard to weapons that are designed to blind, it has been argued that it is better to blind an enemy soldier than to kill him or her. This argument fails to take into account the fact that conventional weapons are not 100% lethal, the psychological impact of sudden blindness,[50] the extent of disability, or the impact on a society of its soldiers returning from battle having been irreversibly blinded. Criteria 1 and 4 apply.

Among other 'non-lethal' weapons which should be studied in the context of the SIrUS Project are chemical agents that render a person confused, demotivated or unconscious for a short period without lasting effects. To such a weapon, if it exists, whether Criteria 1 and 4 apply is arguable. However, there are three additional points to consider: first, 'softening the target' is still an important consideration; second, use of such an agent as a method of warfare is already prohibited under the

---

[48] See Non-Lethal Weapons, above n 23; Lewer and Schofield, above n 23; Coupland, above n 47; M Dando, *A New Form of Warfare: The Rise of Non-Lethal Weapons* (1996).

[49] Non-Lethal Weapons, above n 23; Lewer and Schofield, above n 23.

[50] Doswald-Beck, above 22; See also, E Wittkower and R C Davenport, 'The War Blinded: Their Emotional, Social and Occupational Situation' (1946) 8 *Psychosomatic Medicine* 121.

Chemical Weapons Convention; third, a basic principle of pharmacology is that the only difference between a drug and a poison is the dose and it is unclear how the correct dose can be administered on the battlefield.

One cannot consider the effects of weapons in general without referring to nuclear weapons. Here Criteria 1, 2 and 4 would apply (burns and radiation sickness). The nuclear debate, which is discussed extensively in other fora, is not taken further in this document.

When military utility is being assessed, the primary use of the weapon concerned must be taken into account. Weapons used, for example, to disable tanks or ships must be sufficiently destructive for this purpose. Although the crews themselves are protected by the legal concept of 'superfluous injury or unnecessary suffering', they may still suffer severe injuries associated with high mortality when attacked by such weapons.[51] Criterion 2 apparently applies; however, in this context, it cannot be used as a determination of 'superfluous injury or unnecessary suffering' because of the military need to use such weapons. Criterion 1 definitely applies to an agent or energy form which would cause the crew to suffer, for example, epileptic convulsions.

5.5 *Do not all Weapons Cause 'Superfluous Injury or Unnecessary Suffering'? Is any Weapon Acceptable?*

Can a weapon cause injury which is not superfluous? Is there such a thing as necessary suffering? These questions pose a moral problem for pacifists, those who believe in complete disarmament and the medical profession.

Use of weapons must generate suffering. Whether use of weapons is necessary is a debate that goes beyond the scope of the SIrUS Project which regards weapons as neither acceptable nor unacceptable. The project represents an attempt to limit the types of weapon that might be used in war; this attempt will fail if the criteria are refuted because they do not represent total disarmament.

The SIrUS Project involves drawing a clear and objective distinction between the effects of conventional weapons and the effects of other weapons. Legal and moral judgement can then be applied to this distinction. Endorsement of the SIrUS Project amounts to recommendation that this distinction be recognized by States in meeting their obligations under international law.

In explaining the effects of weapons in an objective and understandable way to lawyers, governments and the military, the medical profession is making neither a moral nor a legal judgement about weapons. The paper adopted by the General Assembly of the World Medical Association states, 'No weapon is medically acceptable to physicians, but physicians can aid in making effective controls against weapons which cause injury or suf-

---

[51] Bellamy 1992, above n 33.

fering so extreme as to invoke the terms of International Humanitarian Law'.[52] The SIrUS Project can help the medical profession to avoid making a moral judgement by recommending the criteria as a means of making a legal judgement. Medical ethics are not breached as this initiative has the potential to prevent specific injury; it is not aimed at preventing all injuries in war.

5.6 The SIrUS Project and Public Opinion

Criterion 1 reflects the question as to whether weapons which target specific biochemical, physiological or anatomical features or weapons which target vital organs or functions should be prohibited.[53] The process whereby knowledge of human form and function is used to develop weapons designed to interfere with that form and function seems to be considered genuinely abhorrent. It is no coincidence then that chemical, biological and blinding laser weapons have been prohibited. This may reflect the distaste for biomedical scientists being involved in weapon design and is linked to the ethical dilemma arising from the fact that much modern weapon design is based on medical knowledge.[54] The measurable and foreseeable effects of conventional weapons provide a baseline, and this baseline pertains to injury and suffering caused by weapons when knowledge of human form and function are not the primary factor in their design. Thus there is an inevitable link between the Martens clause and Criterion 1. As there is proven treatment for the effects of few weapons to which Criterion 1 would apply, there is a link between the Martens clause and Criterion 4 also. Weapons from which a soldier cannot take cover, the use of which may not immediately be detected or which poison, heighten the reaction of abhorrence.

Stigmatization of any weapon system is an important factor in reducing the chance of its use; this applies not only to weapons which have been prohibited but also to napalm and to anti-personnel mines which are not, as yet, deemed illegal by all States. Endorsement of the SIrUS Project would provide an objective and precise means of focusing public opinion so that a new weapon whose effect would clearly be 'abhorrent' or 'inhuman' would not have to be deployed before the public conscience is stirred. The SIrUS Project as an element of public opinion runs parallel not only to the obligation of States to determine the legality of any weapon system they are developing but also to the responsibility of the medical profession to

---

[52] The World Medical Association Inc, *Proposed World Medical Association Statement on Weapons and their Relation to Life and Health*, 48th WMA General Assembly (1996).

[53] ICRC Symposium, above n 2.

[54] Ibid. See also, Doswald-Beck, above n 22; E Prokosch, *The Technology of Killing* (1995); Robin M Coupland, 'The Effects of Weapons: Surgical Challenge and Medical Dilemma' (1996) 41 *Journal of the Royal College of Surgeons of Edinburgh* 65.

educate the public about health matters. The SIrUS Project provides a means for the medical profession to bring weaponry issues objectively into the public domain and at the same time to encourage the international community to recognize the grave implications of continued research and development of new means of warfare.[55]

---

[55] See, Coupland, above n 1; ICRC Symposium, above n 47-9; Lewer and Schofield, above n 23, 24-44. See also Dando, above n 48, Prokosch, above n 54; Coupland, above n 54.

PART IV

Identifying the Law Applicable to Peace Operations

6. Legal Constraints on Military Personnel Deployed on Peacekeeping Operations

1. INTRODUCTION

In early 1997 the ICRC advised that it had been negotiating with the United Nations to prepare a Code of Conduct for peacekeepers. At a number of joint expert meetings in 1995 all the provisions of humanitarian law (in particular those relating to the conduct of hostilities, and to the protection of civilians, detainees and medical personnel) were analyzed in order to determine their applicability to peace-keeping forces, with a view to preparing a draft code of conduct. As a result, a set of Directives for UN Forces Regarding Respect for International Humanitarian Law was jointly prepared, the final text being drawn up in May 1996.[1]

The ICRC advised that the Directives set out the content and scope of the 'principles and spirit' of humanitarian law by which the UN agrees to be bound, and includes a series of provisions covering the various categories of protected persons. The purpose of the Guidelines, according to the ICRC, is to specify the principles and rules of international humanitarian law applicable to UN forces 'conducting operations under UN command and control, when in situations of armed conflicts (either international or non-international) in which they are actively engaged as combatants' (emphasis added). The ICRC characterised the Guidelines as being applicable to both peacekeeping and enforcement operations, where the use of force is authorized either in self-defence or pursuant to a mandate of the Security Council. This characterisation is itself symptomatic of the confusion in this area of the law: it implies that armed conflict law is equally

---

[1] The Code of Conduct has not yet been made public. The ICRC did, however, issue a Press Release, ICRC News 96/1996, dated 15 May 1996, referring to the initiative to negotiate the Code. The guidelines are contained in a document entitled 'Guidelines for UN Forces Regarding Respect for International Humanitarian Law'. It purports to specify the principles and rules of the 1949 Geneva Conventions and their 1977 Additional Protocols applicable to UN forces deployed in areas affected by armed conflicts. The press release can be accessed via the ICRC website at <http://www.icrc.org/unicc/icrcnews.nsf/fc7c477b9b1890bd41256299002e04a2/42483138b7622e44c125632b00534d09? OpenDocument>.

Helen Durham and Timothy L.H. McCormack (eds.), The Changing Face of Conflict and the Efficacy of International Humanitarian Law, 121–139.
© 1999 *Kluwer Law International. Printed in Great Britain.*

applicable to the inherent right of individual self defence, a right which excuses the use of force in circumstances *other* than those governed by armed conflict law, as well as to the other uses of force which may be legally permissible in times of armed conflict or when authorized by a United Nations Security Council mandate.

The ICRC emphasised that the Guidelines do not constitute an exhaustive list of principles and rules of international humanitarian law binding upon military personnel, who, it correctly contends, remain bound by their national laws to respect the principles and rules of international humanitarian law, as may be applicable. The ICRC does however recognize that in case of violation, either of the Guidelines or of rules of international humanitarian law more generally, the alleged violators may be subject to prosecution in their national courts.

The Guidelines, although agreed by the ICRC and the United Nations Secretariat, are not yet public because internal UN procedures have not been completed and, more importantly, it appears that some States have reservations concerning the text. It is unfortunate that they are not available at the time of completion of this paper because exposure would allow a wider public debate and the consequent possibility of rules reflecting the reality of the bulk of the duties of peacekeeping forces. The main issues are capable, however, of identification.

The primary question must be: is there indeed a need for a Code of Conduct for UN peacekeeping troops in the sense of prescribing the laws that must be applied by those troops? If so, what principles should govern its application, what should be its content and what relationship will it have with the laws applied by the troop contributing nations?[2] There can be little doubt that a common basic standard of legal behaviour is highly desirable. In this paper it is proposed to briefly examine the circumstances in which a Code would operate, to highlight some of the legal issues that arise therefrom, the features that would be desirable in any such Code and the perceived obstacles.

---

[2] This includes international law as recognized by each nation. Outside that common body of international law known as customary international law and which binds all nations, international law is different for each nation and depends upon the treaties to which nations are party. The 1977 Protocols Additional to the 1949 Geneva Conventions, for example, form part of Australia's international law obligations because Australia has ratified them whereas they do not impose obligations on either the United States or Iraq which are not States Parties and did not impose obligations upon the United Kingdom at the time of the Gulf War because the UK did not ratify the Additional Protocols until 1998. International law is therefore different for Australia from that for non States Parties to the Additional Protocols.

2. RULES OF ENGAGEMENT

Putting aside for the moment the question of whether the UN or the ICRC can prescribe what law is applicable to national contingents, the negotiations obviously quite clearly (and correctly) recognise that any such Code must identify the legal principles that govern the use of those contingents, the force that they may use and the circumstances in which they use it. Any such Code or set of principles should not, however, be confused with or mistaken for rules of engagement. Rules of engagement, although they must reflect the law, are neither the law nor a subset of the law. They are restrictions placed by government upon the legally permissible actions that their national armed forces may take in performing their operations – in other words they are governmentally imposed parameters within which those forces must operate when carrying out the policy or directions of their government. The relationship of rules of engagement to the law is illustrated in the attached diagram.[3]

Rules of engagement may be governed by other factors in addition to the law, factors such as the need not to risk involvement of neutrals[4] or a desire to ensure that major military engagements will only take place under conditions of superiority[5]. To be effective, precise rules of engagement measures need to be specifically crafted to meet the unique conditions of each operation and, apart from the need to comply with the law, will depend very much upon the particular circumstances of the operation for which they are drawn.

3. DUTIES OF PEACEKEEPING CONTINGENTS

The laws applicable to any deployed body of troops will be dependent, not upon direction from above, but upon the duties and functions they are

---

[3] This diagram, at the end of this chapter, may be familiar. Developed by the author in the course of private study, the Australian, United States, Dutch and Austrian defence forces have used a simplified version in their training in recent years. The simplified version does not have the boxes on the right, which define the various categories of action.

[4] Such as the rule given to Admiral Troubridge, commander of the British squadron hunting the German battlecruiser SMS Goeben in the Mediterranean, just after the outbreak of World War I in August 1914, directing that the squadron was not to approach within 6 miles of the Italian coast. Italy had not entered the war and it was feared that if the British ships breached neutrality by entering territorial waters, even inadvertently, Italy would come in on the side of the Central Powers.

[5] The second substantive rule given to Troubridge was that he was not to engage superior force. The Austro-Hungarian Navy's battle fleet, built around several dreadnought battleships and heavy cruisers was based in Pola in the Adriatic. If the Austrian fleet had engaged Troubridge's squadron of four light cruisers, it would have been likely to annihilate the squadron while providing no strategic, operational or tactical gain for the Entente. The intention of the Admiralty was that Troubridge should withdraw should that fleet come out.

deployed to perform. These duties and functions will be dictated by the particular circumstances into which they are actually deployed. Relevant questions for example are: What is the nature of emergency requiring the deployment? What is the nature of the threat the troops are likely to face? What duties are they likely to have to perform? The answers to these questions will differ according to the specific operation.[6] Applicable laws are likely to differ according to the nature of duties and functions identified in each particular set of circumstances.[7]

In determining the nature of duties to be performed by deployed forces on United Nations operations, the particular mandate is a highly relevant but not necessarily conclusive factor. The actual factual situation on the ground when the forces finally deploy may dictate that those military units take action other than that originally envisaged when the mandate was granted. A UN Mandate may, for example, authorise an action under Chapter VII of the United Nations Charter, but if it is found that the aggressor has ceased its warlike actions when the troops are actually deployed then the UN force may not need to use force as envisaged in Chapter VII. It may only need to use force in self-defence and not in the manner normally required and allowed while in armed conflict. Note, however, that although the mandate may be directly relevant to what duties may have to be performed, it cannot direct what laws govern the operations. This issue will be examined in more depth later in this chapter.

4. PEACEKEEPING CHARACTERISTICS

The advent of mass peacekeeping following the end of the Cold War has involved the deployment of large bodies of military personnel into operations in which they are not normally required, expected or allowed to act in armed conflict (or warlike) roles.[8] Indeed, when deployed in peacekeeping

---

[6] In the Gulf War the forces were deployed to perform armed conflict duties, whilst the military contingents deployed to Somalia as part of UNOSOM were required to provide infrastructure and protection for humanitarian aid and possible reconstruction.

[7] Peacekeeping operations in the 1990s have seen the following activities being undertaken: military, including cease-fire monitoring, cantonment and demobilisation of troops, and ensuring security for elections; policing; human rights monitoring and enforcement; information dissemination; observation, organisation and conduct of elections; rehabilitation and reconstruction of State structures; repatriation and resettlement of large numbers of people; administration during transition of one regime to another; working with or overseeing the operations of regional or non-UN peacekeeping operations. See Ramesh Thakur, 'Introduction: Past Imperfect, Future Uncertain' in Ramesh Thakur (ed), *The United Nations at Fifty: Retrospect and Prospect* (1996) 7.

[8] As stated by a Netherlands Ministry of Defence representative during the NATO Rules of Engagement and Law of War Seminar, Breda, Netherlands on 17 October 1995 (*NATO Seminar*), 'United Nations forces must walk a tightrope. They are not parties to conflicts in which they are deployed but must deal with the parties to the conflict'. John Sanderson

roles it is undesirable that they should do so.[9] The relatively new (on a larger historical scale) use of military forces in peacekeeping roles has created considerable legal confusion. There are several factors that contribute to and perpetuate that confusion. The two major factors are that:

a. traditionally military forces have normally only deployed into armed conflict and have, therefore, been subject to laws of armed conflict when they are deployed; and

b. peacekeeping troops normally deploy into an area because there is or has recently been an armed conflict which, to add to the confusion, is normally an internal armed conflict.

These two factors tend to cloud the issues and disguise the fact that the peacekeepers themselves are not normally deployed in armed conflict. This distinction is important for a number of practical reasons (other than practical *legal* reasons). For example, the laws of armed conflict only apply when an armed conflict is taking place, and only apply to the armed forces of nations (or, in the case of internal armed conflict, factions) actually involved in the armed conflict. When a nation is not in armed conflict, the laws of armed conflict do not apply to the military operations of its armed forces.

5. APPLICABILITY OF LAWS OF ARMED CONFLICT TO MILITARY OPERATIONS

International armed conflict exists when there are official military or paramilitary forces performing acts of war in apparent furtherance of their government's policy, and that government or the government of any country against which the acts are being perpetrated acknowledges that armed conflict is taking place.[10] The criteria establishing the existence of an

---

similarly asserts that for their own protection, an overt display of impartiality by peacekeepers is necessary to establish their credentials as 'honest brokers'. He concludes that, 'peacekeepers are instruments of diplomacy, not of war', see, John M Sanderson, 'Peacekeeping or Peace Enforcement? Global Flux and the Dilemmas of UN Intervention' in Ramesh Thakur, ibid, 186. The UN official doctrine has also emphasised that peacekeeping as distinct from enforcement is based on consent and cooperation, and it is not meant to achieve its aims by force of arms: see United Nations, *The Blue Helmets: A Review of UN Peacekeeping* (2nd ed, 1990) 4-7. See also, Antony Hayward, *Post-Cold War United Nations Peacekeeping and its Evolution: Hostage or Soldier of Fortune* (1995); Karen A Mingst and Margaret P Karns, *The United Nations in the Post-Cold War Era* (1995).

[9] As Major General Dallaire, former UN Advance Mission in Rwanda Commander (UNAMIR) observed, 'if United Nations peacekeeping forces fight ... even to fight their way out of a difficult situation, [they] run the risk that [they] will become party to the fight', NATO Seminar, ibid.

[10] Note that for a state of war to exist customary international law requires that one party to a conflict acknowledge its existence. Common article 2 of the four Geneva Conventions 1949 stipulates that those Conventions apply to a conflict between two Convention parties

internal armed conflict are not as unequivocally a matter of international consensus but for practical purposes, the criteria in article 1, paragraphs 1 and 2 of Additional Protocol II to the Geneva Conventions, although open to interpretation, are sufficient for the purposes of this paper. The said article states that:

> This Protocol, which develops and supplements Article 3 common to the Geneva Conventions of 12 August 1949 without modifying its existing conditions of application, shall apply to all armed conflicts which are not covered by Article 1 of the Protocol Additional to the Geneva Conventions of 12 August 1949, and relating to the Protection of Victims of International Armed Conflicts (Protocol I)[11] and which take place in the territory of a High Contracting Party between its armed forces and dissident armed forces or other organized armed groups which, under responsible command, exercise such control over a part of its territory as to enable them to carry out sustained and concerted military operations and to implement this Protocol.
>
> This Protocol shall not apply to situations of internal disturbances and tensions, such as riots, isolated and sporadic acts of violence and other acts of a similar nature, as not being armed conflicts.[12]

The point is that the Laws of Armed Conflict do not normally apply to military personnel who are not participating in armed conflict. As a senior ICRC lawyer has stated, 'to be applicable, humanitarian law requires the presence of armed conflict.'[13] But there is considerable confusion as to

---

even if one of those parties does not recognize that a state of war exists, see *Geneva Convention for the Amelioration of the Condition of the Wounded and the Sick in Armed Forces in the Field*, 75 UNTS 31 ('*First Geneva Convention*'); *Geneva Convention for the Amelioration of the Condition of Wounded, Sick and Shipwrecked Members of Armed Forces at Sea*, 75 UNTS 85 ('*Second Geneva Convention*'); *Geneva Convention Relative to the Treatment of Prisoners of War*, 75 UNTS 135 ('*Third Geneva Convention*'); *Geneva Convention Relative to the Protection of Civilian Persons in Time of War*, 75 UNTS 287 ('*Fourth Geneva Convention*'). All these conventions entered into force on 21 October 1950, and as at 17 March 1999, there were 188 States Parties.

[11] See *Protocol Additional to the Geneva Convention of 12 August 1949, and Relating to the Protection of Victims of International Armed Conflict*, 1125 UNTS 3; 16 ILM 1391 (entered into force on 7 December 1978) ('*Additional Protocol I*'). As at 17 March 1999, there were 153 States Parties.

[12] See *Protocol Additional to the Geneva Convention of 12 August 1949,and Relating to the Protection of Victims of Non-International Armed Conflicts*, 1125 UNTS 609; 16 ILM 1442 (entered into force on 7 December 1978) ('*Additional Protocol II*'). As at 17 March 1999, there were 145 States Parties.

[13] Toni Pfanner, 'Application of International Humanitarian Law and Military Operations Undertaken Under the United Nations Charter' in Umesh Palwankar (ed), *Symposium on Humanitarian Action and Peace-keeping Operations: Report* (1994) 49, 56. It is clear that in this context 'humanitarian law' is used to refer to the older concept of 'laws of armed conflict'. See also, Astrid J M Delissen and Gerard J Tanja (eds) *Humanitarian Law of*

what constitutes humanitarian law. It is clear that the term 'humanitarian law' in this context was used to mean the older concept of 'laws of armed conflict'. It is submitted, however, that the terminology is no longer capable of such precision (if indeed it ever was) in light of the changing nature of military deployments as a result of large-scale peacekeeping operations.

The ICRC also takes the view that all provisions of international humanitarian law are applicable when United Nations contingents resort to force.[14] The United Nations, on the other hand, is of the opinion that peacekeeping forces should 'observe and respect the principles and spirit of the general international conventions applicable to the conduct of military personnel', including the Geneva Conventions.[15] It is also quite clear that the United Nations has long been of this view and promulgated it as early as 1957 for the United Nations Emergency Force.[16]

If the narrow interpretation of the term 'international humanitarian law' still applies, that is, that international humanitarian law incorporates the laws the purpose of which is to ameliorate sufferings caused by armed conflict, the ICRC view is, with respect, flawed in that it does not provide humanitarian protection for certain classes of people when there is no armed conflict.

If the ICRC view is correct then it must follow that the Geneva Conventions must be applied by peacekeepers (putting aside for the moment the question of whether those Conventions have become customary international law). Common Article 2 stipulates that, as between Parties

> In addition to the [Convention] provisions which shall be applied in peacetime ... [The Convention shall apply to] ... all cases of declared war or any other armed conflict which may arise between two or more High Contracting Parties.

Armed Conflict Challenges Ahead: Essays in Honour of Frits Kalshoven (1991); Frits Kalshoven and Yves Sandoz (eds), *Implementation of International Humanitarian Law* (1989); Jean S Pictet (ed), *Commentary: IV Geneva Convention* (1958).

[14] But what if the United Nations forces have resorted to the use of force purely in a non-armed conflict self defence situation? Surely there is no armed conflict as required by Pfanner, above n 13. There is much confusion in the area.

[15] *Model Agreement Between the United Nations and Member States Contributing Personnel and Equipment to United Nations Peacekeeping Operations*, UN Doc A/46/185, Annex, [28] ('*UN Model Agreement*'). See also, Daphna Shraga and Ralph Zacklin, 'The Applicability of International Humanitarian Law to United Nations Peace-keeping Operations: Conceptual, Legal and Practical Issues' in Umesh Palwankar, above n 13, 43-5.

[16] *Regulations for the United Nations Emergency Force*, UN Doc. ST./SGB/UNEF/1; 271 UNTS 168,184 ('*UNEF*') of 20 February 1957. Regulation 44 states that: 'The Force shall observe the principles and spirit of the general international Conventions applicable to the conduct of military personnel'. See also, Regulation 43 of the *Regulations for the United Nations Force in the Congo*, UN Doc. ST./SGB/ONUC/I of 15 July 1963; Regulation 40 of the *Regulations for the United Nations Force in Cyprus*, UN Doc. ST./SGB/ UNFICYP/I of 25 April 1964.

The reference to peacetime application does not mean that the Conventions generally apply in time of peace. It is not proposed to develop this issue here except to say that, with one possible exception in relation to issues of occupation arising under the Fourth Geneva Convention,[17] those Conventions require the existence of armed conflict before they apply. They were negotiated to apply in times of armed conflict to ameliorate sufferings caused therefrom. It would be premature to argue that, as a matter of customary international law, they apply to military forces that are not involved in armed conflict. Too many nations would resist such a proposition on grounds of national sovereignty for it to be accepted as a matter of customary international law.[18] In any event, it is only comparatively recently that there has been anything approaching consensus that the Geneva Conventions in their entirety represent customary international law applicable in armed conflict.[19]

The point is that the Geneva Conventions themselves cannot be said to apply to a peacekeeping operation unless there is an actual armed conflict applicable to the United Nations forces themselves. Peacekeepers are not normally engaged in armed conflict and the Geneva Conventions, therefore, do not apply to them, however desirable this may be. Peacekeepers would only be engaged in armed conflict if they were deployed to commit

---

[17] The possibility that the Fourth Geneva Convention applies to a partial or total occupation of the territory of a State party to the Convention by forces that are not party to an international armed conflict has been logically advanced by Lt Col Michael Kelly in the well-researched book *Peace Operations: Tackling the Military, Legal and Political Challenges* (1997). Although the argument has been logically and methodically developed, the author of this chapter is not convinced that Kelly's thesis is correct.

[18] During the 1996 Geneva negotiations to amend Additional Protocol II (to include anti-personnel landmines within the 1980 *Convention on Prohibitions or Restrictions on the Use of Certain Conventional Weapons Which May be Deemed to be Excessively Injurious or to Have Indiscriminate Effects*, opened for signature 10 October 1980, 1342 UNTS 137; 19 ILM 1523 (entered into force 2 December 1983) ('*1980 Weapons Convention*') (as at 17 March 1999, there were 73 States Parties), some States including India and Pakistan opposed wording that would have made the amended Protocol apply to non-armed conflict and to internal domestic matters such as law enforcement. They did so, not on the basis that they proposed using anti-personnel landmines in internal and police matters, but on the basis that the Protocol related to what was essentially an international matter; armed conflict. They argued that to extend the provisions to all circumstances (which, by definition would include domestic law enforcement matters) would establish a precedent which would see other law of armed conflict issues, that is, issues relating to international relations, imposed by treaty on internal matters, matters which go to national sovereignty.

[19] It is worth noting that the UN Secretary-General included grave breaches of the 1949 Geneva Conventions in the Draft Statute of the International Criminal Tribunal for the Former Yugoslavia on the basis that the Conventions were widely accepted as representing customary international law: see *Report of the Secretary-General Pursuant to Paragraph 2 of Security Council Resolution 808 (1993)*, UN Doc S/25704 (1993); 32 ILM 1159 ('*Secretary-General's Report*'). The Statute of the Tribunal is found in the Report of the Secretary-General.

acts of war or, in General Dallaire's words, they became 'part of the fight'.[20] To this extent the ICRC view cannot be correct.

There is also a large body of opinion supporting the view that Additional Protocol I forms part of the body of customary international humanitarian law. This opinion is considerably bolstered by the fact that both the United States and the United Kingdom have adhered in practice to the principles and practices espoused by Additional Protocol I.[21] Furthermore, the United Kingdom has recently ratified Additional Protocol I[22] and France has announced its intention to do so.[23] However, this adherence to the principles of Additional Protocol I should not obscure the fact that, on present indications, the United States is unlikely to become party to any international agreement which contains formal Additional Protocol I language that it has formerly refused to accept. The United States consistently asserts that Additional Protocol I is not representative of customary international law. The United States successfully used this argument in the Rome Diplomatic Conference for the establishment of an International Criminal Court (ICC) to avoid any inclusion of Additional Protocol I language it did not already accept in the definition of war crimes. Further, while it is clear that Additional Protocol I incorporates much that is incontrovertibly customary international law, it also contains much that is not. An insistence that Additional Protocol I language be included in any Code of Conduct would increase the reluctance of the United States to accept any such Code, [24] and without the acceptance of the United States there is probably little chance of broader international acceptance. In short, there is very little chance that the nations of the world would accept that the Geneva Conventions or Additional Protocol I should apply except within the pa-

---

[20] General Dallaire, NATO Seminar, above n 8.

[21] The United States' original rationale for refusing to ratify Additional Protocol I was that art 44 (3), by granting combatant status to those who did not distinguish themselves from the civilian population provided they carry arms openly, 'during each military engagement and during such time as they are visible to the adversary while engaged in military deployment preceding the launching of an attack', would encourage terrorists by granting them prisoner of war status. Although US military doctrine adheres to this original objection and teaches that it is a violation of the law of armed conflict to attack enemy while feigning civilian or non-combatant status, the doctrine states that it is nevertheless United States policy to accord such illegal combatants prisoner of war status if they carry arms openly at the time of capture. See The United States Department of Navy, *Commanders Handbook on the Law of Naval Operations* (*NWP 1-14M*) (1995) [12.7]-[12.8].

[22] The United Kingdom became a party on 28 January 1998. The Additional Protocols came into force for the United Kingdom on 28 July 1998.

[23] ICRC Pres Release, ICRC News 11/1998, dated 18 March 1998.

[24] During the 1995-6 negotiations to amend Protocol II to the 1980 Weapons Convention it became clear that the formal incorporation of such language or concepts could be a factor jeopardizing full United States participation in any final Protocol because it would require the United States to accept language that it had already rejected when considering ratification of Additional Protocol I.

rameters of their scope of their applicability already specified in each instrument.

With all due respect to the ICRC and the United Nations Secretariat, the information released to date only serves to highlight the confusion in this area. The draft Guidelines are said to specify the international humanitarian law principles applicable to peacekeeping forces 'when in situations of armed conflicts (either international or non-international) they are actively engaged as combatant'. The problem with this concept is that peacekeeping forces are not normally in situations of armed conflict, nor are they normally engaged as combatants.[25] Accordingly, any code for peacekeeping forces that is drafted to deal only with armed conflict or combatant situations, no matter how accurately it reflects international humanitarian law (in the sense that international humanitarian law is intended to ameliorate the sufferings caused by armed conflict), will be largely theoretical because it will not deal with the normal day to day actuality of peacekeeping operations.

The joint statement of objective also misconceives both the nature of peacekeeping operations and the manner in which the law operates to suggest that the UN can direct what rules and principles are applicable in both peacekeeping and peace enforcement, or to postulate that the use of force in self defence needs to be authorised. This implies that it may be a political or command decision as to what law is to be applied by military personnel in the course of their operations, that politicians, bureaucrats or military commanders may decide what law is applicable. It implies further that a particular mandate, either by careful crafting or characterisation of the situation giving rise to the need for a United Nations deployment, can direct or influence what law must be applied by national contingents.

6. TRIGGERS FOR OPERATION OF LAWS OF ARMED CONFLICT

It cannot be stressed too strongly that whether or not there is an armed conflict is a matter of fact, not a matter of declaration for government or a governing body. The application of international humanitarian law is an automatic consequence of entering or becoming involved in armed conflict. The commencement of its application cannot be retarded, advanced or denied because some person, body or institution has decided or determined that those laws will or will not apply. Once there is armed conflict, the

---

[25] See, eg, Peter Rowe, 'United Nations Rules of Engagement and the British Soldier in Bosnia' (1994) 43 *International and Comparative Law Quarterly* 946, 954, '[The British soldier in Bosnia with UNPROFOR] is not a combatant in the conflict entitled to use whatever force is required to disarm or kill enemy combatants; he is ... limited to acts of self defence'. See also, Gerd J F van Hegelsom, 'The Law of Armed Conflict and UN Peace-Keeping and Peace-Enforcing Operations' (unpublished paper presented at a Conference in The Hague, 19-21 July 1993 - copy on file with author).

appropriate international laws apply automatically (their application being itself automatic as a matter of international law), either by custom or by treaty.[26] The question of what law applies to the actions of military personnel cannot be a political one.

Ethnic cleansing in the Former Yugoslavia is one example of what can happen when military forces allow their political masters, rather than the fact that an armed conflict is happening, dictate what law they must apply. Other examples are the massive genocide that took place under Pol Pot in Cambodia or the massacres in Rwanda. Of course, the best-documented examples (as yet) still come from Hitler's monstrous regime where he directed the Wehrmacht not to apply the law when Germany invaded Russia.

In the so-called Commissar Order of May 13, Hitler required the army to destroy the Soviet leadership by killing all captured political officials and commissars out of hand, an order which, despite the misgivings of individual officers, was circulated in writing by the army High Command. By another directive of May 6, dealing with the treatment of the civilian population in Russia, the High Command ordered the shooting of all local residents who took part in hostile acts or resisted the German armed forces, if necessary 'by collective measures of force against villages from which attacks of any kind have taken place.' Two further decrees exempted German soldiers from prosecution for punishable acts on occupied soil and ordered 'ruthless and energetic action at the slightest sign of restiveness' on the part of prisoners of war. These completed a comprehensive repudiation of military law and the conventions of war demanded in advance by the supreme commander, Adolf Hitler. As the evidence makes clear, they were implemented by the German armed forces, officers and men in their conduct of the war in the east.[27]

The factual situation, not commanders, governments or even the United Nations dictates what international law applies because none of those people or bodies makes international law. Note, however, that while governments cannot direct what law applies, they can direct what actions military forces may take, the only caveat being that the actions so directed must be lawful. It may well be that those actions may have consequences that alter the law applicable to the military operations, (they may, for example, trigger an armed conflict thereby requiring the application of the laws of armed conflict) but this is the only manner in which governments can alter what law is to be governing military operations. Law in this context means international law.

The point is that leaders and commanders cannot mandate what legal regime applies to the deployment of military forces. They can, and should,

[26] See, eg, Geneva Conventions, Common art 2.
[27] Allan Bullock, *Hitler and Stalin: Parallel Lives* (1991) 737-8.

however, identify what regime applies or is likely to apply and train their forces to perform their mandated tasks within the law so identified.

7. POWER OF UNITED NATIONS TO IMPOSE LAW UPON NATIONAL CONTINGENTS

It is also quite clear that not only can the United Nations not direct what laws will be applied by the national contingents contributed to its operations nor create any such laws,[28] but that it also cannot direct member states to take actions which are likely to lead to such a drastically changed status as that of armed conflict. The organisation is the sum total of all its members and while it may, from time to time, take on a life of its own, it cannot interfere in the sovereignty of its members. Constitutionally, it is based on the principle of sovereign equality of all members[29] and it may not intervene in matters 'which are essentially within the domestic jurisdiction of any State'.[30]

Apart from customary international law, which binds all nations, the international laws (generally in the form of treaties or conventions) to which any State becomes party is essentially a matter of domestic jurisdiction and, therefore, not a matter for direction by any organ of the United Nations.[31] Further, actions of State agencies likely to involve that State in armed conflict being directly related to sovereignty are, similarly, not a matter for the United Nations.

The existence of national military forces is a concrete manifestation of the inherent right of a sovereign State to defend its existence and their use is an exercise of sovereignty. Their use always has the potential to create international political consequences for the States to which they belong. States are therefore not likely to allow the United Nations to have such

---

[28] It is quite clear however that the United Nations can be highly persuasive and can influence the development of international law. Rosalyn Higgins, *The Development of International Law Through the Political Organs of the United Nations* (1969) 3-5 states:

> [T]he General Assembly certainly has no right to legislate in the commonly understood sense of the term. Resolutions of the Assembly are not per se binding: ... [They] may [however] command considerable moral force without yet constituting new law. Although ... the Security Council is likely to state that it is basing itself upon the law as it conceives it to be, the line between applying law and legislating becomes thin.

[29] UN Charter, art 2(1).

[30] UN Charter, art 2(7). For a detailed examination of this article, see Higgins, above n 28, 58-108.

[31] See, eg, van Hegelsom, above n 25, who argues that military personnel remain subject to their own national penal laws. The ICRC is also of this opinion.

unfettered command as to allow them to be committed to any action the United Nations deems fit.[32]

The thrust of these issues is that the United Nations has no legal authority to involve national military contingents in armed conflict because to do so is likely to embroil the contributing countries in armed conflict, an action that goes to the root of sovereignty. Sovereign States are the only entities that can involve their own military forces in acts of war or warlike acts. In a similar vein, the United Nations cannot negotiate a binding international law treaty on behalf of any nation without that nation's active participation and consent.

Because of the question of sovereignty, it would appear that any proposed Code, or Directives, (unless negotiated and agreed in the normal manner in which multilateral treaties and conventions are agreed) could only be said to establish a minimum standard of behaviour expected of peacekeeping forces. Any such instrument could only be binding in a contractual sense in that contributing States would undertake that their military contingents would comply and a failure of any military contingent member to comply would be a matter for resolution by the courts of that State to which the contingent belongs. Such a Code could not impose international law obligations (additional to customary international law obligations) upon members of a State's military forces, obligations which may conflict with the laws of that State.

On the question of the content of any Code, the point is that international humanitarian law in the narrow sense of law intended to ameliorate the sufferings of warfare (which appears to be the sense in which the proposed Code uses it) does not govern the operations of a military force unless that force is in fact involved in right of its State in armed conflict. It is a fact that peacekeeping forces, although deployed in circumstances of great tension, are normally not deployed to perform armed conflict duties. The Code must therefore address wider issues and to ascertain those issues it is necessary to analyse the nature of duties performed by peacekeepers.

---

[32] UN Model Agreement, art 7 provides that national forces will be under full command of the UN. No nation however gives UN full command. The greatest power given by any nation to the United Nations is what is called operational control. States are also reluctant to concede full command of their armed forces for reasons other than sovereignty. In recent years, it has become a matter of major concern for member States taking part in a peacekeeping operation that such operation may turn into a more active military one through a later Security Council Resolution. There is an unwillingness of contributing States to leave the Secretary General or any UN military commander different free options [of action], especially if they involve some risks for the security of troops: Giorgo Gaja, 'Use of Force Made or Authorized by the United Nations', in Christian Tomuschat (ed), *The United Nations at Age Fifty: A Legal Perspective* (1996) 54-6.

8. HUMAN RIGHTS ISSUES

Peacekeeping forces are regularly in confrontation with people in situations that, while they involve tension, do not involve them in a state of armed conflict with those people. When dealing with people in circumstances requiring them to exercise some form of control (which is why military forces are used) they must apply, not armed conflict law, but law that has more of a human rights flavour. Indeed, human rights law is becoming a matter with which military commanders must be familiar because of the phenomenon already mentioned, that most UN deployments are to operations in which the military forces are not performing armed conflict roles and therefore do not involve the application of laws of armed conflict. Where does human rights law fit in to the general legal scheme as it applies to military operations?

Both human rights and the laws of armed conflict are part of a larger scheme of international humanitarian law, as it is developing to meet the needs of the post-Cold War world. The laws of armed conflict which govern behaviour in armed conflict pre-suppose the division of people into combatants and non-combatants; accept that military force may automatically be used against objects and places if they can be legitimately categorized as military objects; accept the concept of legitimate military targets; prescribe behaviour in relation to enemies and situations affected by enemy, and are, generally speaking, relevant only to armed forces. Human rights law governs peacetime behaviour, does not involve any concept of combatant, does not recognize the legitimacy of any use of force except for the narrow purpose of self-defence, does not incorporate any concept of military targets, prescribes behaviour towards all people but more particularly the behaviour of the powerful towards the relatively more powerless sections of the community (women, children, prisoners, those accused of crimes etc) and is, in the normal course of events, relevant only to law enforcement and authorities. It is, however, highly relevant to UN peacekeeping forces because the greater part of their day to day duties have historically involved these human rights issues.

The recognition, however, that human rights principles are relevant to the manner in which peacekeeping forces comport themselves highlights another thorny issue. The question of universally applicable human rights for United Nations peacekeepers is likely to be controversial and not readily resolved. Even the question of what are fundamental human rights is problematical, bearing in mind that different cultures have different approaches to human rights and there is an increasing international insistence that human rights are a matter of domestic policy.[33] The issue is even

---

[33] Note Australia's strong objection to the recent European Union (EU) attempt to require Australia to comply with EU human rights standards as a condition of a trade treaty between Australia and the EU. Australia claimed that human rights matters are internal Australian

more basic than that and, I submit, revolves around what each nation believes are the fundamental humanitarian principles that form the root of the laws that that nation (and, consequently, its armed forces) should apply. It is submitted that it is those principles from which all aspects of humanitarian law (including human rights law and international humanitarian law) are derived. Unfortunately, despite much wishful thinking, it is unlikely that there will be a substantive regime of universally accepted fundamental human rights for some time.[34]

9. IDEAL CONTENTS OF A CODE

Any proposed Code, which fails to recognise that peacekeeping forces may have to apply laws other than international humanitarian law in the traditional sense, would be dangerous. The use solely of armed conflict terms – terms such as 'combatant', 'prisoner of war' and 'neutrals' – without making the clear distinction between armed conflict situations and situations not involving armed conflict is likely to suggest to peacekeeping forces that they are always in an armed conflict role and that any action taken by them is an armed conflict action governed by the laws of armed conflict. This is dangerous because there are legal matters other than humanitarian ones, which automatically apply when in armed conflict. Of most concern is the fact that when in armed conflict, combatants may automatically be attacked upon identification (unless subject to one of the humanitarian law exceptions).

Concentration upon armed conflict and recourse to its terminology alone could create the undesirable result that peacekeeping troops may believe that there will always be combatants and non-combatants, military objects

---

policy and law issues, a matter of sovereignty. Australia's position seems remarkably similar to that espoused in China's 1991 White Paper, *Human Rights in China* (1991) when it stated that, 'Despite its international aspect, the issue of human rights falls by and large within the sovereignty of the States', 11. There is a strong argument that the 1983 statement by Yougindra Khushalani to the effect that, '[F]rom the practical experience in many developing States, it is evident that in most States in the world, human rights as defined by the West are rejected or, more accurately, are meaningless' in 'Human Rights in Asia and Africa' (1983) 4 *Human Rights Law Journal* 403, 414, remains valid.

[34] Professor Yash Ghai asserts:

  Claims of universality and indivisibility of rights are hard to sustain in the face of the West's history of the oppression of its own people and others, with slavery which once enjoyed religious approbation, abuse of child labour, the exploitation of colonies and the other depredations of imperialism and racism. [There is no reason] why the contemporary concerns and fads in the West should define the parameters of international discourse in and aspirations of human rights.

'The Politics of Human Rights in Asia' (unpublished). Paper presented at a seminar on 'The United Nations: Between Sovereignty and Global Governance', La Trobe University, July 1995.

and civilian objects and, as a result, that people need to be categorised as belonging to one category or the other. A likely tendency would be to treat hostile people as enemy combatants, increasing the likelihood that the peacekeeping forces could apply armed conflict notions of the use of force at all times even when the much narrower peacetime principle that force may only be used in self-defence is the proper applicable lawful rule.[35]

A Code which fails to distinguish between the two situations and concentrates upon or emphasises the rules applying in armed conflict will only increase the risk of peacekeeping forces treating all hostile people as enemy combatants with the consequence that they may illegally use force against them and exacerbate an already tense situation, or become "part of the fight" rather than a restraining influence. The danger of such misconception would be especially great in respect of armed forces from those States that do not provide comprehensive legal training in all laws affecting the operations of their forces. Further, such a Code is likely to diminish the admirable restraint that UN peacekeeping troops have shown in the past when confronted by hostile people who are nevertheless not in armed conflict with the UN troops.

It would therefore seem that, in addition to spelling out armed conflict considerations, an effective Code would need to provide guidelines for peacekeepers who are not in armed conflict. It would need to spell out those humanitarian principles that must be applied when the powerful are dealing with the weak, the occupiers (no matter how benevolent the intention behind the occupation) are dealing with the occupied, and those who are secure and certain of their security are dealing with those who are insecure and confused.

10. THE NEED FOR UNIVERSALITY

A compounding conundrum in this matter, in addition to establishing common international ground on applicable human rights principles, is the clear need to identify the universal international legal principles that govern the actions of military forces when they are not deployed to armed conflict. A Code that does not reflect legal principles that are reasonably

---

[35] Allegations of murder and torture of Somalis by Canadian, Belgian and Italian forces during Operation Restore Hope seem to indicate a failure to inculcate the correct legal principles in those forces. In addition, it is alleged that, after the failed attempt to capture General Aideed, United States helicopter gunships (which had nothing to do with the actual United Nations peacekeeping troops) randomly fired cannon and machine guns into houses in Mogadishu – actions appropriate in armed conflict if those houses were legitimate military targets. While there had been fighting and killing, there was no armed conflict and the actions, if occurring as alleged, were most inappropriate and probably illegal. See 'UN Soldiers of Mercy Murdered and Tortured by Somalis', *The Weekend Australian*, (Melbourne, Australia), 5 July 1997, 18.

common to all nations (perhaps even customary international law) is un-likely to either gain common acceptance or be effective.[36] Military forces cannot be expected to behave in a manner that does not reflect the values of the societies from which they are drawn.[37] Any national contingent whose society values are not reflected in the Code is unlikely to honour it.[38]

The whole question would therefore seem to revolve around a re-evaluation of what constitutes international humanitarian law. It is submit-ted that in the years after 1989 that body of law has been subjected to considerable turbulence, if not substantive change, and it is arguable that it has expanded substantially beyond the traditional concept which incorpo-rated only those laws which ameliorated the suffering caused by armed conflict and now incorporates, *inter alia*, human rights laws and princi-ples.[39] Once underlying principles, which have the status of customary international law,[40] have been identified, then the creation of a realistic and effective Code for peacekeepers, in the sense of identifying the minimum standard of legal behaviour in all likely situations, would be much more probable. To write a Code without that evaluation and identification proc-ess is likely to create a document of very little practical use, although it would be of significant academic interest.

---

[36] '[T]he universality of international humanitarian law is a *sine qua non* for its effective application', Yves Sandoz, 'Humanitarian Law: Priorities for the 1990s and Beyond' in William Maley (ed) *Shelters from the Storm: Developments in International Humanitarian Law* (1995) 15.

[37] '[S]ocieties cannot expect their militaries to behave in ways which are in fact superior to the values of the societies themselves; ... if humanitarian values and human rights values are not a part of a society, then it is most likely that the military will behave accordingly', John Sanderson, 'International Humanitarian Law and the Role of Military Establishments', in William Maley (ed) above n 36, 57.

[38] '[I]t is not enough to teach soldiers humanitarian law. International humanitarian law is part of humanitarian law and can only be a reality in a society which respects human rights', Dorab Patel, 'Comment', in William Maley (ed) above n 36, 23.

[39] It also includes other areas such as refugee law but that is outside the scope of this paper.

[40] No matter how laudable a particular principle may be, merely by saying that a principle has become customary international law does not make it so. 'The law [as evidenced by the practice of States] is what States do, not what professors think they should do' D W Bowett, (Reviewing Fernando R Teson's, *Humanitarian Intervention: An Inquiry into Law and Morality,* 1988) in (1988) 59 *British Yearbook of International Law* 263, 264. See also, Anthony D'Amato who says, 'I think that we must ... recognize that [what] States do, and not what we [in academic legal argument] want them to do, constitutes international law' in 'The Concept of Human Rights in International Law' (1982) 82 *Columbia Law Review* 1110, 1148.

11. Conclusion

Because of national sovereignty, any Code of Conduct for peacekeeping forces, unless formally accepted as a treaty, would bind no nation and could impose no legal obligations upon the national military contingents supplied as peacekeeping troops. A Code could however establish the minimum standards of legal behaviour that the United Nations expects that contributing States will enforce upon their military contingent. It is clear that there is a need for such a Code or set of Directives.

Any such Code must recognise that peacekeeping forces are but rarely involved in armed conflict and that, consequently, humanitarian law in its traditional sense of ameliorating the suffering caused by armed conflict should not form the sole basis for and topic of such a Code. The Code should encompass matters beyond UN forces conducting operations when in situations of armed conflict they are actively engaged as combatants. To be of any practical effect it must also govern those operations where UN forces are active but are themselves not involved in armed conflict although conflict may be going on around them. This latter area is most deserving of attention because the major part of peacekeeping has been in this area rather than in participating in armed conflict in the capacity of combatants. To concentrate solely upon armed conflict considerations in a Code is dangerous because it could give poorly trained contingent members the belief that there will always be enemy combatants and that force may be used merely upon identification of a person as hostile.

Just as legal principles governing the conduct of armed conflict and commonly accepted by the international community have been identified, so too is there a need to identify what are the universally accepted international humanitarian law principles applicable to the use of military force when not in armed conflict. If such principles are not commonly accepted they will not be observed. Once this evaluation and identification process has taken place it will be possible to create a more realistic and, therefore, effective Code.

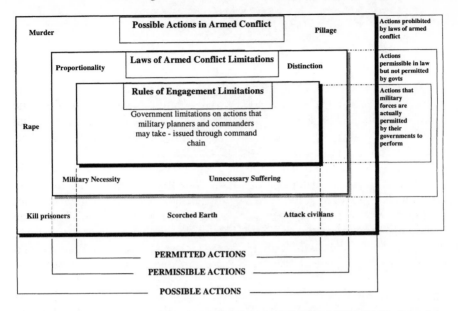

| | Possible Actions in Armed Conflict | | | Actions prohibited by laws of armed conflict |

Murder | Pillage

Laws of Armed Conflict Limitations

Proportionality | Distinction

Actions permissible in law but not permitted by govts

Rules of Engagement Limitations

Government limitations on actions that military planners and commanders may take - issued through command chain

Rape

Actions that military forces are actually permitted by their governments to perform

Military Necessity | Unnecessary Suffering

Kill prisoners | Scorched Earth | Attack civilians

PERMITTED ACTIONS

PERMISSIBLE ACTIONS

POSSIBLE ACTIONS

Notes: In armed conflict the range of possible actions open to combatants is limited only by imagination. Laws of armed conflict however seek to ameliorate suffering by limiting those actions to legally **permissible** actions. Governments limit options open to their armed forces further by the use of rules of engagement (ROE). While there may be a broad range of actions that it is legally permissible for those armed forces to perform, they may only be **permitted** by their government to perform some of those legal actions. Governments will use, inter alia, ROE to control the actions of their armed forces.

© G.J. Cartledge

Diagram 1: Relationship between rules of engagement and laws of armed conflict – effect upon military action

MICHAEL J. KELLY

7. Responsibility for Public Security in Peace Operations

Peacemaking and peace-keeping operations, to be truly successful, must come to include comprehensive efforts to identify and support structures which will tend to consolidate peace and advance a sense of confidence and well-being among people. Through agreements ending civil strife, these may include disarming the previously warring parties and the restoration of order, the custody and possible destruction of weapons, repatriating refugees, advisory and training support for security personnel, monitoring elections, advancing efforts to promote human rights, reforming or strengthening governmental institutions and promoting formal and informal processes of political participation.

Former UN Secretary-General Boutros Boutros-Ghali[1]

1. INTRODUCTION

The issue of public security on peace operations has arisen because the context in which they take place has more and more frequently been one of internal conflict. These internal conflicts have resulted in or been a product of the disintegration of a 'civil society'. A common feature in the cause of the conflict has been the insecurity felt or attacks endured by one particular ethnic, religious or national group. This is often because the group has lost confidence in the administration of justice to secure their human rights, protect their cultural identity and guarantee their physical security. In these cases or in the case of rebellion against an autocrat the problem has been that the mechanisms of 'justice' have been the instruments of repression in the first place. Addressing the issue of the administration of justice therefore goes to the heart of the conflict resolution objective on a peace operation.

---

[1] Boutros Boutros-Ghali, 'An Agenda for Peace', *United Nations Department of Public Information* (1992) 32.

Helen Durham and Timothy L.H. McCormack (eds.), The Changing Face of Conflict and the Efficacy of International Humanitarian Law, 141–172.

In addition, the peace operation is focused on leaving behind a viable state entity whose institutions will be self-sustaining and from which they can depart as quickly as possible. Justice reconstruction issues are also centrally tied to this objective. Having an effective public security environment encourages responsible leadership to step forward. It enables economic activity to develop as no one will work when they know that the fruits of their labour will end up in the hands of a rapacious bandit organisation or be siphoned off by a corrupt administration. Another common feature of these conflicts is property disputes, which should be addressed by an appropriately formed resolution forum. If this is not done the seeds will be sown for future conflict.

In order to deal with the public security function a peace operation must be provided with a framework of legitimacy tailored to the particular circumstances of the operation. Without this legitimacy a peace operation can rapidly lose credibility, focus, rationale and support – both internationally and locally. Without a framework the forces will be left to flounder and will be prone to descend to summary justice measures as occurred in Somalia with the Canadian, Belgian, Italian and other contingents. To begin with a broad mandate from the UN is clearly required. Beyond this, however, it is essential to have a more detailed framework that can form the point of reference to justify actions taken to the international community and the local population. This can either be in the shape of a framework agreement amongst the warring parties and the intervening force or where no agreement has been possible then existing international law provisions should be exploited, particularly in the collapsed state scenario.

The framework having been settled it is then necessary to determine how the mission will be structured. In theory, to rebuild a justice system it would be logical to attempt to mobilise civilian experts in the field. Three things militate against this, at least in the initial phases of an operation. The environment may be such that the security threat is still beyond that which civilian police forces could cope with. States generally do not have a spare capacity of civilian policing as these personnel are fully engaged in daily policing at home. As a consequence, the police contribution may be of the wrong category (ie border police) or they are from jurisdictions that have an inferior human rights record. It has proven extremely difficult to recruit civilian police for peace operations. This has proven true for other civilian elements. Many important opportunities are lost in the early phases of an operation for this very reason. The military offers certain institutional advantages in this regard which includes: potential speed of mobilisation, greater logistic and equipment capability, spare capacity as troops are often engaged in ongoing training rather than operations and an ability to operate in harsh and threatening environments.

If the military are the best source for the short term in addressing public security issues this does not mean that they are perfectly adapted for it. This is merely to say that the potential is there. In order for that potential to be maximised, the troops must have appropriate Rules of Engagement (ROE) and operating guidelines, they must be properly trained, and the force must be properly structured with the public security function in mind. This may involve placing the emphasis on Military Police, Engineers, Civil Affairs, Psychological Operations and Special Forces.

2. THE PUBLIC SECURITY PROBLEM

What are some of the common trends relating to the public security function in recent peace operations? Some brief examples where the public security function was in issue are very instructive and illustrated below.

2.1 *Former Yugoslavia*

The Yugoslavia War Crimes Tribunal was established on 25 May 1993 to deal with crimes occurring after 1 January 1991.[2] The establishment of the tribunal further expanded the humanitarian tasks of the UN and IFOR/SFOR, carrying implications for operations on the ground concerning recording violations, apprehending offenders and prosecuting them. The apprehension of offenders in particular carries significant implications for the military. It will raise issues not only of how the operation is to be effected but how to manage the possibility of resultant security threats to the whole operation. Often the figures to be apprehended will have some tie-in to organised forces which themselves must be neutralised before apprehension can occur. The work of investigators would also require the provision of security. The most significant aspect of the tribunal was that it was a Chapter VII operation, carrying with it the potential for compulsion to ensure the viability of its operation.

2.2 *Rwanda*

Rwanda had been experiencing on-going internal conflict for many years prior to the 6 April 1994 fateful plane crash that killed the leaders of Rwanda and Burundi. That date, however, was significant as the commencement of the destruction of at least 500,000 and probably closer to 1,000,000 people.[3] With the passing of Resolution 965 of 30 November

---

[2] *Statute of the International Tribunal for the Prosecution of Persons Responsible for Serious Violations of International Humanitarian Law committed in the Territory of the Former Yugoslavia since 1991*, SC Res 827, 48 UN SCOR (3217th mtg), UN Doc S/Res/827 (1993); 32 ILM 1203 ('*Statute of the ICTY*').

[3] *Preliminary Report of the Independent Commission of Experts on Rwanda Established Pursuant to Security Council Resolution 935 (1994), released by the UN Secretary General* in *Letter Dated 4 October 1994 from the Secretary-General Addressed to the President of the Security Council*, S/1125/1994, [43] ('*Preliminary Report of Expert Commission on*

1994, the UN force's (UNAMIR) mandate in Rwanda was extended to include the provision of security to the personnel of the ICTR and for assistance in the establishment and training of a new, integrated, national police force.[4] This outgrowth began as a simple observation mission until the Rwandan Government requested assistance in the creation of a new police force. On 16 August 1994, 103 volunteer students of differing ethnic and social backgrounds began training in basic law enforcement. The former police 'observers' also were required to assume responsibility for monitoring the activities of the police and civil authorities with respect to human rights violations.[5]

By 6 February 1995 some civil administration had been restored in Rwanda with the exception that there was still no judiciary, a situation made more difficult by the fact that the intelligentsia had been particularly devastated.[6] Reports persisted of summary executions, secret detention, torture and banditry. Law and order and human rights were once more assuming centre stage as the refugee crisis began to subside. The Secretary-General stated at that time that:

> A professional police force and functioning judiciary are essential to the establishment of internal security. Yet, at present, Rwanda's court system does not function, its prisons are overcrowded and thousands of suspects await trial. Of the 1,100 magistrates working in the judiciary before April 1994, only 100 are still in the country today and of 100 prosecutors, only 12 are still available. There is also an acute shortage of trained personnel to investigate alleged crimes.[7]

Fear remained the key factor as to why refugees were reluctant to return to their homes and the Security Council Mission in February 1995 clearly identified the need for assistance to the Rwandan government in the restoration of an effective judiciary and police force as the chief means of addressing this fear. They supported the increase in the civilian police

---

Rwanda'); and *Final Report of the Independent Commission of Experts on Rwanda,* 9 Dec 1994 [55] ('*Final Report of Expert Commission on Rwanda'*).

  [4] SC Res 965, 49 UN SCOR (3473rd mtg), UN Doc S/Res/965 (1994).

  [5] *Progress Report of the Secretary-General on the UN Assistance Mission for Rwanda Submitted Pursuant to paragraph 17 of Security Council Resolution 925 (1994),* S/1133/1994, [39]-[40]. In his Progress Report of 16 Feb 1995, the Secretary-General recommended the number of police observers be increased to 120: *Progress Report of the Secretary-General on the UN Assistance Mission for Rwanda,* S/107/Add I/1995, [1].

  [6] *Report of the Secretary-General on the UN Assistance Mission for Rwanda Submitted Pursuant to paragraphs 17 and 11 of Security Council Resolutions 925 (1994) and 929 (1994) respectively,* S/924/1994, [3]. See also, *Progress Report of the Secretary-General on the UN Assistance Mission for Rwanda Submitted Pursuant to Security Council Resolution 965 (1994),* S/107/1995, [2] ('*Progress Report 107/1995'*).

  [7] Progress Report 107/1995, [9]. See also, *Canberra Times* (Canberra, Australia), 27 July 1994, 13; S Honeysett, 'Law and Order the Priority In Rwanda', *The Australian* (Sydney, Australia), 4-5 March 1995.

component from 90 to 120.[8] In the meantime it was estimated that up to 50,000 Rwandans were being detained in various prisons and makeshift facilities under appalling conditions, as the restoration effort fell alarmingly behind the needs of the country.[9] By August 1995 it was estimated that there were still more than 200 deaths per month in these prisons.[10] Attempts to commence trials in April 1995 had been thwarted by the inability to muster prosecution witnesses, notwithstanding admissions of guilt on the part of some of the accused,[11] indicating the deficiencies of the prosecutorial and investigative capability. A plan was finally adopted by the UN, which sought to expand the prison capacity by 21,000 and dispatch 50 legal experts to assist the justice system.[12]

A *Commission de Triage* was established to screen those held in prison. An investigative and prosecutorial unit was established in Kigali to begin the work of the International Tribunal. In the meantime UNAMIR troops moved into the law and order role as they tentatively scoured some refugee camps within Rwanda to remove disruptive elements and enable the refugees to return home. In one operation 44 people were detained and handed over to Rwandan Government authorities.[13] The investigation into the genocide, however, suffered from lack of funds and great delays in recruiting personnel.[14] There were also reports that those investigators who had been deployed were not working effectively to record evidence that was steadily being lost.[15] The Tribunal was not able to issue its first indictments until late 1995.

The Rwanda operation demonstrates how an attempt to avoid commitment and costs at an early phase of a conflict can lead to far greater expenses later on when remaining uninvolved becomes totally unconscionable. It also demonstrated once again the pitfalls of an uncoordinated, *ad*

---

[8] Progress Report 107/1995, [35].

[9] '50,000 Rwandans Detained: Amnesty', *The Australian* (Sydney, Australia), 7 April 1995, 8. Eventually 130,000 people were being held in Rwandan prisons on allegations of genocide.

[10] *Progress Report of the Secretary-General on the UN Assistance Mission for Rwanda Submitted Pursuant to Security Council Resolution 997 (1995)*, S/678/1995, [26].

[11] J Bedford, 'Rwandan Trial Defendant Says He Killed 900', *Canberra Times* (Canberra, Australia), 8 April 1995, 12.

[12] *Letter from the Secretary-General Addressed to the President of the Security Council*, 31 August 1995.

[13] Progress Report 107/1995, [26].

[14] *Progress Report of the Secretary-General on the UN Assistance Mission for Rwanda Submitted Pursuant to Paragraph 1 of Security Council Resolution 965 (1994)*, S/457/1995, [5].

[15] Interview with Major B Oswald, Australian Contingent Legal Officer in Rwanda from Aug 1994-Jan 1995, (20 March 1995); A Purvis, 'Will There be Justice in Rwanda', *Time*, 3 October 1994, 57; S Peterson, 'UN Soldiers Pray Among the Corpses', *Weekly Telegraph* (London, UK), 23 September 1994, 16.

hoc and tardy response capability.[16] The Rwanda case further stoked the claims by some to re-establish a UN trustee or conservatorship system as the best way to cope with the key priorities of law and order, right down to fundamental social units, reconstruction, institutional reform and amendment of societal attitudes through education. This case demonstrates that resettlement of refugees and the creation of confidence in minorities is based on the guarantee of law and order and human rights.[17]

It is clear also that there was a reluctance to take a robust approach in security measures in the refugee camps within Rwanda and the general environment because of confusion over the mandate. Debates have focused on whether the mission came under Chapter VI or Chapter VII of the UN Charter (the resolutions being silent on this point as regards UNAMIR) rather than looking at the terms of the mandate and seeking to fulfil them. In reality the specified mandate required assertive action in certain key respects without the consent of the parties and so was clearly a Chapter VII operation.[18] The confusion and uncertainty of the involvement of the international community in Rwanda highlights the need for appropriate frameworks to address key law and order and human rights issues. The need for a framework was implied by mandates to establish safe havens, investigate the genocide, regulate camps, rebuild an efficacious system of justice (including police, prisons and judiciary), and establish a tribunal.[19] Chapter VII could provide the overall authority but something more akin to the Paris Accords without its deficiencies or the Dayton Agreement would have been preferable. An agreement or framework that in effect laid down a temporary regime of law and order and responsibilities was needed.

2.3 *Mozambique*

UN forces, to be known as ONUMOZ, were deployed into Mozambique following conclusion of the General Peace Agreement in Rome of 4 October 1992. The mission was to assist in the demobilisation and disarmament

---

[16] See 'Editorial', *New Statesman and Society*, 29 July 1994; G Dinmore, 'Planeloads of Supplies Too Late for Many', *Canberra Times* (Canberra, Australia), 27 July 1994, 13; 'Current Affairs Report on CARE Australia', *Channel Nine Television*, Australia, 26 February 1995.

[17] A Purvis, 'All the Hatred in the World', *Time*, 13 June 94, 22-3; J Waterford, 'Taking up the "Burden" of Rwanda not Easy', *Canberra Times* (Canberra, Australia), 25 June 1994, 14.

[18] Interview with Major B Oswald, Australian Contingent Legal Officer in Rwanda from Aug 1994-Jan 1995, (23 March 1995).

[19] An International Tribunal was established in 1994. See *Statute of the International Tribunal for the Prosecution of Persons Responsible for Genocide and Other Serious Violations of International Humanitarian Law Committed in the Territory of Rwanda and Rwandan Citizens Responsible for Genocide and Other Violations Committed in the Territory of Neighbouring States, between 1 January 1994 and 31 December 1994*, UN Doc S/RES/955 (1994), 49 UN SCOR (3453rd mtg); 33 ILM 1598 ('*Statute of the ICTR*').

of the various armies and militias and to facilitate the institution of an electoral process.[20] Pursuant to this mission 70,000 troops were demobilised by 31 August 1994 while 100,000 weapons were collected from troops and 50,000 from militia.[21] An expansion of the mandate occurred however when the parties to the Agreement requested the UN to monitor all police activities in Mozambique along with some additional tasks. Security Council Resolution 863 of 13 September 1993[22] responded positively to the requirement and requested the Secretary-General to investigate. Under Security Council Resolution 898 of 23 February 1994,[23] a plan to deploy a civilian police contingent of up to 1,114[24] personnel was approved. As the election dates were fixed for October, the Security Council stressed the importance of the cooperation of the parties with, and facilitation of, the role of the police contingent.[25]

The tasks of the police contingent included; monitoring the activities of the Mozambique National Police and other law agencies, monitoring observance of human rights, providing technical support to the National Police Commission, verifying that private security agencies did not violate the peace agreement, verifying the strength and material of government police forces, monitoring and verifying the re-organisation and retraining of the quick reaction police including weapons and equipment, and the proper conduct of the election campaign. In addition they were required to ensure that political rights were respected in accordance with the Rome Agreement and the electoral law.[26] The UN was also confronted with the task of attempting to coordinate its mission with 140 different NGOs in Mozambique.[27] The mission in Mozambique has proved to be one of the UN's most successful with an effective election process taking place on 27, 28, and 29 October 1994 and the ONUMOZ mission winding up on 31 January 1995.[28]

---

[20] See SC Res 782, 47 UN SCOR (3123rd mtg), UN Doc S/Res/782 (1992); SC Res 797, 47 UN SCOR (3149th mtg), UN Doc S/Res/797 (1992); SC Res 818, 48 UN SCOR (3198th mtg), UN Doc S/Res/818 (1993); SC Res 850, UN SCOR (3253rd mtg), UN Doc S/Res/850 (1993).

[21] *UN Secretary-General's Report on the Working of the Organisation,* 2 September 1994, [593].

[22] SC Res 863, 48 UN SCOR (3247th mtg), UN Doc S/Res/863 (1993).

[23] SC Res 898, 49 UN SCOR (3338th mtg), UN Doc S/Res/898 (1994).

[24] J Rixon, 'The Role of Australian Police in Peace Support Operations', Hugh Smith (ed), *Building on Cambodia* (1994) 123.

[25] SC Res 916, 49 UN SCOR (3375th mtg), UN Doc S/Res/ 916 (1994).

[26] Rixon, above n 24, 121-2.

[27] James C Ingram, 'The Politics of Human Suffering' (1993) *The National Interest,* 64.

[28] See SC Res 957, 49 UN SCOR (3458th mtg), UN Doc S/Res/957 (1994).

2.4 *Burundi*

In Burundi the same tensions that produced the Rwandan catastrophe are present, with up to 100,000 people being killed in the immediate aftermath of the aforementioned plane crash of 6 April 1994. It appeared as though the power sharing agreement of 10 September 1994 stabilised the situation but underlying fissures were too deep for this to occur. The Security Council Mission to Burundi in February 1996 noted that the situation was potentially explosive with extremist elements in and outside the country undermining the viability of the government while Palipehutu guerillas were operating in the hinterland. Further to this, the security forces remained a Tutsi preserve and independent power base that could not be relied upon to remain on the sidelines. The Mission noted that the judicial system had largely collapsed and was often perceived as being partial in any event. The Mission recommended augmenting UN presence to assist in the areas of building an impartial justice system, civilian police training, impartial investigations and support services especially in urban centres and establishing an effective administrative presence in the provinces. They called for more OAU and Human Rights observers to encourage restraint.[29] This call was echoed by the media in April 1995 as violence increased with the need for more military observers from the OAU to add to the 46 already there, more human rights monitors and a more concentrated effort to rebuild the country's judicial system, being identified.[30]

---

[29] *Report of the Secretary-General on the Situation in Burundi Pursuant to Security Council Resolution 1040 (1996)*, S/116/1996, [6], [14]-[18], [21]-[24].

[30] P Smerdon, 'Burundi's Violence Endemic: Envoy', 'Red Cross Fears Crisis', *Canberra Times* (Canberra, Australia) 7 April 1995, 12; 'Only Urgent UN Action Can Prevent African Bloodbath', *The Australian* (Sydney, Australia), 6 April 1995, 10; 'Burundi Coup Threat', *The Australian* (Sydney, Australia), 2 February 1995; S Kiley and S Weizman, 'Hutu Leader's Death Fuels Burundi Tensions', *The Australian* (Sydney, Australia), 14 March 1995; 'Hutus Slaughtered in Burundi', *Canberra Times* (Canberra, Australia), 27 March 1995, 8; J Bedford, 'Burundi Massacre Has Echoes of Rwanda', *The Australian* (Sydney, Australia), 27 March 1995, 19; J Bedford, 'Tribal Bloodbath Threatens Burundi', *The Australian* (Sydney, Australia), 28 March 1995, 11; 'War Fears in Burundi', *Canberra Times* (Canberra, Australia), 28 March 1995, 6; L T de la Llosa, 'UN Chief Urges Scrutiny of Burundi Crisis', *The Australian* (Sydney, Australia), 29 March 1995, 9; J Bedford, 'Burundi PM to Combat Violence with Ghettos', *Canberra Times* (Canberra, Australia), 29 March 95, 11; S Kiley, 'Burundi Risks Dual Genocide, Leader Warns', *The Australian* (Sydney, Australia), 5 April 1995, 8; S Arnold, 'Burundi Massacres Worsen', *Canberra Times* (Canberra, Australia), 5 April 1995, 11; P Smerdon, 'Rwanda Recalls Horror as Burundi Toll Mounts', *The Australian* (Canberra, Australia), 6 April 1995, 10; J Bedford, 'Burundi Government in Crisis After New Wave of Violence', *Canberra Times* (Canberra, Australia), 30 March 1995, 6; 'Thousands Wait for Border to Open: Refugees Flee Burundi as Violence Escalates', *Canberra Times* (Canberra, Australia), 2 April 1995, 6; K Austin, 'Rwanda Repeat', *The Jerusalem Post* (Jerusalem, Israel), 14 December 1994; H Nevill, 'Hutu Refugees Trapped in Camps', *The Australian* (Sydney, Australia), 6 April 1995, 10.

2.5 *Liberia*

In Liberia a bitter civil war raged through the early 1990s killing an estimated 150,000. In March 1995 fighting spread all across Liberia as the
cease-fire of 28 December 1994 collapsed and strain began to tell on the
hard pressed contributors to the Economic Community of West African
States (ECOWAS) peacekeeping force.[31] The Cotonou Agreement which it
was hoped would end the conflict was flawed, as Trevor Gordon Somers,
the UN Special Representative in Liberia concedes, 'there are aspects we
did not pay sufficient attention to. For one, we did not address the issue of
the internal security arrangements in the country.' He indicated that there
was an insufficient security structure of customs, police and immigration to
assume some of the key responsibilities and no planning for the future
army. As another UN official stated, '[t]here needs to be a state, an economic and social structure for fighters to embrace, so they can resume a
life that doesn't depend on the power of a gun for food. We have never had
to create a state before.'[32]

Other familiar features of the situation were: the inclusion of the establishment of safe havens in the Abuja Agreement of 19 August 1995,[33] the
banditry problem of factional troops not under effective command and
control, and an ineffectual or non-existent police force and justice administration. In fact, the maintenance of law and order was being performed to
some extent by the ECOWAS force where it was present. Once again the
Secretary General called for technical and logistic assistance in this area.[34]

3. THE LEGAL FRAMEWORK

Having noted the problem in the context of collapsed states in particular,
what then are the possibilities in terms of legal frameworks to establish the
legitimacy of the actions a peace operation may be required to take to
restore an efficacious regime of public security? One regime under general
international law is particularly relevant and useful, that being the law of

---

[31] 'Liberia Crisis as Ceasefire Collapses', *The Australian* (Sydney, Australia), 21 March
1995, 13.

[32] C Shiner, 'The Authority Vacuum', *Africa Report*, (1994) 23.

[33] This agreement provided for the creation of a Council of State representing all the
warring factions, to organise free and fair elections. This was the eleventh peace agreement
since the conflict began in 1989: SC Res 1014, 50 UN SCOR (3577th mtg), UN Doc
S/Res/1014 (1995). See also, *Twelfth Progress Report of the Secretary- General on the UN
Observer Mission in Liberia UNOMIL,* S/781/1995, [38] ('*Twelfth Progress Report*').

[34] Twelfth Progress Report, [42].

occupation. The key embodiment of that law is the Fourth Geneva Convention of 1949.[35]

3.1 *The Advent of the Fourth Geneva Convention*

Following World War II a broad review of the laws of armed conflict occurred through a series of conferences initiated largely through the efforts of the ICRC, culminating in the Diplomatic Conference of Geneva from 21 April to 12 August 1949. Given the experiences and the behaviour of the Axis forces in territories they occupied during World War II, and issues arising from the occupations of World War I, a central element of this review was the law regulating the rights and obligations of an occupant.[36] The result was the greatly embellished provisions of the Fourth Geneva Convention of 1949. This was part of the first attempt to provide for the systematic protection of civilians in light of their greater exposure to danger and abuse with the advent of total war. There are 188 States Parties to all four Geneva Conventions of 1949,[37] making them the most universally adopted international humanitarian law codes. The Fourth Convention is broken up into four parts dealing with: General Provisions; General Protection of Populations Against Certain Consequences of War; Provisions Common to the Territories of the Parties to the Conflict and to Occupied Territories; and Execution of the Convention. Of most concern in this work are Part I, which contains the important application and derogation provisions, Part III, which contains the substantive provisions dealing with occupation, and Article 154 of Part IV which preserves the relevant provisions of the Hague Regulations of 1907.[38] The questions that arise in relation to the Fourth Geneva Convention are; (a) in what circumstances will the Convention apply and in particular does it apply to peace enforcement under Chapter VII of the UN Charter? and, (b) when does the Convention cease to apply?

---

[35] *Geneva Convention Relative to the Protection of Civilian Persons in Time of War*, 75 UNTS (entered into force on 21 October 1950) (*'Fourth Geneva Convention'*) 287. As at 17 March 1999, there were 188 States Parties.

[36] Jean Pictet (ed), *The Geneva Conventions of 12 August 1949 - Commentary on the IV Geneva Convention Relative to the Protection of Civilian Persons in Times of War* (Ronald Griffin and C W Dumbleton trans, 1958), 3-9.

[37] The other Geneva Conventions being the *Geneva Convention for the Amelioration of the Condition of the Wounded and the Sick in Armed Forces in the Field*, 75 UNTS 31 (*'First Geneva Convention'*); *Geneva Convention for the Amelioration of the Condition of Wounded, Sick and Shipwrecked Members of Armed Forces at Sea*, 75 UNTS 85 (*'Second Geneva Convention'*); *Geneva Convention Relative to the Treatment of Prisoners of War*, 75 UNTS 135 (*'Third Geneva Convention'*). All these conventions entered into force on 21 October 1950) and as at 17 March 1999, there were 188 States Parties.

[38] *Convention Concerning The Laws and Customs of War on Land (Hague IV)*, signed at The Hague, 18 October 1907, 205 CTS 277. The Regulations are annexed to the Convention.

3.2 *The Application of the Convention*

The introduction of the Fourth Convention was to radically alter the application and shape of the legal regime regulating military presence in foreign territory. It would no longer be accurate to refer to the law of belligerent, or non-belligerent occupation. This resulted from the expansion of the Convention's coverage to all forms of non-treaty occupation, regardless of whether there was an armed conflict. The Convention was designed to regulate the relationship between foreign military forces and a civilian population where the force exercises the sole authority or is the only agency with the capacity to exercise authority in a distinct territory. As Adam Roberts puts it:

> One might hazard as a fair rule of thumb that every time the forces of a country are in control of foreign territory, and find themselves face to face with the inhabitants, some or all of the provisions on the law on occupations are applicable.[39]

How does the Fourth Geneva Convention produce this result and what did the framers have in mind when they so expanded this area of law? The answer to the first question lies in an analysis of Article 2 of the Convention where the application of the laws set out in the Convention is defined. To appreciate the Fourth Geneva Convention fully it must be understood that it has different levels of application. The four Conventions of 1949 were drafted with the object in mind of addressing all forms of armed conflict in some way, as by that time the experience of undeclared and civil wars had already been evident.[40] For example Common Article 3 to all the Conventions addresses all forms of armed conflict not of an international character while paragraph 1 of Common Article 2 applies the remaining provisions in the Conventions to all international armed conflicts, whether a state of war exists or not. We also can see that certain non-conflict situations were to be addressed in the Fourth Geneva Convention in particular, dealing as it does with the protection of civilian populations and their relationship with foreign armed forces. The Geneva Conventions also create certain peacetime obligations. It is important at this point to set out the exact wording of Common Article 2:

> In addition to the provisions which shall be implemented in peacetime, the present Convention shall apply to all cases of declared war or of any other armed conflict which may arise between two or more of the High

---

[39] Adam Roberts, 'What is A Military Occupation' (1984) 55 *British Yearbook of International Law* 249, 250.

[40] Denise Plattner, 'Assistance to the Civilian Population: the Development and Present State of International Humanitarian Law' (1992) 288 *International Review of the Red Cross* 249, 258.

Contracting Parties, even if the state of war is not recognised by one of them.

The Convention shall also apply to all cases of partial or total occupation of the territory of a High Contracting Party, even if the said occupation meets with no armed resistance.

Although one of the Powers in conflict may not be a party to the present Convention, the Powers who are parties thereto shall remain bound by it in their mutual relations. They shall furthermore be bound by the Convention in relation to the said Power, if the latter accepts and applies the provisions thereof.[41]

Paragraph 2 of the Article contains the key formula, for the purposes of this work, providing the expanded coverage of the provisions regulating occupations. The wording to note here is the expression, '[T]he Convention shall *also* apply' (emphasis added), meaning that it also applies to the following outlined circumstances *other than* a state of war or armed conflict between or among High Contracting Parties as mentioned in paragraph 1. The additional application is to, '*all* cases of *partial or total* occupation of the territory of a High Contracting Party, *even* if the said occupation meets with *no armed resistance*'[42] (emphasis added). The form of words adopted in the Report on the Work of the Conference of Government Experts, convened by the ICRC in Geneva in 1947,[43] would have made this clearer as it stated that the Convention should apply 'also in the event of territorial occupation in the absence of any state of war.'[44] The Conference of Experts' Report elaborated its intention in this respect by its commentary on the draft provision, stating that, 'this Article was adopted in order to make the Convention applicable to ... every occupation of territories, even should this occupation not be forcible.'[45] Nevertheless, Pictet states, regarding paragraph 2 of Article 2 of the 1949 Geneva Convention, that:

---

[41] Geneva Conventions, Common art 2.

[42] This was not intended to discourage armed resistance to an invader or reflect a belief that it was improper to expect civilian populations to resist, as such action was given legitimate belligerent status, provided certain qualifications were met, in arts 13(2) of the First Geneva Convention and 4A (2) of the Third Geneva Convention. The absence of the requirement for resistance reflected only the desire to simplify the *de facto* qualifications for the application of the Convention to ensure the protection of civilian populations in the widest range of relationships with foreign armed forces in positions of authority. See Georg Schwarzenberger, *International Law as Applied by International Courts and Tribunals* (1968) Vol 2, 325-7.

[43] This conference was convened to review draft re-workings developed by the ICRC in 1937 of the earlier Geneva Conventions and was an important preliminary step towards the final drafting of the Geneva Conventions of 1949 at the Diplomatic Conference of that year. See 'Report of the Work of the Conference of Government Experts for the Study of the Conventions for the Protection of War Victims (Geneva, April 14-26, 1947)', *International Committee of the Red Cross* (1947) ('*Conference of Experts' Report*').

[44] Conference of Experts' Report, 272. See also, Pictet, above n 36, 18.

[45] Ibid.

The sense in which the paragraph under consideration should be understood is quite clear. It does not refer to cases in which territory is occupied during hostilities; in such cases the Convention will have been in force since the outbreak of hostilities or since the time war was declared. The paragraph only refers to cases where the occupation has taken place without a declaration of war and without hostilities, and makes provision for the entry into force of the Convention in those circumstances.[46]

This general category of occupation is distinct from occupations occurring as a result of armistice or capitulation that is covered by paragraph 1of Article 2. Pictet's commentary explains the distinction as follows:

(A) simultaneous examination of paragraphs 1 and 2 leaves no doubt as to the latter's sense: it was intended to fill the gap left by paragraph 1. The application of the Convention to territories that are occupied at a later date, in virtue of an armistice or a capitulation, does not follow from this paragraph, but from paragraph 1. An armistice suspends hostilities and a capitulation ends them, but neither ends the state of war, and any occupation carried out in war time is covered by paragraph 1.[47]

The historical reference the framers had in mind was the German occupation of countries in relation to which there had been no declaration of war, the first of which was the occupation of Czechoslovakia which occurred even before the outbreak of general hostilities in 1939.[48] Also relevant was the experience of the Allies in occupying territory of friendly countries where they had to provide interim administration, such as in France, Holland and Belgium. It was clear therefore that the Convention was not concerned with the *circumstances* of the coming together of military forces and civilian populations foreign to each other in a relationship of authority and submission, but with the *fact* of its occurrence. As Roberts states, 'the broad terms of common Article 2 establish that the 1949 Geneva Conventions apply to a wide range of international armed conflicts and occupations – including occupations in time of so-called peace.'[49] This is further reflected by the terms expressed in Article 4 referring to protected persons where it talks of 'a conflict *or occupation*' and 'a Party to the conflict *or Occupying Power*' (emphasis added). In addition Article 6, which defines the beginning and end of the application of the Convention, states that the Convention will apply, 'from the outset of any conflict *or occupation* mentioned in Article 2'[50] (emphasis added). The practical effect is that, for the parties to it, the Convention will apply to a wide range of situations that were hitherto not within the contemplation of the formal

---

[46] Pictet, above n 36, 21-2.
[47] Ibid.
[48] Ibid 21.
[49] Roberts, above n 39, 253.
[50] Pictet, above n 36, 59-60.

codes or would have been covered by the less prescriptive law of non-belligerent occupation.[51]

The test is whether the force present is not just passing through, is not engaged in actual combat and is in effect the sole authority capable of exercising control over the civilian population, or any remaining authority requires the approval or sanction of the force to operate. The test is not based on whether the force has established a formal administrative framework or military government. This would be contrary to the intention of Article 4 of the Convention which defines protected persons, in relation to whom the rights and obligations of the Convention relate, as those simply 'in the hands' of the occupying power.[52] The way of avoiding the application of the Convention is by simply leaving the occupied territory as there is no requirement of any kind for the force to remain. Indeed the whole thrust of this law is that the situation is temporary, seeking only the regulation of the relationship between the force and the population while the force is present.

Given the transformation that has been wrought by the Fourth Geneva Convention it now seems possible to identify the circumstances that will attract the application of this body of law. Adam Roberts has set out four basic elements in this respect:

(i) there is a military force whose presence in a territory is not sanctioned or regulated by a valid agreement, or whose activities there involve an extensive range of contacts with the host society not adequately covered by the original agreement under which it intervened; (ii) the military force has either displaced the territory's ordinary system of public order and government, replacing it with its own command structure, or else has shown the clear physical ability to displace it; (iii) there is a difference of nationality and interest between the inhabitants on the one hand and the forces intervening and exercising power over them on the other, with the former not owing allegiance to the latter; (iv) within an overall framework of a breach of important parts of the national or international legal order, administration and the life of society have to continue on some legal basis, and there is *a practical need for an emergency set of rules to reduce the dangers which can result from clashes between the military force and the inhabitants.*[53] (emphasis added)

These elements were to be found in reference to the UNTAC operation in Cambodia, the IFOR/SFOR operation in Bosnia (although those operations were governed by formal agreements) and, in particular, in the UNITAF and UNOSOM operations in Somalia. Other recent situations that have often contained these elements are 'safe haven' operations. Usually a

---

[51] Eyal Benvenisti, *The International Law of Occupation* (1993) 173.
[52] Pictet, above n 36, 47, 617.
[53] Roberts, above n 39, 300-1.

safe haven will involve a force being deployed into a clearly demarcated area. Within the safe haven the deployed force may be required to undertake the restoration and maintenance of public order. The force may find itself the predominant authority with the varying degrees of breakdown in civil authority, including the total lack thereof, that may occur in these areas.

From the above analysis and using Roberts' basic elements there can be no doubt that the Fourth Geneva Convention will apply to most of these operations where there is no consent or formal agreement with the State in which the action is taken. Clearly, for example, the Fourth Geneva Convention applied to the safe haven in Northern Iraq during Operation Provide Comfort and to Southwest Rwanda in Operation Turquoise.

3.3 *Termination of an Occupation*

The time at which the law of occupation ceases to apply is also an important issue. As stated above, this body of law is intended to cover what is an essentially temporary state of affairs. The underlying assumption is that the temporary measures provided for in the law of occupation should end, and the status of the territory be resolved, as soon as possible. There is, however, no defined limit to an occupation notwithstanding the fact that it is 'temporary', as illustrated in the prolonged circumstances of the Israeli control of the West Bank, Gaza and Golan Heights or the Allied occupations of Germany and Japan. In this sense the law of occupation in its current state should be read in the context of the UN Charter, as the Charter governs issues of dispute resolution, contains prohibitions against territorial aggrandisement and regulates the transition of territories and colonies under trusteeship including assistance to statehood or peaceful incorporation into new state entities. There is nothing specified or implied in either the Fourth Geneva Convention, or the customary law of occupation that *requires* the force to remain. It is not, for example, a requirement that the force must remain until normal civil life or order is restored. The force is only required to work towards this end as far as it is within its capacity for the period during which it is in the territory. The force is free to depart at any time of its own pleasing and all its legal obligations with respect to that territory end with this departure.[54] The only circumstance where the force may be obliged to remain is where a genocide is occurring, in which case there may be an obligation on the force, and indeed the

---

[54] 'Belligerent occupation is, after all, a question of fact. It seems to the writer that an occupation would be terminated at the actual dispossession of the occupant, regardless of the source or cause of such dispossession': G von Glahn, *The Occupation of Enemy Territory: A Commentary on the Law and Practice of Belligerent Occupation* (1957) 29. See also, Doris Appel Graber, *The Development of the Law of Belligerent Occupation, 1863-1914: A Historical Survey* (1968) 64, for the historical roots of this reasoning.

international community at large, under the Genocide Convention to take preventati've action.[55]

The Fourth Geneva Convention will cease to apply when the military force departs or when it is forcibly evicted. If during the occupation a legitimate sovereign government is constituted to which the force by agreement hands over all authority, then this will terminate the relationship which the convention regulates. It will also cease to apply when the force has effectively lost control of the territory or part of it due to widespread and effective armed resistance by the local population. In this situation the Convention ceases to apply because the force 'is presumed to have lost capacity to exercise authority.'[56] Clearly the resistance referred to would have to be dramatic and not just a random campaign of terror or widespread lawlessness.

The termination of the application of this body of law is clear in the case of the departure, eviction or loss of control by the occupying force. There is, however, a complicating gradation of application provided for in the Fourth Geneva Convention based on the changing nature of the military presence. Article 6 specifies that in the case of occupied territory occurring in a conflict situation the general application of the Convention ceases one year after the close of military operations.[57] While the occupation continues, however, and to the extent that the occupying power exercises the functions of government, a number of articles remain applicable. This was a provision apparently drafted with the Allied post World War II experience in mind, but went against the initial impulse in the drafting process to end application when the occupation ended.[58] This then poses the question

---

[55] *Convention on the Prevention and Punishment of the Crime of Genocide*, opened for signature 9 December 1948, 78 UNTS 277 (entered into force 12 January 1951) (*'Genocide Convention'*), art 2. As at 17 March 1999, there were 129 States Parties. Article 1 of the Convention states, 'The Contracting Parties confirm that genocide, whether committed in time of peace or in time of war, is a crime under international law which they undertake to prevent and to punish.' The prohibition of genocide will be binding on all states regardless of whether they are signatories to the Convention as this prohibition has attained the status of *jus cogens*.

[56] Graber, above n 54, 259.

[57] Fourth Geneva Convention, article 6 reads:

The present Convention shall apply from the outset of any conflict or occupation mentioned in Article 2.

In the case of occupied territory, the application of the present Convention shall cease one year after the general close of military operations; however, the Occupying Power shall be bound, for the duration of the occupation, to the extent that such Power exercises the functions of government in such territory, by the provisions of the following Articles of the present Convention: 1 to 12, 27, 29 to 34, 47, 49, 51, 52, 53, 59, 61 to 77, 143.

Protected persons whose release, repatriation or re-establishment may take place after such dates shall meanwhile continue to benefit by the present Convention.

[58] Pictet, above n 36, 62.

as to what provisions apply to a non-belligerent occupation, whether the application of the provisions change at any point and when they cease altogether. Pictet comments on this issue as follows:

> Article 6 does not say when the Convention will cease to apply in the case of occupation where there has been no military resistance, no state of war and no armed conflict. This omission appears to be deliberate and must be taken to mean that the Convention will be fully applicable in such cases, so long as the occupation lasts.[59]

This produces the result that more provisions will continue to apply to an occupation which begins as non-belligerent, while fewer provisions would apply in relation to an occupation which began in a conflict situation, even though it may have acquired the same character as a non-belligerent occupation one year after the cessation of military operations. This anomaly was addressed by Additional Protocol I.[60] For those states party to it, Additional Protocol I alters the termination provisions of Article 6 of the Fourth Geneva Convention by clearly stating, without qualification or elaboration, in Article 3 (b) that the relevant provisions of the Additional Protocol and Convention will cease to apply 'on the termination of the occupation.'[61] For those few remaining nations who have not yet adopted Additional Protocol I, such as France or the United States, the Article 6 anomaly in the Fourth Geneva Convention will remain an issue and pose interoperability questions.

The utility of the law of occupation is extensive in relation to the public security issue, including guidelines for dealing with the local law and the parameters for departing from this law when necessary. It also provides well for the temporary administration of justice where there is no local capability. The measures for security of the force and relief operations are clearly spelled out as is the authority for reconstructing the local justice administration.[62]

---

[59] Ibid 63.

[60] *Protocol Additional to the Geneva Convention of 12 August 1949, and Relating to the Protection of Victims of International Armed Conflict,* 1125 UNTS 3; 16 ILM 1391 ('*Additional Protocol I*'). As at 17 March 1999, there were 153 States Parties.

[61] Fourth Geneva Convention, art 3(b) reads:

> The application of the Conventions and of this Protocol shall cease ... in the case of occupied territories, on the termination of the occupation, except ... for those persons whose final release, repatriation or re-establishment takes place thereafter. These persons shall continue to benefit from the relevant provisions of the Conventions and of this Protocol until their final release, repatriation or re-establishment.

[62] See Michael J Kelly, *Peace Operations - Tackling the Military, Legal and Policy Challenges* (1997).

3.4 *The Current Status of Non-Belligerent Occupation*

Recent examples of pacific occupation by agreement include the United Nations Transitional Authority for Cambodia (UNTAC) experience in Cambodia. The Paris Agreement of 23 October 1991 under which the UN forces deployed constituted the temporary transfer of key areas of sovereignty to the UN.[63] As we have seen however there were many areas which

---

[63] See the *Agreement on a Comprehensive Political Settlement of the Cambodia Conflict, Agreement concerning the Sovereignty, Independence, Territorial Integrity and Inviolability, Neutrality and National Unity of Cambodia, 23 October 1991*; (1991) 40 ATS. Article 3 of the Accords vested sovereignty in a Supreme National Council (SNC) composed of representatives of the Cambodian factions. Article 6 then went on to state:

> [T]he SNC hereby delegates to the United Nations all powers necessary to ensure the implementation of this Agreement, as described in annex 1.

> In order to ensure a neutral political environment conducive to free and fair general elections, administrative agencies, bodies and offices which could directly influence the outcome of elections will be placed under direct United Nations supervision or control. In that context, special attention will be given to foreign affairs, national defence, finance, public security and information. To reflect the importance of these subjects, UNTAC needs to exercise such control as is necessary to ensure the strict neutrality of the bodies responsible for them. The United Nations, in consultation with the SNC, will identify which agencies, bodies and offices could continue to operate in order to ensure normal day-to-day life in the country.

Under Article 16 UNTAC was given responsibility for fostering an environment of respect for human rights, also governed by the provisions of annex 1. Annex 1, Section A, paragraph 1 assigned to UNTAC the powers necessary to ensure the implementation of the Agreement. Paragraph 2 put in place a mechanism for resolving issues by requiring UNTAC to comply with the advice of the SNC, provided there was a consensus in the SNC and the advice was consistent with the objectives of the Agreement. If there was no consensus then SNC President Norodom Sihanouk was empowered to make the decision on what advice should be offered UNTAC which it was bound to follow, once again, only if it was consistent with the objectives of the Agreement. If the President was not in a position to make such a decision then the power transferred to the Special Representative of the Secretary-General (SRSG). The determination of whether the advice of the SNC or President was consistent with the Agreement was a matter for the SRSG to determine. Section B of annex 1 dealt with civil administration and through paragraph 1 placed under the direct control of UNTAC 'all administrative agencies, bodies and offices acting in the field of foreign affairs, national defence, finance, public security and information'. More specifically, paragraph 4 gave the SRSG the power to:

(a) Install in administrative agencies, bodies and offices of all the Cambodian Parties, United Nations personnel who will have unrestricted access to all administrative operations and information;

(b) Require the reassignment or removal of any personnel of such administrative agencies, bodies and offices.

Paragraph 5 (b) went on to grant the SRSG the authority to determine, in consultation with the Cambodian Parties, the civil police necessary to perform law enforcement. In this respect it was provided that:

> All civil police will operate under UNTAC supervision or control, in order to ensure that law and order are maintained effectively and impartially, and that human rights and

remained the source of much contention and uncertainty under the necessarily broad terms of the Agreement. The customary law of pacific occupation will fill any such voids left by an Agreement of this sort and certain fundamental principles can be applied to help clarify uncertainties.[64] One example of an area the customary law can illuminate is the right of the force to take measures for its own security.[65] Another of the principles discussed above that would also be applicable in the case of occupation by agreement relates to the aspect of control. For example, in the case of UNTAC the UN force was never able to exert its authority in the areas controlled by the Khmer Rouge. The Khmer Rouge were clearly a force exercising sole control over a part of Cambodia such as to enable them to carry out sustained and concerted military operations.[66] The customary laws of pacific occupation therefore did not apply to that particular area of Cambodia, as the occupying force had no control there.

Another recent experience of pacific occupation was that established by the Dayton Agreement involving the warring parties in the Former Republic of Yugoslavia, NATO, the Organization for Security and Cooperation in Europe (OSCE) and the UN.[67] This Agreement provided for the deployment of a large NATO Implementation Force (IFOR) for a period of one year pursuant to UN Security Council authorisation and Chapter VII of the UN Charter.[68] IFOR was empowered to 'take such actions as required, including the use of necessary force, to ensure compliance with the ... (agreement) and to ensure its own protection', a point to be emphasised throughout the document.[69] There were a number of other provisions assigning authority to the IFOR commander and various agencies, approximating an occupation condition.

Of particular interest was the development of the role of an International Police Task Force (IPTF) building on the experience in numerous recent

---

fundamental freedoms are fully protected. In consultation with the SNC, UNTAC will supervise other law enforcement and judicial processes throughout Cambodia to the extent necessary to ensure the attainment of these objectives.

Under Section D, UNTAC was empowered to organise and conduct the election and to establish a system of laws, procedures and administrative measures for this purpose. (Paragraphs 1, 3(a)). UNTAC was also tasked to make provisions for the investigation of human rights complaints, and, where appropriate, corrective action. (Section E).

[64] Kelly, above n 62, 22– 36.

[65] Ibid.

[66] The test is used here as an indicative guide for determining when effective control by the occupant ceases.

[67] *General Framework Agreement for Peace in Bosnia and Herzegovina*, S/999/1995 (1995) ('*Paris Peace Agreement*').

[68] Paris Peace Agreement, Annex 1-A, arts I(1) and VI(1). SC Res 1031, 50 UN SCOR (3607th mtg), UN Doc S/Res/1031 (1995), subsequently provided full authorisation for the Agreement under Chapter VII including UN responsibilities arising from the International Police Task Force and the High Representative for relief matters.

[69] Paris Peace Agreement, Annex 1-A, art I(2).

deployments. The management of this operation was assigned to the UN, headed by a Commissioner appointed by the Secretary General in consultation with the Security Council. It was coordinated by and came under the guidance of the High Representative. The Commissioner was permitted to receive and request personnel, resources and assistance from States as well as international and non-governmental organisations.[70] In carrying out their functions they were to act in accord with international standards but were to respect local laws and customs.[71]

The tasks of the IPTF included: monitoring, observing, and inspecting law enforcement activities and facilities, including associated judicial organizations, structures, and proceedings; advising law enforcement personnel and forces; training law enforcement personnel; facilitating, within the IPTF's mission of assistance, the Parties' law enforcement activities; assessing threats to public order and advising on the capability of law enforcement agencies to deal with such threats, advising governmental authorities in Bosnia and Herzegovina on the organization of effective civilian law enforcement agencies; and assisting the Parties' law enforcement personnel as they carried out their responsibilities, as the IPTF deemed appropriate.[72]

To fulfill these tasks they were to have complete freedom of movement and be allowed access to any site, person, activity, proceeding, record or other item or event in Bosnia and Herzegovina. This was to include the right to monitor, observe and inspect any site or facility at which it believed police, law enforcement, detention, or judicial activities were taking place.[73]

Clearly pacific occupation is alive and well and is finding new modes of application and relevance as it is employed by the international community to meet the challenges of the diverse security crises that threaten international peace and stability. This is clearly being driven by the need to address the source of this threat, which is not primarily that of tackling cross border invasions but internal disintegration and violence. It is important, however, that the terms of a pacific occupation be sufficient to allow a robust approach to establishing an efficacious public security administration. Both the Paris Accord in particular and to a lesser extent the Dayton process have not fully measured up to this test. It is only through action that equates to occupation that such internal strife can be effectively addressed, if addressed at all. It also requires a realisation that the commitment needs to be over a number of years.

---

[70] Paris Peace Agreement, Annex 11, art II(2).
[71] Paris Peace Agreement, Annex 11, art II(5).
[72] Paris Peace Agreement, Annex 11, art III.
[73] Paris Peace Agreement, Annex 11, art IV(3).

3.5 *The Proper Use of Force*

The dilemma that faces any peace operation is the appropriate use of force in dealing with the public security aspect. This becomes an even more complicated issue when there is no law enforcement agency of any form or civil authority capable of enforcing a code of law. The troops will often, in these circumstances, be caught between the force appropriate for combat situations and something more akin to civil policing.[74] This difficult circumstance places emphasis on two aspects of military preparation: the training of the troops and the Rules of Engagement. It was clear in Somalia that some troops were better prepared for the complexity of the operation than others were. The Canadian Airborne Regiment Battle Group (CARBG) was able to achieve much good work in the Belet Weyn area but its reputation was tarnished by the inappropriate manner in which the unit dealt with the issues of base security and crowd control. This deficiency was a consequence of disciplinary problems within one of the sub-units, poor leadership and command attitude in relation to ROE standards, inadequate training of at least one sub-unit and the lack of a proper framework for effecting the ROE.[75] It is not advisable to deploy assault units of this kind into a situation like Somalia without careful supplementary training.

---

[74] M Maren, 'The Tale of the Tape' (1993) 38 *The Village Voice* 23, 24.

[75] The Board of Inquiry into the CARBG of 31 August 1993, the Toronto Star investigative piece of 10 July 1994 and Canadian Television (CTV) investigative reports revealed the extent of the disciplinary problems of 2 Commandos of the Airborne Regiment. These included challenges to the authority of unit and sub-unit formal leadership, inappropriate initiation rituals, racist attitudes and practices, steroid usage and a tendency to unharnessed aggression. These problems were identified before deployment by the then CO of the unit Lieutenant Colonel Paul Morneault. He recommended that 2 Commando not be sent to Somalia. Soon after passing on this advice Lieutenant Colonel Morneault was relieved of command and Lieutenant Colonel Carol Mathieu was appointed CO. 2 Commando's preparation was not ideal. It was put through what amounted to a collective punishment exercise in an attempt to correct its discipline problems and had suffered a high turnover in junior personnel. It fell behind 1 and 3 Commandos in specific mission training for Somalia as a result, focusing instead on 'general purpose combat training.' In an attempt to remedy the training deficiency, 2 Commando was put through a one-week crash course immediately prior to departure for Somalia.

Once in Somalia a number of training, leadership and ROE issues arose. The troops began referring to the Somalis using derogatory epithets such as 'gimmes, niggers, smufties and nig-nogs' and this was not stamped out by the unit leadership. Despite the use of force regime laid out by the UNITAF ROE, the CO on 28 January 1993 issued instructions that any Somali caught in the perimeter stealing equipment was to be shot. Major Seward, the 2 Commando Officer Commanding (OC) wrote in his diary concerning this instruction that,

> he has amended the rules of engagement ordering us to open fire on individuals pilfering the camp. These individuals are teenaged Somalis. His direction ... amounts to killing children ... I will not willingly accept murdering boys stealing water, rations and even military kit.

P Cheney, 'Death and Dishonor in Somalia', *The Toronto Sunday Star* (Toronto, Canada), 10 July 1994, Section F. Major Seward also expressed concern over the subsequent killing

This was recognised, for example, in the preparation of the 1st Battalion, Royal Australian Regiment (1 RAR) before it deployed to Somalia. While this unit was also trained for intense and aggressive combat, in the two years prior to the Somalia deployment it had been coming to grips with more complicated mission concepts. These revolved around low level conflict scenarios in Northern Australia and Services Protected Evacuations of Australian citizens in such circumstances as internal conflicts and the disintegration of law and order. In the course of this training the soldiers were trained to deal with varying levels of threat and the discriminating use of force. The training was in reference to two simple states of restraint based on a 'red' and 'amber' card. The cards are plastic and carried permanently in the soldier's basic pouch. The cards themselves would be meaningless of course without appropriate training. This training was conducted by taking, for example, a rifle platoon and having members of the platoon play act a scenario with props in an outdoor setting. The remainder of the platoon would observe as the scene was played out. Afterwards the soldiers would be queried as to appropriate responses and given the opportunity to ask questions and discuss the issues. The scenarios would then be varied to present gradations of the problem. In subsequent exercises the troops would be exposed to civilians, sometimes their own families, who had volunteered to participate. Also encountered were delegates of the ICRC who have been incorporated into major Australian exercises since 1989.

This soldier level regime of standard response is called Orders For Opening Fire (OFOF) to distinguish it from higher level ROE reserved for commanders in control of significant weapon systems which focus more on the strategic implications of conflict. The OFOF training emphasises certain key elements of the soldier's decision making reference. The first is the clear identification of the target. This was a fundamental discipline in Somalia, which the soldiers adhered to exceptionally well.[76] This concept places soldiers under the stricture that they must be able to identify the target to be fired upon as hostile or the source of a hostile act (depending

---

of an intruder in pursuance of this policy: 'I was disgusted by what seemed to be a recce (reconnaissance) platoon-hunting trip. The succession of shots and the anticipatory tone of voices makes me conclude that the killing was a murder' (Ibid).

Later instructions were issued by the sub-unit leaders, including Major Seward, to physically 'abuse' captured intruders in order to deter them. This resulted in the torture and death of a Somali. On 17 February 1993 there was a demonstration by some Belet Weyn inhabitants against Lieutenant Colonel Mathieu's selection of locals for reconstruction committees which excluded some clans from representation. In handling the demonstration, 12-gauge shotguns were fired into the crowd by the Canadian troops killing one Somali and critically injuring three others: See, CARBG Board of Inquiry, Vol XI, 3287, 3306-10, 3313-8, 3321, 3328-9, 3345. CTV news reports, video recordings up to January 1995 provided to author by CTV.

[76] Ascertained by the author in reviewing all casualty-producing incidents caused by the Battalion in Somalia.

on the circumstances) and not open fire indiscriminately or engage, for example, in 'reconnaissance by fire'.[77] The element emphasised and debated most extensively in the training is the issue of self-defence and proportionate or necessary force. Here, through demonstration and discussion, the soldier is made intimately familiar with the concepts of this legal standard and the parameters set by the courts. The goal here is two fold. First, to reduce the hesitation of the soldier which might otherwise result in their death or the death of a person it is their duty to protect, secondly, to minimise the risk to innocent bystanders and, finally, to equip them with the means of explaining and accounting for their actions in any subsequent review.

In training, the concept of the proportionate use of force is carefully explored. The focus here is providing soldiers with guidelines as to the options they might use when confronted with particular situations. The first distinction that is drawn is whether the soldier faces a lethal or non-lethal threat. If they face a non-lethal threat which nevertheless has the potential to cause physical injury then methods of responding are canvassed such as the use of batons, warning shots or Riot Control Agents (RCA). The application of force they are instructed to apply in this circumstance must be no more than is required to neutralise the threat and not to kill or cause more bodily harm than is absolutely necessary. In response to a lethal threat, the soldier is authorised to use whatever means they can to counter the threat including the employment of lethal force subject only to the requirement to attempt to minimise the risk of death or injury to innocent bystanders. When 1 RAR was warned for deployment to Somalia, the troops were put through refresher OFOF training, modified according to the known facts about the operational environment, the specific ROE for the mission and the law and order role.

They were permitted to employ the level of firepower considered necessary to neutralise the threat, restricted by consideration of the proportional risk to civilians. In this respect the training of the soldiers in the Laws of Armed Conflict and discussion in the acted out scenarios assisted them in judging the issue of proportionality. This training and the command philosophy of the Commanding Officer (CO) also highlighted the individual responsibility of the soldier and the standards of behaviour expected of them when dealing with civilians. This training was validated when members of the contingent reported observed violations of these standards committed by members of another contingent resulting in disciplinary action.[78] The CO very quickly acted upon any reports of an inclination towards lack of respect for the local population. The combination of train-

---

[77] This term refers to clearing an area in front of troops by massive use of firepower, without regard to what may be under the fire.

[78] The Australian contingent Commander, Colonel Mellor, reinforced this by writing to the soldiers concerned, commending them for their actions.

ing, realistic ROE, command philosophy, the creation of a law and order regime relying on the law of occupation and a civic action programme, explains the remarkable good will enjoyed by the Australian contingent with the local population. No progress in rehabilitating the public security function can be made without maintaining the good will of the population.

It is therefore imperative for common standards to be developed in the application of force and the Laws of Armed Conflict for all troops that are nominated to become part of a peace operation with a public security dimension. To this end it is a matter of some urgency that a training package be created and adopted by the UN and regional military cooperation organisations that focuses on the essential elements of behaviour and the application of force for peace operations. This would not be a 'Code of Conduct' such as has been mooted, but a formal training programme. This package should then be provided to every prospective troop contributing nation and a training regime commenced for those forces that have been nominated as part of the standby force arrangements between the UN and participant countries. The UN should have a permanent training officer who can advise on the implementation of this training and monitor the standards attained. The advice of this officer could then be obtained as to whether a contingent being offered for a mission had achieved a satisfactory level of training in this respect, measured against the nature of the operation. Such a package could form the basis of a general standard to apply to all armed forces in the same manner as UN Rules relating to standards of criminal justice. Training should also be put into effect to prepare troops to operate in accord with the particular ROE for a given mission. When ROE are promulgated to supplement or alter original ROE, then the onus is on commanders to ensure there is proper briefing and training for troops expected to adapt to new operating conditions.[79] As Colonel Kenneth Allard of the US Army has put it, 'a single unwise tactical move by a soldier on patrol can instantly change the character of an entire operation and, when broadcast by the ever-present media pool, can also affect strategic considerations.'[80]

It is also important that the commanders of the contingents examine carefully the management of the application of force in peace operations.[81] In this respect the commanders must appreciate the differing circumstances of operations so that they will understand that most peace operations are closer in nature to what used to be termed 'Counter Insurgency' operations, now given the generic term Low Intensity Conflict.

---

[79] F M Lorenz, 'Rules of Engagement in Somalia: Were They Effective?' (Paper submitted for publication in the *Naval Law Review*, January 1995). See also M S Martins, 'Rules of Engagement for Land Forces A Matter of Training, Not Lawyering' (1994) 143 *Military Law Review* 3; Kenneth Allard, *Somalia Operations: Lessons Learned* (1995) 37-8.

[80] Allard, ibid, 6.

[81] Ibid 8-9.

Those commanders who are not sensitive to the subtleties of such operations should not be appointed. This was one of the major lessons to emerge from the Canadian experience in Somalia, much of the explanation for which stems from the attitude of the Airborne Regiment leadership at the time. The employment of firepower must also be highly selective and confined. The circumstances of peace enforcing occupations and humanitarian interventions dictates a standard higher than would apply in a state of war and therefore it is incumbent on commanders to adopt tactical options that offer a more surgical approach. This once again places emphasis on the need for the assets to open up such options, including Special Forces and intelligence.

3.6 *Justice Reconstruction and Interim Measures*

We have seen how important an effective justice reconstruction programme was to the overall success the Somalia intervention hoped to achieve and how this was not reflected in the urgency, resources or efficiency with which the issue was approached. The recurrence of this central problem in peace operations requires that the international community find a way of addressing it at the outset of the contemplation of a mission. The two crucial aspects of creating an effective international response are funding and physical capability. The programme in Somalia suffered firstly because of the fact that the funds to support it could not come from the peacekeeping budget for the mission. Funds had to come instead from donors. Perhaps the UN may have had greater success in raising funding support had it used the argument that the troop contributing countries had obligations in this respect under the laws of occupation. In missions of this nature in the future, where it is clear that the re-establishment of a justice regime is going to be involved, an estimate should be provided as to the costs involved. This cost should then be factored into the determination by the Security Council and contributions assessed against member states in accordance with their assessed proportional contributions to the UN in general. In 'contracted out' operations, which appear to be the most likely for the foreseeable future, participating states should be required in the authorising resolution to organise an effective means of dealing with such reconstruction issues in tandem with UN and other agencies.

Having noted the difficulty of quickly deploying civilian experts in a peace operation, what is the interim solution? It is essential that some nations who are intending to offer stand-by forces to UN operations develop a deployable civil affairs capability geared to address the restoration and maintenance of law and order. Such units could deploy rapidly, at less cost and in harsher environments than civilian alternatives. Once circumstances permit, these units could either hand over to civilians or to local authorities who had resumed functioning. They would have the capability to establish interim measures such as military courts to hear cases involving major offenders against the force and public order. Such units would also be equipped and staffed to conduct investigations to support the work of international criminal tribunals including the International Criminal Court when it is operational, or assist local prosecution efforts against major violators of international humanitarian law. These units could use as their reference the provisions of the laws of occupation and international standards established by conventions, general principles and published UN Rules. Under these authorities a basic code could be drawn up which could serve as an interim regime in the worst case of no local code capable of application. Primarily the focus should be on rehabilitating pre-existing local codes pursuant to the obligations of the law of occupation. The world is predominantly divided into criminal law traditions derived from the Napoleonic Code, the English Common Law and/or *Sharia* Law. The nation called upon to contribute civil affairs unit to a mission could be selected on the basis of a tradition or capability matching the assisted country so that familiarisation on deployment will be quicker. The NGO community could also be drawn into such efforts.

Apart from the failure of UNOSOM to deal effectively with justice reconstruction for reasons of funding and capability, it was critically undermined by the approach taken during the UNITAF phase to the issue and the restoration and maintenance of order in general.[82] This stemmed from the reluctance to recognise the need for a framework for the interim administration of justice and the rejection of the laws of occupation for this purpose. One option in this early phase, according to Brigadier Ahmed Jama, would have been to have foreign judges come in to operate courts until a transitional government was formed and enough judges found, trained and vetted to take over. He believed this was necessary at least in Mogadishu where it would take some time for the people to accept that a Somali judge would not be clan biased. He believed the foreign judges would have been required for at least a year.[83] This would have created problems for UNITAF and UNOSOM because of the uncertainty both experienced over the authority for taking such action. This authority was clearly available under the law of occupation. This option has been partially adopted in the pacific occupation arrangements of the Dayton Agreement where non-nationals have been nominated to the role of Human Rights Ombudsman and on the panel of the Human Rights Chamber.

The failure to establish any form of law and order regime by either UNITAF or UNOSOM led directly to the frustration that emerged among the troops of contingents where no alternative had been attempted similar to the Australian initiatives. This frustration led to incidents which would only further alienate the troops from the population and which seriously damaged the international image of the operation. The frustration of troops

---

[82] I Alexander, 'There Oughta Be a Law' [1994] *National Review* 32-3.
[83] Interview with Brigadier Ahmed Jama (3 January 1995).

who have their initial motivation to help restore order checked and the loss of faith of a population which has high expectations of what the force will do to restore security to their lives, combines to produce a tragic atmosphere of bitterness, futility and the decay of morale. There was also confusion for the commanders trying to come to grips with the complexity of the operation. In considering the detainee issue, the Canadian Board of Inquiry into the CARBG made what was a common error in Somalia; looking for guidance on the handling of detainees from the Third Geneva Convention, rather than the Fourth Geneva Convention.[84] All troop-contributing governments and the UN have a responsibility to ensure that the men and women of their armed forces are never placed in such a position again. No mission into a failed state or to establish a safe haven should proceed without an interim administration of justice plan and a concept of operations with the appropriate resources and assets for the longer term restoration of the local capability.[85]

---

[84] CARBG, Board of Inquiry, above n 75, 3332.

[85] Ibid 3288:

> 2 Commando was also given the task of re-creating the local police force. This was a part of the normalisation process and supported the UNITAF Phase Three integral task of re-establishing non-partisan institutions at the local level, as the basis for a return to effective government. Although the task of training the Somali police force was assigned to the Battle Group by UNITAF through the CJFS (Canadian Joint Force Somalia) headquarters, there were major policy deficiencies and potential legal command and control problems associated with this project. These problems could have been resolved only at the UN/UNITAF level', ibid 3281-2; 'It was to be expected that OPERATION DELIVERANCE (the Canadian name for its participation in UNITAF) would at some point lead to the detention of Somalis. This was contemplated in the ROE in that they specified that detainees would be handed over to the appropriate military authorities. UNITAF Headquarters were formally queried the first week of January 1993, as to the procedures necessary to comply with this direction, but no practical solution was provided. There were, in fact, significant jurisdictional problems which were beyond the authority of the in-theatre commanders to resolve.

Ibid 3331:

> This was peacemaking, which might informally be described as falling somewhere between peacekeeping and low-intensity war. As noted in the statement by the Board, there was no government in Somalia, and no administrative, legislative or judicial structures in place. This new challenging environment posed problems to all levels of command who had not, in the opinion of the Board, fully contemplated, nor provided the required policy direction. This did have an effect on the actual application of the ROE in theatre. For example, the ROE clearly anticipated the requirement for the detention of Somali persons. They directed that detainees be handed over to "appropriate military authorities". However, within the CJFS, clear legal authority to detain Somali persons on a long-term basis did not exist. A detainee was certainly not a prisoner of war because Canada was not at war with Somalia. Nor could the detainee be considered subject to The Criminal Code of Canada, or the Code of Service Discipline. The Commander CJFS' attempt to obtain clarification from UNITAF, his next higher headquarters in the operational chain of command, resulted in a verbal response to simply avoid

Such plans do not necessarily imply the commitment of vast sums of money and personnel. The Australian experience in Baidoa proved that much can be achieved with little and, in fact, the best approach is to rely as much as possible on what can be gleaned locally. For example, it was not necessary to bring large numbers of police trainers to Somalia. In many cases the trainers that were brought in had inferior training to the formerly highly competent Somali force. This in itself was something of an insult to the locals. The Australian approach of locating survivors from the old police academy and putting them to work doing the training in coordination with members of the former Somali CID and Somali judges was the better approach and would have saved much time and money. Similarly, weapons could have been issued from the confiscated stock and buildings restored from the least damaged available. The police could have been equipped with vehicles from confiscated technicals or the vehicles of bandits. All that may have been needed then was some basic office equipment, stationery, communications gear, generators and uniforms to supplement what was salvaged from Somali stock in Kenya.

Another measure that should have been adopted to help finance the operation in terms of pay for the police and judges was the commencement of some form of rudimentary taxation once the markets, farms and livestock trade were functioning again in areas where councils were established. The SDM council in Baidoa had wanted to commence taxation for this purpose towards the later period of the Australian presence. As the justice system was providing a secure environment for the economy to revive the measure would have had moral logic. The authority that could have been used to provide a framework for taxation was the laws of occupation. Under these provisions the force may gather revenue for the administration of the territory and take measures necessary for the welfare of the population. As long as the taxation was applied solely for paying local personnel it would have been easily justified. In this way the officials would be paid in accordance with what the economy could bear and there would be no difficulty of sustainability after UN departure or lowering of expectations. One less string to the cycle of dependency could be severed. To avoid any acrimony developing with the population from the UN gathering the revenue this could have been left to the re-established councils acting in accord with UN guidelines, under UN supervision and financial monitoring.

Perhaps the key issue a law and order regime would have had to contend with, had it been established, is the position to be taken towards the warlords. It was advocated in some quarters that all the warlords, who had been guilty of committing grave atrocities during the civil war, should have

---

detaining Somali persons for any length of time. The Board concludes that this was an indication that the same problem was recognised at that level.

been arrested *en masse* and placed on trial.[86] Prosecution action greatly assisted the long-term objectives of the Australian contingent in Baidoa. This poses the question as to what should have been the approach taken to the warlords. For the seizing of the warlords to have been effective, in the sense of being seen to be even handed and pre-empting conflict with any particular faction, all the warlords would have to have been arrested simultaneously. Clearly this would have been extremely difficult and fraught with great risk. There is also the important consideration that there ought to be some evidence connecting particular individuals with specific acts, in the possession of the force, which would justify every arrest if it were intended to bring the warlords to trial. Such evidence would not have been available, if at all, until after careful investigation. More legally sustainable would have been the detention of the warlords on the grounds of the threat they represented to public safety and the safety of the force. This would still have carried grave operational risk and would have been difficult to execute.

A more feasible approach would have been the establishment, once the force was effectively and securely established, of a humanitarian law violations investigation operation to gather evidence of atrocities committed during the civil war. Initially, regional bandits such as Gutaale in Baidoa, and Jess and Morgan in the south, could have been targeted for possible prosecution (as opposed to the approach taken in the hunt for Aideed). Once sufficient evidence was available the warlords could have been arrested, when the opportunity presented, as quietly as possible without announcing before hand that these individuals were being sought. Targeting the lesser regional figures would have sent a powerful message to the major faction leaders to cooperate lest the same fate befall them. It would have had the added benefit of eroding the regional support for these main players. This proved to be the case with the warlord Gutaale who was tried and executed in Baidoa and whose demise resulted in a reduction in revenue and support for Aideed.

The idea of an international tribunal to try such figures is fine in theory, however, the difficulty in establishing the ICTY/ICTR indicates that these instruments cannot be rendered operable within at least a year. The other problem with a tribunal in the Rwandan circumstance is that it focuses attention and funding on an external legal mechanism rather than on reviving the local system. The Rwandan Tribunal could only prosecute at best a small number of perhaps the key figures in the genocide. In the meantime thousands languish in appalling conditions in Rwandan prisons awaiting trial. Many of these people have had accusations leveled against them which have not and will not be supported by further evidence but who have been nominated by the word of a single complainant who may

---

[86] 'The Bandits on Their Donkeys', *The Economist* (London, United Kingdom), 1 May 1993, 40-1.

have had particular motives for making the accusation, such as acquiring the land of the accused.[87] While the trial of the key figures by the Tribunal is desirable, the real problem is the ability of the system to handle the languishing thousands. An Argentinean team working in Ethiopia,[88] concentrated on enabling the Ethiopians themselves to handle the investigation and prosecutions relating to the atrocities committed by the Mengistu regime.[89] In Somalia the priority should have been in equipping Somalis to

---

[87] Major B Oswald and Major C McConaghy, legal officers attached to the Australian contingent in Rwanda, 1994-5. See also, the Australian ABC Television 'Foreign Correspondent', investigative report by Jonathon Holmes, *Rwanda Justice*, on the prison situation in Rwanda and the Rwandan International Tribunal, 6 June 1995.

[88] 'From 1974 to 1991, the Dergue regime led by now-exiled Colonel Mengistu Haile Mariam, was responsible for human rights violations on a massive scale. Tens of thousands of Ethiopians were tortured, murdered or "disappeared."' Tens of thousands of people were killed, as a result of humanitarian law violations committed during Ethiopia's many internal armed conflicts. Many others, perhaps more than 100,000, died as a result of forced relocations ordered by the Mengistu regime. These violations are documented in Human Rights Watch/Africa, *Evil Days: 30 Years of War and Famine in Ethiopia* (1991). In May 1991, the Ethiopian People's Revolutionary Democratic Front (EPRDF) and the Eritrean People's Liberation Front (EPLF), overthrew the Mengistu regime: see Human Rights Watch/Africa Report, *Accountability and Justice of Transitional Government* (1994).

[89] See Australian ABC Television 'Foreign Correspondent', report *Terror on Trial*, from BBC Assignment program on Ethiopian atrocities investigation, 19 July 1994. See also, US State Department Report, *Human Rights in Ethiopia* (1995):

> On October 25, the Special Prosecutor's Office (SPO) handed down long-awaited indictments against the first group of defendants to be tried for serious crimes, including for crimes against humanity during the "Red Terror" and forced resettlement and villagization, committed during the Mengistu dictatorship from 1974 to 1991. The SPO was established in 1992 to create an historical record of the abuses during the Mengistu government and to bring to justice those criminally responsible for human rights violations and corruption. The trial of the first 66 defendants began on December 13 (1994). In this first group, the Government is trying 21 of the 66 in absentia, including the former president, Colonel Mengistu Haile Mariam, who is in exile in Zimbabwe. It may eventually charge and try more than 3,000 defendants in connection with these crimes; some government officials expect the trials to go on for 3 to 5 years. In 1994 the Government arrested 25 former Air Force personnel for having bombed civilian targets during the civil war. Over 1,600 suspects remained in detention without charge at year's end, some of whom have been detained for more than 3 years.

Human Rights Watch /Africa Report, above n 88:

> The people of Ethiopia and the international community have waited many years for the process of accountability and justice to begin in Ethiopia," said Paul Hoffman, one of the report's authors and a member of the California Committee of Human Rights Watch. "It is essential that those accused of serious human rights crimes be brought to justice under internationally recognized fair trial procedures as a foundation for the creation of a judicial system in Ethiopia based on the rule of law. These trials offer a unique opportunity for national reconciliation and remembrance that should contribute to the development of democratic institutions in Ethiopia.

Unfortunately the new government is beginning to evince characteristics that suggest it may not be committed to furthering human rights standards in its own dealings, US State Department Report, above.

prosecute the bandits and warlords. Major figures, beyond the capability of the locals to handle, could have been tried by the domestic courts of one of the troop contributing states where there was evidence of such persons having committed grave breaches of common Article 3 of the Geneva Conventions of 1949. With no Somali sovereignty left to offend, and these figures having passed into the hands and authority of the occupying power, this would have been justifiable.

With the establishment of the International Criminal Court another option will emerge for bringing to justice major violators of international humanitarian law. This will be a useful mechanism for dealing with major figures that need to be removed from the scene to facilitate the peace-building process. Notwithstanding this development, the priority of effort should always be in rehabilitating the municipal justice administration to salvage and revive collapsed states. This approach is better for the long-term viability of such states.

Justice reconstruction should not focus solely on the issue of maintaining order, however. As the Australian experience in Baidoa and the operations in Haiti and Rwanda have demonstrated, an integral factor in laying the foundations for long term order is the need to address the attempted supplanting of ownership of land and property, often accompanied, as in Baidoa, by genocidal activities.[90] It is essential to include a mechanism for resolving land and property disputes in many operations and this may include establishing a special tribunal. The same logic as was discussed in relation to crimes tribunals applies here in that effort should be directed primarily at creating an indigenous capability to deal with these matters, albeit perhaps with close supervision. This can help take the heat out of potentially explosive situations. Once again the framework for proactive intervention in this area can be provided by the laws of occupation under the provisions governing the restoration of order and public life.

The mission in Somalia could have achieved a great deal more had the international community been fully committed to the long-term view finally expressed in Security Council Resolution 814 of 26 March 1993,[91] from the first day the troops hit the beach and sent in the assets capable of carrying it out with them. In principle it is possible to restore a Somalia, a Rwanda, a Burundi, a Liberia, an Ethiopia, a Mozambique, a Cambodia and many other situations like them. The world learned how to go about such a task in Germany and Japan after World War Two and is re-learning in Haiti and Bosnia. Internal civil wars and/or social breakdown pose much greater difficulties but they are not insurmountable. Resolution of such conflicts depends on the ability of the intervening force to manage and

---

[90] Lee V Cassanelli, 'Somali Land Resource Issues in Historical Perspective', in Walter Clarke and Jeffrey Herbst (eds), *Learning From Somalia: The Lessons of Armed Humanitarian Intervention* (1997) 67, 68-75.

[91] SC Res 814, 48 UN SCOR (3188th mtg), UN Doc S/Res/814 (1993).

begin the resolution of inherent grievances, guarantee security and to create mechanisms that will give all parties confidence that this guarantee will continue on the departure of the force.

When intervening in a collapsed state scenario the idea that laboratory solutions produced in western think tanks can be automatically and inflexibly applied should be dispelled. Similarly the concept that all developing States should be made over in the image of western economies and societies is destructive of the social fabrics that must be built upon for long term results and usually cannot be sustained by the environment or resources of the assisted country. The failure of the instant 'short sharp shock' remedies applied to some post cold war eastern bloc countries has demonstrated the counter productive consequences of this approach. An intervention should deploy with a capability and with experienced staff in key positions but should be prepared to be flexible and imaginative, adapting the mission to the circumstances and being as inclusive of the local population and sensitive to their culture and laws as possible. In this context the broad framework of the laws of occupation provides the best basis for the interim regulation of the relationship between the force and the community and upon which to build an environment of law and order from which many other desired outcomes will flow. Accepting the application of the laws of occupation will also lead to the realisation that a force must come equipped and prepared to assume administrative functions normally the preserve of the sovereign.

PART V

Enforcing the Rules of International Humanitarian Law

GILLIAN TRIGGS

8. National Prosecutions of War Crimes and the Rule of Law

1. INTRODUCTION

Failure to enforce the law, whether international or national, is fatal to its
credibility. Indeed, failure to enforce the law is antithetical to the notion of
the rule of law itself. Herein lies one of the fundamental difficulties with
international humanitarian law. Prosecution of war crimes or of 'grave
breaches' of the Geneva Conventions[1] and Protocols[2] is seen as either not
happening at all, or as one of the spoils of victory. There is, in short, an
echoing chasm between aspiration and achievement.

My task is to discuss national approaches to enforcement of international humanitarian law.[3] As this is a dismal tale to tell, I am pleased that
other contributors will present a more positive view of the future by dis-
cussing the *ad hoc* tribunals established by the United Nations Security
Council at The Hague[4] (ICTY), and Rwanda[5] (ICTR) and the Rome Statute
of the International Criminal Court[6] (ICC).

---

[1] See *Geneva Convention for the Amelioration of the Condition of the Wounded and the
Sick in Armed Forces in the Field*, 75 UNTS 31 ('*First Geneva Convention*'); *Geneva
Convention for the Amelioration of the Condition of Wounded, Sick and Shipwrecked
Members of Armed Forces at Sea*, 75 UNTS 85 ('*Second Geneva Convention*'); *Geneva
Convention Relative to the Treatment of Prisoners of War*, 75 UNTS 135 ('*Third Geneva
Convention*'); *Geneva Convention Relative to the Protection of Civilian Persons in Time of
War*, 75 UNTS 287 ('*Fourth Geneva Convention*') All these conventions entered into force
on 21 October 1950, and as at 17 March 1999, there were 188 States Parties.

[2] *Protocol Additional to the Geneva Convention of 12 August 1949, and Relating to the
Protection of Victims of International Armed Conflict*, 1125 UNTS 3; 16 ILM 1391 (entered
into force 7 December 1978) ('*Additional Protocol I*'), as at 17 March 1999, there were 153
States Parties; and *Protocol Additional to the Geneva Convention of 12 August 1949,and
Relating to the Protection of Victims of Non-International Armed Conflicts*, 1125 UNTS
609; 16 ILM 1442 (entered into force 7 December 1978) ('*Additional Protocol II*'), as at 17
March 1999, there were 145 State Parties.

[3] For examples of war crimes prosecutions by municipal courts see Rudiger Wolfrum,
'The Decentralized Prosecution of International Offenders Through National Courts' in
Yoram Dinstein and Mala Tabory (eds), *War Crimes in International Law* (1996) 233.

[4] *Statute of the International Tribunal for the Prosecution of Persons Responsible for
Serious Violations of International Humanitarian Law committed in the Territory of the*

*Helen Durham and Timothy L.H. McCormack (eds.), The Changing Face of Conflict and the Efficacy of International
Humanitarian Law*, 175–191.
© 1999 *Kluwer Law International. Printed in Great Britain.*

After signature by the Allies of the London Charter[7], which established the Nuremberg Tribunal as an international court with universal jurisdiction to try war crimes, came the inspirational dicta: 'crimes against international law are committed by men, not abstract entities, and only by punishing individuals who commit such crimes can the provisions of international law be enforced.'[8]

The Nuremberg and Tokyo Tribunals were successful in developing the jurisprudence of international criminal law and individual responsibility for war crimes. The general perception was that the trials had achieved their objectives of justice, retribution, deterrence and education.[9] Despite the progressive lead shown by these international proceedings, domestic rather than international tribunals have conducted war crimes trials since then. A new catalyst, the atrocities of civil war following the break up of Yugoslavia and the war in Rwanda, have prompted the Security Council to create by resolution, two *ad hoc* tribunals to prosecute war crimes. As we observe the current trials at The Hague,[10] and consider the Rome Statute for a Permanent International Criminal Court, it may be useful to assess the difficulties experienced by national courts in their efforts to prosecute war crimes. While it is unlikely that the lessons of domestic law can easily be

---

Former Yugoslavia since 1991, SC Res 827, 48 UN SCOR (3217 [th] mtg), UN Doc S/Res/827 (1993); 32 ILM 1203 ('*Statute of the ICTY*').

    [5] *Statute of the International Tribunal for the Prosecution of Persons Responsible for Genocide and Other Serious Violations of International Humanitarian Law Committed in the Territory of Rwanda and Rwandan Citizens Responsible for Genocide and Other Violations Committed in the Territory of Neighbouring States, Between 1 January 1994 and 31 December 1994*, UN Doc S/RES/955 (1994), 49 UN SCOR (3453rd mtg); 33 ILM 1598 ('*Statute of the ICTR*').

    [6] *Rome Statute of the International Criminal Court*, adopted by the United Nations Diplomatic Conference of Plenipotentiaries on the Establishment of an International Criminal Court on 17 July 1998; 37 ILM 1002. The whole of the Statute is also located at <http://www.un.org/icc/romestat.htm> ('*Statute of the ICC*').

    [7] *Agreement for the Prosecution and Punishment of Major War Criminals of the European Axis, (London Agreement)*, 8 August 1945, 82 UNTS 279. The Charter of the International Military Tribunal is appended to the Agreement ('*Charter of the IMT*').

    [8] *Trial of the Major War Criminals before the International Military Tribunal*, Nuremberg (1945-1946), Judgment, 41; reprinted in 'Judicial Decisions' (1947) 41 *American Journal of International Law* 17, 221.

    [9] See, M Cherif Bassiouni and Ved P Nanda, *A Treatise on International Criminal Law* (1973) vol 2.

    [10] *Prosecutor v Dusko Tadic (Jurisdiction) (Decision of the Appeals Chamber, 2 October 1995)* 105 ILR 419, 453. See also, Peter Rowe, 'The International Criminal Tribunal for Yugoslavia: the Decision of the Appeals Chamber on the Interlocutory Appeal on Jurisdiction in the *Tadic Case*' (1996) 45 *International Comparative Law Quarterly* 691, 691-701, also summarised in (1997) 91 *American Journal of International Law* 718; Virginia Morris, *Prosecutor v Kanyabashi* (Decision of 18 June 1997) [1996] ICTR-96-15-T summarised in (1998) 92 *American Journal of International Law* 667. On 2 September 1998, the ICTR found Jean-Paul Akayesu, (former mayor of the village of Taba), guilty of genocide for the slayings of 2,000 minority Tutsis who had sought his protection. On 24 April 1998, 22 people were executed by Rwandan firing squads after their conviction for genocide.

translated to an international court, some of the difficulties experienced by national war crimes trials might be avoided in the future.

Domestic war crimes trials, relating to the Second World War and the conflict in Vietnam, have been held in France, Australia, Austria, Israel, Canada, The Netherlands, Spain, United Kingdom, United States, USSR, Eastern Europe and Germany.[11] These trials have been subject to trenchant criticisms which employ as their benchmark the ideal of the rule of law; an ideal which is taken to require consistency, legality and impartiality.

Oft-repeated criticisms are that national war crimes trials are:

- merely the victors' justice;
- partial, biased and selective;
- lacking in legal precision;
- retroactive in their criminal laws;
- procedurally unfair, resulting from unjustified delay in trials, difficulties in witness testimony and gathering of evidence;
- conducted without benefit of traditional defenses such as superior orders and act of State;[12]

An examination of domestic legislation and experiences of national tribunals provides ample support for these criticisms and demonstrates that the rule of law in domestic war crimes trials has been strained and distorted. Paradoxically, the rule of law has ultimately triumphed because most recent prosecutions have failed to gain convictions. Demjanjuk was acquitted for lack of convincing identification evidence;[13] the two Australian prosecutions of Berezowsky,[14] and Polyukovich[15] were fatally hampered by unavailability or unreliability of witnesses; the French collaborator Bousquet was shot and killed prior to trial;[16] Dusko C was acquitted by an Austrian jury;[17] Rauca Sujectto died in prison prior to trial;[18] Wolfgang

---

[11] German Courts are reported by Alfed Streim, Head of the Documentation Center on Nazi crimes in Ludwigsburg, to have conducted 6,494 trials of Nazi War criminals since 1945: *The Associated Press*, 13 February 1996.

[12] See especially in this context, Gerry J Simpson, 'War Crimes: A Critical Introduction' in Timothy L H McCormack and Gerry J Simpson (eds), *The Law of War Crimes* (1997) 4-28.

[13] *State of Israel v John Demjanjuk* Crim Case No 373/86 (District Court of Israel), overturned in *Demjanjuk*, Crim App No 347/88 (Supreme Court of Israel, 29 July 1993) reprinted in Landau (ed), *The Demjanjuk Trial* (1991) ('*The Demjanjuk Trial*').

[14] *Mikolay Berezowsky*, File No 91/25241 (Adelaide Magis Ct, 16 July 1992) 9 (DC Gurry SM) ('*Berezowsky Case*').

[15] *Director of Public Prosecutions v Ivan Timofeyevich Polyukhovich*, No S 3782 (Sup Ct of South Australia, 22 December 1992) (Cox J) (*Polyukhovich*). See also, Gillian Triggs, 'Australia's War Crimes Trials: All Pity Choked', in McCormack and Simpson, above n 12, 130-2.

[16] Charges against Christian Bousquet were brought in 1990, but he was killed in 1993.

[17] *Dusko C's* appeal against a jury finding of not guilty has been appealed by the Austrian Prosecutor in 1995. The Salzburg Offfice of Public Prosecutions had filed charges of genocide, murder and arson: *Amklageschrift der Staatsanwaltschaft Salzburg*, 8 St 4570/94, 27 July 1994.

Otto was acquitted for lack of evidence;[19] Rühl was too sick to take part in his German trial and charges were dropped in 1984 and extradition requests have been denied by Chile and Argentina.[20]

2. WHY HAVE MANY RECENT NATIONAL WAR CRIMES TRIALS FAILED?

National efforts to prosecute war crimes have been the victim of changes in national moods and priorities. At the end of the Second World War, the pressure was strong to prosecute immediately, whether by international or domestic tribunals. This post war period was followed by the practical need to get on with the challenges of the New World. Governments decided to 'close the chapter'[21] on war crimes trials and to move on to build new lives or, less positively, to engage with the 'real' enemy, communism. After 20 or so years of relative peace and prosperity, there was a growing fear that the young understood little of the Nazi holocaust. Political and community groups became convinced that war criminals who were still alive should be prosecuted. Little consideration appeared to have been given to the possibility that such trials might be partisan and selective. Rather, the prosecution of remaining Nazi war criminals was driven by a deeply felt moral imperative. The strength of the moral arguments overbore a wider view of the rule of law as nations proceeded to draft their new laws for prosecution.

Many of the trials which followed failed, not because the legislation was partial or narrow in application, but for the practical reason that trials 40-50 years after the event are not able to satisfy basic principles of procedural and evidentiary fairness. It was, in short, too late to do what might have been done 20-30 years earlier. This paper seeks to examine the main criticisms of national war crimes trials, particularly those, which have been instituted over the last decade or so.

---

[18] Rauca Sujectto died in prison in 1983 after his extradition to Germany from Canada.

[19] Wolfgang Otto was acquitted due to inadequate proof of fault in 1989: Rousseau, *Chronique des Faits Internationaux* (1989) 93 RGDIP 104.

[20] Rühl, who was alleged to have experimented in the effects of poison gas on concentration camp prisoners, was too sick to participate in the German trial and the charges were dropped in 1984; Chile denied a request from the UK for his extradition, Walter Rauff, *Le Monde*, (Paris, France) 16 May 1984. Note that charges have been brought against *Szymon Serafinwicz* by the UK in 1995*, International Herald Tribune*, 17 July 1995.

[21] Commonwealth of Australia, *Parliamentary Debates*, H of R 22 March 1961, 451; see also, A Menzies, *Review of Material Relating to the Entry of Suspected War Criminals into Australia* (1987) 9 ('*Menzies Report*'). For discussions on the Menzies Report see, Gillian Triggs, 'Australia's War Crimes Trials: A Moral Necessity or Legal Minefield?' (1987) 16 *Melbourne University Law Review* 382; McGinley, 'War Crimes Legislation and the External Affairs Power' (1990) 14 *Criminal Law Journal* 342; O'Neil, 'Prosecuting War Criminals in Australia' (1991) 16 *Legal Services Bulletin* 20; Starke,'The High Court and the War Crimes Legislation' (1991) 65 *Australian Law Journal* 701.

3. SELECTIVITY AND PARTIALITY

A predominant issue arising from national war crimes trials is the perception that they have been highly selective and partial as to the war with which they have been concerned, as to the geographical place of the crime, as to the choice of criminal acts for which prosecutions can be made and as to the time span within which the act must have occurred. The prosecutions of war crimes after the Second World War were especially subject to the criticism that they were ideologically selective with a focus on Nazi prosecutions rather than the prosecution of war crimes in the course of other conflicts.

Australia's *War Crimes Act*,[22] justified by the Government on the grounds of universal jurisdiction is the best example of highly selective legislation. It applies only to war crimes committed in Europe, during a war or occupation occurring between 1 September 1939 and 8 August 1945. The narrow sliver of time during which this legislation applies, the limitation of the geographic location of the offence to Europe, and the paucity of any relevant connection with Australia (other than the residence or citizenship of the accused at the time of the prosecution, though not at the time of the offense) raise doubts as to the legal and moral validity of the legislation. Any illusion of universality and even-handedness vanished when the first draft of the proposed legislation, which was sufficiently wide to allow prosecution of Australians for acts in the Pacific region, created such a political furore that the bill was amended to restrict trials to acts committed in Europe, thereby excluding acts in the region where Australian Defence Personnel were alleged to have committed war crimes.

The legislative history of the United Kingdom's *War Crimes Act* 1991 [23] was also stormy. The House of Lords rejected the Bill twice on the grounds that it was retroactive and selective. The legislation was finally passed, using the powers under the 1949 Parliament Bill. The Act applies only in cases of murder, manslaughter and homicide, excluding crimes without lethal consequences. It does not apply to Japanese war criminals, officials of regimes installed or tolerated by the Nazis, members of the allied forces, or German prisoners of war outside Germany or German held territory. No war crimes trials have yet been held under this legislation, though it is reported that trials are soon to be commenced.[24]

France participated actively in the prosecution of war criminals and collaborators after the Second World War under laws and tribunals estab-

---

[22] *War Crimes Act* 1945 (Cth) as amended by *War Crimes (Amendment) Act* 1988 (Cth).

[23] *An Act to Confer Jurisdiction on United Kingdom Courts in respect of Certain Grave Violations of the Laws and Customs of War Committed in German-Held Territory During the Second World War and for Connected Purposes* 1991 (UK) ('*War Crimes Act*').

[24] Axel Marschik, 'The Politics of Prosecution: European National Approaches to War Crimes' in McCormack and Simpson, above n 12, 89.

lished with special jurisdictional competence. These trials came to an end with the statutory limitations in the early 1970s.[25] The trial against the former Gestapo chief of Lyon, Klaus Barbie,[26] much later in 1987, was based on the finding of the Cour de Cassation that certain crimes against humanity, embodied in the Statute of the Nuremburg Tribunal, were directly applicable in French Law.[27]

The first of two Frenchman to be tried for crimes against humanity during the Second World War was Paul Touvier, a former militia chief, who was sentenced to life for ordering the execution of six Jews in 1944. He died in jail while serving this sentence. More recently, in April 1998, a French Assize Court in Bordeaux convicted 87 year old Maurice Papon, a former French official of the Vichy regime during the Second World War, (who later became the budget minister in the cabinet of former President Valery Giscard d'Estaing), for crimes against humanity. He was sentenced to 10 years jail, after a six-month trial. As the appeal process is now underway, it is thought unlikely that he will serve a sentence. One of the central jurisprudential questions for the court was whether Papon was a 'middleman' and functionary for his superior, Maurice Sabatier, now dead. The conviction indicates that superior orders will not necessarily provide a defence under French law.

While the jurisprudence of French criminal law was advanced by recognition of crimes against humanity as part of French law, French law remains open to the criticism that it is selective because charges under the Code can be brought only in relation to Nazi crimes. The Code will not apply to crimes against humanity committed in the later Algerian war of independence or in the Vietnam conflict. The French Government reaffirmed an amnesty for all French military infractions during the Algerian war, only days before enacting a statute declaring crimes against humanity to be 'imprescriptible' under the Statute of Limitations.[28]

---

[25] Ibid 82.

[26] *Federation Nationale des Deportes et Internes Resistants et Patriotes contre Klaus Barbie,* reprinted in (1986) 90 RGDIP 1024. See also, A Finkielkraut, *Remembering in Vain: The Klaus Barbie Trial and Crimes Against Humanity* (R Lapidus trans, 1992); Guyora Binder, 'Representing Nazism: Advocacy and Identity in the Trial of Klaus Barbie' (1989) 98 *Yale Law Journal* 1321; Doman, 'Aftermath of Nuremberg: The Trial of Klaus Barbie' (1989) 60 *Colorado Law Review* 449.

[27] The successful prosecution by France of Barbie was followed by only two other fruitful French trials, those of Paul Touvier, who was found guilty in 1994 and sentenced to life imprisonment, and Maurice Papon in 1998. Papon was found guilty of crimes against humanity and sentenced to 10 years imprisonment on 2 April 1998. The jury found him guilty of complicity in organising the round-up and detention of Jews during World War II, but acquitted him on charges of complicity in the deaths of the Jews, most of whom perished at Auschwitz: see Christopher Henning, '*Papon* Trial: Guilty of Crimes Against Humanity', *The Sydney Morning Herald* (Sydney, Australia), 3 April 1998, <http://www.smh.com.au/daily/content/980403/world/world6.html>.

[28] Simpson, above n 12, 27.

The supremacy of French domestic laws, rather than international law, was upheld in the trial of Boudarel, a French Vietnam war veteran, for serving the Viet-Minh between 1952 and 1954. The Cour de Cassation held that his acts did not constitute a crime against humanity and that all other criminal acts were protected by the general amnesty in relation to the French war of independence in Vietnam in 1966. While too much cannot be deduced from this decision, it illustrates the extreme reluctance of States to take war crimes prosecutions beyond trials of Nazi criminals or collaborators.

The Netherlands took a strong stand against German Nazi war criminals but no prosecutions have been attempted in relation to evidence of acts of Dutch armed forces against Indonesia 1945-1949.[29] The attitude of Spain to war crimes trials has been described as 'reserved'.[30] The trial in 1997 by an Italian military court of former Nazi SS Capt. Erich Priebke was successful in gaining a conviction for his role in the execution of 335 men and boys at the Ardeatine Caves in Italy during the Second World War.[31] His sentence was reduced to 5 years jail on the basis of certain mitigating circumstances, presumably including the fact that Priebke was 83 years old. While he will serve little more than 18 months in jail, as he has been held in custody for the last three and a half years, the essential point is that a conviction for crimes against humanity has been achieved.

The erstwhile Federal Republic of Germany and the Democratic Republic of Germany and Austria, conducted thousands of war crimes trials against their own citizens after the Second World War, though with varying degrees of enthusiasm and often-minor penalties. The highly publicized trial by Germany of the supervisors and guardians of the concentration camp at Maidanek, Poland were, for example, disappointing because, after six years of hearings, only one life sentence was given in 1981, and all other penalties were described as light.[32]

The Soviet Union punished Nazi war criminals severely, and continued to do so as recently as 1987, when Fedorenko was found guilty of treason

---

[29] See the report on the public confessions of several Dutch soldiers, which revealed details of major humanitarian crimes against the local Indonesian population, in *Die Presse*, 15 February 1995; also see Marschik, above n 24, 89-90.

[30] Marschik, above n 24, 90.

[31] Erich Priebke was extradited from Argentina to Italy in November 1992. Priebke, an 82-year-old German citizen, was charged with taking part in the slayings of 335 people in 1944 at the Ardeatine Caves outside Rome to avenge a bombing that killed 32 German soldiers, 'Trial of ex-Nazi Unlocks Horror of "Past and Present"' The Detroit News (Detroit, USA) 9 May 1996 <http://www.detnews.com/menu/stories/47147.htm>. See also, Cousigli, Marchisio and Martines, 'The Case of Erich Priebke' (1998) 1 *Yearbook of International Humanitarian Law* 341–361.

[32] Marschik, above n 24, 74.

and murder and executed aged 79.[33] Soviet war crimes trials have, none-theless, been restricted to Nazi war criminals.

Canada's history in relation to war crimes prosecutions is similar to that of Australia's. The Deschênes Report of 1986 led to amendment of the Criminal Code of Canada on 16 September 1989 to enable prosecutions of war crimes and crimes against humanity. However, the Canadian Code differs in significant ways from Australia's *War Crimes Act* because it is not restricted in time to the Second World War, but applies to any defined crimes, whenever committed.[34] Prosecutions to date have also been con-fined to war crimes of the Second World War.

Israel enacted the 1950 *Nazi and Nazi Collaborators (Punishment) Law*,[35] which applies only to crimes 'during the period of the Nazi regime.' It adopts offences that are substantially similar to those of the Nuremberg Charter, though there is no requirement that the offense should have been committed as a crime of war. The Nazis (Punishment) Law was based, in part, on universal jurisdiction, but, like the Australian and Canadian legis-lation, it applies only to crimes against a specific group, the Jewish people, and focuses on Israel's personal, rather than universal experience of geno-cide.[36]

The trial of Adolf Eichmann,[37] while successful in gaining a conviction, was not free from criticism. Israel, in effect, condoned the illegal abduction of Eichmann and there was a perception that justice would have been better served had a trial been conducted by an international tribunal rather than by courts representing the victims of the holocaust. Eichmann's prosecu-tion displayed many elements of a 'show trial' and was clearly used for educational and ideological purposes, beyond trial of the guilt of the ac-cused. Justification for the trial lay in the fact that no international tribunal existed (nor was in prospect) at the time and no other State wanted the responsibility or cost of conducting such a trial. Understandable though prosecution of Eichmann by Israel was at the time, and scrupulous though the procedures were reported to be, this national trial of a major war crimi-nal, stood in stark contrast with the earlier Nazi war crimes trials on behalf of the Allies (if not the international community). The Eichmann trial

---

[33] Ibid 91. In light of the civil war following the breakup of Yugoslavia, it is interesting to note that the Yugoslav Penal Code provided in Chapter XVI for the prosecution of genocide and grave breaches of the Geneva Conventions and these have remained in the codes of the new Republics.

[34] Sharon A Williams, 'Laudable Principles Lacking Application: The Prosecution of War Criminals in Canada' in McCormack and Simpson, above n 12, 159.

[35] 57 *Sefer Hachukim*, 9 August 1950 ('*Nazis (Punishment) Law*'), 281.

[36] Jonathan Wenig, 'Enforcing the Lessons of History: Israel Judges the Holocaust', in McCormack and Simpson, above n 12, 106.

[37] See *Attorney General of the Government of Israel v Adolf Eichmann*, (1961) 36 ILR 5 ('*The Eichmann Case*').

raised serious concerns for the rule of law and demonstrated the need for justice to be seen to be done by a more objective international tribunal.

It should be recognised, however, that Israel attempted to act evenhandedly by prosecuting its own war criminals under the Nazis (Punishment) Law which permits charges against the *Judenrat*, the Jewish Council[38] and the *Kapos*, the Jewish policemen in the concentration camps. Such prosecutions caused great national anguish and few prosecutions were made; the only reported case resulting in an acquittal.[39]

In summary, national war crimes trials have been highly selective in the sense that they deal only with Nazi or Nazi related crimes during the Second World War. With rare exceptions, no attempt has been made to prosecute crimes arising in other conflicts.[40]

4. RETROACTIVITY

It is a principle of domestic criminal law, common to most national legal systems, and of international law, that an act cannot be made criminal if it was not a crime at the time it was committed. This is described as the principle of retroactivity. National war crimes trials have been required to consider whether the legislation under which the prosecutions were being instituted might be invalid on the grounds that the offenses they describe offend the principle against retroactivity.

There was a unique problem of retroactivity in the *Eichmann Case* because the State did not exist at the time of the criminal acts. It was thus impossible to argue that the crimes had existed under pre-existing Israeli law. The Supreme Court argued, in support of the validity of the Nazis (Punishment) Law, that laws concerning acts that were neither innocent nor indifferent at the time they were committed did not offend any rule against *ex post facto* criminal laws. This analysis begs the question whether the act is a war crime, a crime against humanity or a crime which is contrary to a natural universally accepted law, at the time it was committed.

---

[38] The *Judenrat* were to organise the relocation of the Jewish community to the ghettoes. See Lichenstein, *Himmlers Grune Helfer: Die Schutz – Und Ordnungspolizei Im Dritten Reich* (1990).

[39] Wenig, above n 36, 120.

[40] Ironically, some of the most successful national cases in relation to alleged war criminals were not trials of criminality but have arisen as hearings on denaturalisations and deportations. The United States, for example, has not attempted war crimes trials, preferring to denaturalise and deport persons for reasons only indirectly linked to war crimes. This approach, which has also proved successful in Canada, where future legal action against alleged war criminals are likely to be confined to deportation and revocation of citizenship. See John Francis Stephens, 'The Denaturalization and Extradition of Ivan the Terrible' (1995) 26 *Rutgers Law Journal* 821; Williams, above n 34, 170.

The United States courts in the later *Demjanjuk Case*[41] found that, as criminality of the acts did not depend on the Nazi (Punishment) Laws, the issue of retroactivity could be avoided.

The legislation of Canada and Australia was drafted to avoid the criticism of retroactivity by adopting the device that the act or omission must have been a crime both at international law and under domestic law at the time it was committed. Nonetheless, the Australian legislation was challenged on the ground that it was retroactive in its operation, though the constitutional dimensions of the issue dominated analysis. Justice Brennan argued in *Polyukovich*[42] that his 'real objection' to the War Crimes Act was that it adopts a municipal law definition of war crimes which operates retrospectively.[43] He acknowledged, though obliquely, that, if the acts did not constitute a criminal offense under international law at the time they were committed, the *War Crimes Act* places Australia in breach of Article 15 of the International Covenant on Civil and Political Rights 1966,[44] which provides: '[n]oone shall be guilty of any criminal offence on account of any act or omission which did not constitute a criminal offence, under national or international law, at the time when it was committed.'

Justice Brennan concluded that crimes against humanity were not clearly established in international law independently of war crimes when the Nuremberg Charter was drafted.[45] He thus concluded, in a minority opinion, that the means adopted under the War Crimes Act:

> [N]ot only trample upon a principle which is of the highest importance in a free society, namely, that criminal laws should not operate retrospectively, but also select[s] a specific group of persons from a time long past out of all those who have committed, or are suspected of having committed, war crimes in other armed conflicts.

The other Justices did not need to consider the issue because, for one reason or another, they agreed that the legislation adequately reflected international law during the Second World War.[46]

As was the case in the constitutional challenge in *Polyukovich*, resolution of the retroactivity question is most likely to arise in relation to crimes against humanity, which is the offence most vulnerable to the charge that it

---

[41] *Demjanuk*, 612 F Supp 544, (ND Ohio 1985), *Demjanik* (6th Cir), 612 F Supp 571 (ND Ohio), aff'd, 776 F 2d 571, (6th Cir 1985); Landau (ed), *The Demjanuk Trial* (1991).

[42] *Polyukhovich v Commonwealth*, (1991) 172 CLR 501, 572. The constitutionality of the *War Crimes Act* was challenged by *Polyukhovich* in the High Court of Australia after he had been charged with various offences under the Act. The High Court determined that the Act was constitutionally valid.

[43] Ibid.

[44] *International Covenant on Civil and Political Rights*, opened for signature 19 December 1966, 999 UNTS 171, 6 ILM 368 (entered into force 23 March 1976) ('*ICCPR*'). As at 17 March 1999, there were 144 States Parties.

[45] *Polyukhovich*, above n 42, 587.

[46] Triggs, above n 15, 141-4.

was not established as a rule of customary international law before the Second World War.[47] As substantive international criminal law develops, and has developed over the years since the Second World War, it is less likely that the retroactivity issue will present such a serious jurisprudential problem for future international war crimes tribunals.

5. PROCEDURAL FAIRNESS

The legislative and jurisdictional problems of national war crimes trials have, in recent cases, been overshadowed by the practical difficulties of collecting evidence and securing eyewitness identifications more than fifty years after the criminal acts were committed. Indeed, it is a common feature of most national trials that they foundered on the rocks of procedural unfairness. It proved to be difficult to meet the necessary levels of proof; most witnesses were very old at the time of trial and very young at the time of the criminal acts; a fatal evidentiary combination. This is especially true of Australia's experiences in the *Wagner, Berezowsky* and *Polyukovich* cases. Courts have considered themselves bound to refuse requests to take evidence on commission from witnesses overseas. The fear was that evidence taken in this way would threaten the defendant's rights to confront and question witnesses directly. In certain Canadian and Australian war crimes trials, for example, the right to take commission evidence was rejected. As evidence of key witnesses was not available, the prosecutions were stayed. Moreover, judges seemed disturbed on occasion by the feebleness, infirmity or illness of the accused.[48]

The Canadian experience has been similar to that of Australia. The Government established a team of investigators to recommend prosecution, or deportation proceedings as a 'secondary option'. The Justice Department's Progress Report of 1993,[49] states that in most cases investigated there was not enough evidence to request extradition from the USSR or Eastern European States. Four cases were prosecuted in 1988-90, the most important of which was that of *R v Imre Finta*[50] in 1988, in relation to crimes against humanity and war crimes committed in Hungary. Finta was acquitted; a finding which was not reopened by the Supreme Court of

---

[47] For a detailed discussion on this issue see, M Cherif Bassiouni, *Crimes Against Humanity in International Criminal Law* (1992) 114-29.

[48] Triggs, above n 15, 129-34.

[49] Crimes Against Humanity and War Crimes Section, Department of Justice, Canada, *Progress Report of the Investigation of War Crimes in Canada* (1993) ('*Canadian War Crimes Progress Report*').

[50] (1989) 50 CCC (3rd) 247; (1989) 61 DLR (4th) 85, confirmed by the Ontario High Court on Appeal (1992) 73 CCC (3rd) 65 and by the Supreme Court of Canada in March 1994, 69 OR (2nd) 557 ('*Finta Case*').

Canada in applications for a rehearing in 1994.[51] The case against Reistetter[52] in 1991 was dismissed on the death of critical witnesses and the prosecution of Pawlowski[53] in 1992 also failed when witness were not available to testify and applications to take evidence on commission were refused.

It is notable that the same problem of evidence was fatal in the first prosecution by a Swiss tribunal in criminal proceedings based on universal jurisdiction over war crimes. In April 1997, a military tribunal considered alleged violations of the laws and customs of war under the Swiss Military Penal Code by G G, in the prisoner of war camps of Omarska and Keraterm in Bosnia-Herzegovina in 1992. The accused was acquitted because the evidence was insufficient to establish that he was in the camps at the times of the crimes. As Zeigler comments:

> The cultural differences, the geographical and temporal distance, the surviving witnesses' fear of testifying and the chaotic circumstances at the time of the crimes make it extremely difficult to achieve that level of proof beyond a reasonable doubt normally expected to support a guilty verdict in criminal proceedings.[54]

Thus it seems that the length of time after the crime is not the only cause of evidentiary problems in subsequent war crimes trials.

A significant contribution by the Swiss Military Tribunal to the jurisprudence of war crimes trials was that the rules of international conflict also applied to the conduct of Bosnian Muslims in prisoner of war camps in Bosnia in a non-international conflict. The conclusion of the tribunal was by no means to have been expected because most of the Geneva Convention rules are applicable only in international armed conflicts. Indeed, two of the judges of the trial chamber of the subsequent ICTY in the *Tadic Case* reached opposite views on this issue.[55]

Demjanjuk's trial by the Israeli District Court of Jerusalem was similarly dominated by questions of evidence, notably identification of the accused. By the time the matter reached the Supreme Court, the defence was able to raise a reasonable doubt that the accused was in fact Demjanjuk, and he was acquitted 'because time permitted doubt to erode what might once have seemed certain'.[56]

Whatever doubts one might have about the selectivity of national war crimes legislation or the jurisdictional bases of trials, the determination of

---

[51] Williams, above n 34, 165.

[52] Canadian War Crimes Progress Report, 15.

[53] *Regina v Pawlowski*, (1992) 13 CR (4th) 228 (Ont CJ (General Division).

[54] Andreas R Zeigler, 'In re G' (1998) 92 *American Journal of International Law* 78,82.

[55] *Prosecutor v Dusko Tadic*, (*Decision of Trial Chamber II, 7 May 1997*) IT-94-1-T; 36 ILM 908; summarised in (1997) 97 *American Journal of International Law* 718 ('*Tadic Judgment*').

[56] Wenig, above n 36, 117.

national courts to ensure that high standards of procedural fairness are afforded the accused, has been a signal feature of national trials. It is arguable that, to bring a prosecution fifty years after the criminal act was committed, is *ipso facto* an abuse of process. While Justice Cox, in the Australian prosecution in *Polyukhovich*,[57] regarded the 51 year delay as 'enormously long – of unprecedented length'[58] he remained confident that 'countervailing steps'[59] could be taken to warn the jury of any potential risk to a fair trial. In fact, he stayed proceedings in relation to one of the counts before him on the basis that, on the totality of the evidence, the accused could not be assured of a fair trial. Thus, while the passing of the legislation was an uncomfortable parliamentary endorsement of the validity of the trial, which could not be questioned by the Court, a remedy for injustice lay in the rules of criminal procedure. Ultimately, Polyukovich's case came to an end when the indictments were quashed for a lack of evidence.

In *Demjanjuk* the Israeli court was compelled, as we have seen, to acquit the accused because a reasonable doubt had been raised as to his identity as 'Ivan the Terrible'. This was so despite a finding by the District Court that, 'the powerful store of impressions which these people kept within themselves relating to the image of Ivan the Terrible, is strong, and has been preserved through the course of time.'[60] Similarly, in the German and Austrian war crimes trials, there were difficulties with the collection of evidence arising from the passage of time and with extradition. In the recent *Dusco C.* trial, Austria's main difficulty was, again, one of adducing evidence.

As with the problem of retroactivity, it is to be hoped that the problems created by extreme delays in bringing war crimes trials will be less likely to arise in the future if trials can be commenced before a permanent international tribunal, soon after the criminal acts have been committed

6. Substantive Legal Content of War Crimes

A severe impediment to national war crimes prosecutions has been the 'underdeveloped'[61] and ill-defined nature of international criminal law, particularly the category of crimes against humanity. As Simpson points out, the definition of a war crime might vary to include:

- a lay person's notion of an abhorrent act;
- a technical breach of the 'laws of war';

---

[57] *Polyukhovich*, above n 15.
[58] Ibid 11.
[59] Ibid 10.
[60] Landau, above n 41, 198-9.
[61] Simpson, above n 12, 12.

- the 'grave breaches' enumerated in the 1949 Geneva Conventions;
- the Statute of the War Crimes Tribunal for Former Yugoslavia 'violations of the laws and customs of war'; or
- the use by the International Law Commission of the term 'exceptionally serious war crimes' in the Draft Code on Crimes Against the Peace and Security of Mankind. [62]

It was, for example, important to both Justices Toohey and Brennan in the Australian constitutional challenge to the *War Crimes Act* that crimes against humanity were proven to be crimes at customary international law at the time that they were committed. That these Justices differed in their findings on questions of proof only compounds the central difficulty of ascertaining the rules of substantive international criminal law.

There are other problems of legal definition, including the various ways in which defences can be relevant, the inapplicability of much of the body of international humanitarian law to civil wars and the difficulty of establishing the subjective 'intent to destroy' in Article II of the Genocide Convention.[63] The Canadian prosecution in the *Finta Case* was fatally flawed when the court searched for an element of 'culpability', on the ground that something more was necessary to constitute a war crime. (With the failure of this prosecution, there are not thought likely to be any further prosecutions by Canada of Nazi war criminals under the Code).[64]

A notable feature of national war crimes legislation in Canada, Australia and the United Kingdom has been the means adopted to define a war crime. It was thought necessary first, to define war crimes by reference to international law and secondly, to provide a reference back to domestic laws. This two-pronged approach was intended partly, as mentioned earlier, to ensure that the prohibition against retroactivity was met by ensuring that the offence was not only an offence at international law but was also clearly known as an offence within domestic law at the relevant time. Another objective of this drafting technique was to provide a practical way of defining a war crime for domestic judges who are not usually trained in the methodology and substance of international law.

It was a curious feature of the Australian legislation that, while a judge could rely on known and clear local criminal laws, they would be required to look to the principles of international law to determine whether a defence might apply.[65] The circular process seems ineffective to the extent that the primary drafting intent was to avoid the need for proof of international law.

---

[62] Ibid.

[63] *Convention on the Prevention and Punishment of the Crime of Genocide*, opened for signature 9 December 1948, 78 UNTS 277, (entered into force 12 January 1951) ('*Genocide Convention*'), art 2. As at 17 March, there were 129 States Parties.

[64] Williams, above n 34, 170.

[65] *War Crimes Act* 1945 (Cth), s 17(2).

The clear definition by the Rome Statute of war crimes, crimes against humanity and aggression for the purposes of the International Criminal Court will make a significant contribution to the development of the jurisprudence of international criminal law and avoid the drafting problems faced by national legislatures.

7. DEFENCES: SUPERIOR ORDERS AND ACTS OF STATE

A common defence in war crimes trials is that the defendant either committed the act under superior orders or that the act was carried out as an act of State and in the absence and ignorance of the accused. The defences of superior orders and act of State were not available during the Nuremberg or *Eichmann* trials. Under the Australian *War Crimes Act*, evidence of superior orders can be considered only at the sentencing stage.

By contrast, in the United States trial of its national, Lt Calley, counsel argued that any defence of superior orders, which is made dependent upon the accused's ability to distinguish reasonable orders from aberrant ones, is unworkable in the battlefield.[66] The defence of superior orders was made available to Calley, but on the basis of an impractical criterion.

Not only is there inconsistency in admitting defenses, either to the substantive crime or in mitigation of sentence, but also there are differing practices in war-time and in peace. For example, while the defence of State immunity was not available to defendants at Nuremburg, the United States courts have found that State immunity continues to apply where claims are brought under the *Torture Victim Protection Act*.[67] These problems are compounded by the traditional rule of international law that one sovereign may not sit in judgment upon another. Trial by an international tribunal provides a solution to the problem of sovereign equality as the tribunal sits in judgment in the place of the State, though admittedly as the creation of other sovereign States.[68] The lesson for the future is that any international tribunal should clarify the role and function of defences.

8. VICTOR'S JUSTICE

A perception of war crimes trials is that victory brings the power to prosecute war crimes and that national prosecutors do not always come to court with clean hands. Examples in support of the 'victor's justice' criticism abound in history and, more recently, in the Nuremberg and Tokyo trials. Simpson argues that the 'victor's justice' objection to war crimes trials is

---

[66] *US v Calley*, 46 CMR 1131 (1971), aff'd, 22 USCMA 534, 48 CMR 19 (1973).

[67] 106 Stat. 73, printed at 28 USC § 1350 (1991).

[68] See discussion by Simpson, above n 12, 15.

misplaced, particularly in recent war crimes trials. In fact, most war crimes trials have been conducted by nations against their own nationals or, in the cases of *Polyukovich* and *Eichmann*, where there has been only a tenuous relationship between the victorious and the vanquished. Moreover, war crimes usually take place before military tribunals in secret; a curious fact in light of the asserted educational and deterrent rationalizations for war crimes trials. Finally, the tribunals established in relation to Rwanda and Former Yugoslavia are intended to deal with war criminals on all sides in the conflicts, not only those of a victorious side.

Despite these recent instances of evenhandedness, there has been a dearth of examples of the victors, as distinct from the defeated, bringing war crimes prosecutions against their own nationals. This is true in relation to acts of the Allies in the Second World War. It is also true for other wars in Algeria, Korea, Vietnam, Middle East and the Gulf War. The proposed war crimes trials in Cambodia will be a rare exception.

9. Conclusions

National war crimes trials over the last 20 years or so have been ineffective and sometimes an abuse of process. They have typically failed to secure convictions and have raised the specter of ethnic discrimination in multi-cultural communities. The selective and partial nature of the legislation on which trials have been conducted have tarnished respect for the rule of law, risking both procedural unfairness and breach of the prohibition against retroactive crimes. The well-intentioned, moral and legal imperatives to prosecute war crimes have been followed by the disbanding of the Australian War Crimes Investigation Bureau in 1993 with termination of each prosecution and French anguish over the *Touvier* and *Papon* trials.

National attempts to prosecute war crimes and crimes against humanity, nonetheless, signal some ways forward. There are needs:

- to develop clear substantive international criminal laws and defences;
- for an international tribunal which will be less vulnerable to national needs to provide credibility and ideological education or satisfy domestic political priorities;
- to create new internationally recognized rules to ensure procedural fairness
- to avoid trials more than (say) 25 years after the event, (despite the position taken by the United Nations and national legislatures that the statute of limitations does not run against war criminals);
- to develop an international criminal legal profession.

The encouraging prospect for the future, stimulated by public condemnation of the brutality in Former Yugoslavia and Rwanda, has been a preference for *ad hoc* tribunals and, more recently, the adoption on 20 August

1998 of the Statute of the International Criminal Court. The Statute will come into force with the ratification by 60 States.[69]

The new court is intended to complement national criminal jurisdiction and will have jurisdiction only where a nation is unwilling or unable genuinely to carry out the investigation or prosecution of persons alleged to have committed crimes. This brief survey of national approaches to war crimes trials suggests that such a permanent court and a developed jurisprudence might better maintain the rule of law.

---

[69] Statute of the ICC, art 126(1).

9. International Criminal Law and the *Ad Hoc* Tribunals

1. HISTORICAL BACKGROUND

> The privilege of opening the first trial in history for crimes against the peace of the world imposes a grave responsibility. The wrongs we seek to condemn and punish have been so calculated, so malignant and devastating that civilization cannot tolerate their being ignored because it cannot survive their being repeated.[1]

Thus spoke Justice Robert Jackson in his opening address at the Nuremberg trials on 20 November 1945. Over 50 years later – it is obvious with heart-breaking clarity that civilisation continues to tolerate devastating acts during times of armed conflict and in times of "peace" – in the former Yugoslavia, Rwanda, Afghanistan, Zaire, former Soviet Union – the list goes on. In the face of continuing horrors what has the international community done to date?

In August of 1945 the four major victorious Allies of World War II in London agreed upon the Charter for an International Military Tribunal.[2] This Tribunal was empowered to try major German officials accused of war crimes. Not long after a similar Tribunal was established in Tokyo to try Japanese officials accused of breaching international humanitarian law.[3] Despite being deemed victors' courts these were the first international criminal proceedings and for many years they were the last.

It is with ease that a critical perspective may be taken on both these Tribunals – in relation to rules of evidence and procedure Nuremberg had

---

[1] Telford Taylor, *The Anatomy of the Nuremberg Trials* (1992) 167.

[2] *Agreement for the Prosecution and Punishment of Major War Criminals of the European Axis*, 8 August 1945, 82 UNTS 279 (*'London Agreement'*). The Charter of the International Military Tribunal is appended to the Agreement (*'Charter of the IMT'*).

[3] *Charter of the International Military Tribunal for the Far East*, 19 January 1946, revised 26 April 1946 (*'The Tokyo Charter'*), reproduced in C Bevans, *Treaties and Other International Agreements of The United States of America 1776-1949* (1970) vol 4, 27.

Helen Durham and Timothy L.H. McCormack (eds.), The Changing Face of Conflict and the Efficacy of International Humanitarian Law, 193–203.
© 1999 *Kluwer Law International. Printed in Great Britain.*

limited guidance.[4] However the impact of these Tribunals on the development of international law cannot be underestimated. Indeed the Statutes of the current *ad hoc* Tribunals,[5] as well as the Statute of the International Criminal Court,[6] rely heavily upon the Charter of the IMT.

Concepts currently accepted in all areas of international law, that individuals have international duties which transcend their national obligations, were extremely radical in the 1940s. Commentators on the consequences of international criminal proceedings expressed grave fears; 'What the prosecution is doing ... in the name of the world community ... is destroying the spirit of the State'.[7]

The spirit of the State is alive and well, and the debate has moved on from 'if' the international community is able to trump state sovereignty to when and to what degree? These issues relate back to the essence of why the international community sees the need for international criminal trials.[8] I want to very briefly examine this area of the debate.

2. A Case for War Crimes Tribunals

There is a plethora of legal, intellectual and emotional arguments as to why international criminal proceedings are important.[9] Perhaps the most obvi-

---

[4] 'Rules of Procedure of the International Military Tribunal' (1945) 1 *Trial of Major War Criminals* 19-23.

[5] See *Statute of the International Tribunal for the Prosecution of Persons Responsible for Serious Violations of International Humanitarian Law Committed in the Territory of the Former Yugoslavia since 1991*, SC Res 827, 48 UN SCOR (3217th mtg), UN Doc S/RES/827 (1993); 32 ILM 1203 ('*Statute of the ICTY*'); *Statute of the International Tribunal for the Prosecution of Persons Responsible for Genocide and Other Serious Violations of International Humanitarian Law Committed in the Territory of Rwanda and Rwandan Citizens Responsible for Genocide and Other Violations Committed in the Territory of Neighbouring States, Between 1 January 1994 and 31 December 1994*, UN Doc S/RES/955 (1994), 49 UN SCOR (3453rd mtg); 33 ILM 1598 ('*Statute of the ICTR*').

[6] *Rome Statute of the International Criminal Court*, adopted by the United Nations Diplomatic Conference of Plenipotentiaries on the Establishment of an International Criminal Court on 17 July 1998; 37 ILM 1002. The whole of the Statute can also be accessed at <http://www.un.org/icc/romestat.htm> ('*Statute of the ICC*').

[7] H King, 'The Limitations of Sovereignty from Nuremberg to Sarajevo' (1994) 20 *Canada-United States Law Journal* 167, 167.

[8] In this context, Draper asserts, '[T]he enthusiasm to bring war criminals, as newly defined, to trial may so increase that jurisdiction will be seen as a matter not of competence or legal power but of legal obligation to exercise it': G I A D Draper, 'The Modern Pattern of War Criminality' in Yoram Dinstein and Mala Tabory (eds) *War Crimes in International Law* (1996) 141, 147.

[9] See, eg, ibid; Theodor Meron, 'Is International Law Moving Towards Criminalization?' (1998) 9 *European Journal of International Law* 18; Lyal S Sunga, *The Emerging System of International Criminal Law: Developments in Codification and Implementation* (1997); Timothy L H McCormack, 'From Sun Tzu to the Sixth Committee: The Evolution of an International Criminal Law Regime' in Timothy L H McCormack and Gerry J Simpson

ous argument is the assistance international criminal law provides as a deterrent for unlawful behaviour during conflict and to break cycles of violence and reprisals. These arguments correlate with the *raison d'être* for domestic criminal jurisdictions and for that reason it is unnecessary for me to expand upon them.

A second reason often cited is the role international criminal trials play in developing international humanitarian law. As Professor Theodor Meron asserts; 'the reaction of the international community to the appalling abuses in the former Yugoslavia has brought about certain advances – in international criminal and humanitarian law.'[10]

Many international legal norms are currently articulated but not tested and trials allow practical application. The argument that the norms of international humanitarian law are discredited if they are never enforced, has some validity (ie there has never been a prosecution for genocide contrary to the Genocide Convention[11] since that Convention was concluded[12]). So, the capacity to give international law teeth and application other than mere academic validity is vital.

Another argument is the role that international criminal proceedings play in the healing of both individual victims and the healing or reconciliation of States ravaged by war. There is no doubt that many survivors of war crimes (be it rape, torture, ill treatment in camps) and families of those who are killed demand justice. This is not necessary for individual revenge but for acknowledgment of the crime suffered and to work against the apathy, disbelief and complacency that is rampant in the world today.

Whatever the Nuremberg and Tokyo Trials did or did not do, they created a mass of documented history in minute detail which now makes it difficult to deny the atrocities that occurred during World War II.[13] One wonders whether Pol Pot's reign of terror, or the Afghan conflict or even the events in East Timor could have become part of the daily dialogue of international humanitarian law if they had been the subject of detailed prosecutions. Gerry Simpson has cautioned us against the development of this argument too far, particularly in view of the post World War II sce-

---

(eds), *The Law of War Crimes: National and International Approaches* (1997) 31. See also, 'Report of the Working Group on the Question of an International Criminal Jurisdiction,' (1992) *Report of the International Law Commission on its Forty-Fourth Session,* 47 UN GAOR, UN Doc A/47/10 (Supp 10) (1992) [419]-[424] ('*ILC Report 1992*').

[10] Theodor Meron, 'War Crimes in Yugoslavia and the Development of International Law' (1994) 88 *American Journal of International Law* 76, 87.

[11] *Convention on the Prevention and Punishment of the Crime of Genocide*, opened for signature 9 December 1948, 78 UNTS 277, (entered into force 12 January 1951) ('*Genocide Convention*'), art 2. As at 17 March 1999, there were 129 States Parties.

[12] ILC Report 1992, [419].

[13] 'The public trials of [Nazi] criminals have played an important role in educating the public regarding the Holocaust and undermining the propaganda of the Holocaust deniers'; Efraim Zuroff, *Occupation: Nazi-Hunter – the Continuing Search for Perpetrators of the Holocaust* (1994) 224.

nario. He illustrates this by identifying the 'complexity and precariousness of th[e] process by which good and evil are sharply defined.'[14] This is an important caution. The use of precise legal documentation, provided it has been taken from all sides in the conflict, may assist in the accurate representation of historical events. In the construction of history, there is still a need to view international criminal jurisdiction beyond the strict legal parameters and through the eyes of psychologists, historians and politicians.

The issue of national reconciliation is strongly recognised as another pointer to enhance the case for international criminal jurisdiction. The Rwandan Government, during debates at the creation of the *ad hoc* Tribunal, stated that it is impossible to build a state of law and arrive at true national reconciliation without eradicating the culture of impunity.[15] The need to not only stop revenge but to help construct a new society based on issues of social justice and respect for fundamental human rights is advanced greatly through international criminal jurisdiction. However, such proceedings must be undertaken with integrity and due process.

Another example of the range of roles that international criminal law plays in re-constructing society after conflict is the case of the Former Yugoslavia. Diplomats advise of the dramatic impact of the indictments of certain Serbian politicians and one can witness people carrying around placards in the streets of Belgrade stating that 'X is a war criminal, send him to The Hague'. Ths gives validity to the voices of people wishing to change the domestic *status quo*. Rather than one country's isolated attempts to deal with its past, there are some over-arching international legal institutions involved in the process. These are very complex matters. However, they must be considered when dealing with the enforcement of international humanitarian law, if such enforcement is to be truly valid.

3. CASE AGAINST WAR CRIMES TRIBUNALS

Of course, there are also arguments against international criminal courts and tribunals. Some commentators claim that such cases are stumbling blocks in potential efforts to create peace. It cannot be ignored that many perpetrators are those in government or heads of state. Thus, potential defendants may be the only ones with the control to cease violations. The

---

[14] Gerry Simpson, 'War Crimes: A Critical Introduction' in McCormack and Simpson, above n 9, 1, 22.

[15] Payam Akhavan, 'Current Developments' (1996) 90 *American Journal of International Law* 204.

instigation of proceedings against such individuals may not cease the problem but rather entrench the conflict.[16]

Other arguments raised against international criminal jurisdiction include very large number of technical difficulties involved. Issues such as a fear of erosion of State sovereignty, the political will to implement such jurisdiction and the requirement of large economic resources are all raised. Former Air Commodore, Geoff Skillen, also deals with many of these issues, vital to the success of international criminal law in the following chapter.

4. THE ICTY AND ICTR

I would now like to move on to an examination of the current *ad hoc* Tribunals with a particular focus upon their establishment. The ICTY was established by the Security Council pursuant to Resolutions 808 of February 1993 and 827 of May 1993.[17] These resolutions were adopted pursuant to Chapter VII of the United Nations Charter and accordingly create a binding obligation on all member States to assist and cooperate fully with the Tribunal, if so requested.[18] The Tribunal has attempted to balance States' concerns over issues of sovereignty, against responding appropriately to the international outcry of the violations of international humanitarian law committed in the former Yugoslavia. Thus, the Tribunal has concurrent jurisdiction with the national courts in relation to war crimes and crimes against humanity committed in their territory since 1991.[19] However, whilst such concerns have been attempted to be dealt with within the structure of the Tribunal, there are criticisms from many States of the process used to create this Tribunal. The decision of the Security Council represents the opinion of only a very few States. To impose such a Tribunal, to which all States are technically bound to assist, raises a number of concerns. Furthermore, in appropriate circumstances, the Tribunal can exercise primacy over national courts.[20] It is also important to note that the Federal Republic of Yugoslavia (Serbia and Montenegro) and other key parties to the Balkan conflict strongly oppose the establishment of the Yugoslav Tribunal.

In November of 1994, pursuant to Security Council Resolution 955, a similar international criminal Tribunal was created to try breaches of international law in Rwanda.[21] Although the Security Council established

---

[16] Anthony D'Amato, 'Peace vs. Accountability in Bosnia' (1994) 88 *American Journal of International Law* 500, 502.

[17] See above n 5.

[18] Statute of the ICTY, art 29.

[19] Statute of the ICTY, art 91.

[20] Statute of the ICTY, art 92.

[21] See above n 5.

separate Tribunals for these two regions, it recognised the need to make institutional and organisational links. Thus, the Appeals Chambers of both Tribunals are the same and the Prosecutor for the ICTY also serves as the Prosecutor for the ICTR, although extra staff are available and Rwanda has a separate Deputy Prosecutor. The two International Criminal Tribunals also share the same Rules of Procedure and Evidence.[22] It is interesting to note that, unlike with the former Yugoslavia, the Rwandan Government supported, at least initially, the establishment of an *ad hoc* international criminal jurisdiction within its own territory. Rwanda eventually voted against the creation of the ICTR in the Security Council due to the institution's non-inclusion of the death penalty. Here rises another irony in the inter-face between domestic and international war crimes prosecutions. In countries like Rwanda, those prosecuted and found guilty by domestic courts are eligible to receive the death penalty, whilst those convicted by the ICTR are eligible to face life imprisonment at the most.

Prior to the creation of both Tribunals, the Security Council had mandated a Commission of Experts to examine the evidence of international humanitarian law violations on the ground.[23] This Commission assisted in ascertaining whether or not there was enough documentation to proceed with the development of the International Tribunals. Due to the method of drawing up the *ad hoc* Tribunals through the speedy process of Security Council resolutions rather than the drafting of a treaty, there were limited opportunities for lengthy debate on much of the legal technicalities. The vast bulk of drafting for both the Tribunals was done by the United Nations Department of Legal Affairs, thus accounting for the greater influence of the Common Law rather than the Civil Law.[24]

Perhaps an area where the Tribunals differ most is with regard to subject matter jurisdiction. Both Tribunals have the capacity to try individuals for genocide, and the definition is reproduced from the Genocide Convention.[25] They can try individuals who perpetrate crimes against humanity,

---

[22] See, eg, *International Tribunal for the Prosecution of Persons Responsible for Serious Violations of International Humanitarian Law Committed in the Territory of the Former Yugoslavia Since 1991,'Rules of Procedure and Evidence'*, as amended, UN Doc IT/32 Rev 11 (1997).

[23] See *Final Report of the Commission of Experts Pursuant to Security Council Resolution 780 (1992)*, 47 UN SCOR (3119th mtg), UN Doc S/Res/780 (1992); 31 ILM 1476, UN Doc S/674/1994 Annex (1994) ('*Final Report*').

[24] Paul Tavernier, ' The experience of the International Criminal Tribunals for the Former Yugoslavia and for Rwanda' (1997) 321 *International Review of the Red Cross* 605, 609.

[25] Genocide Convention, art 2 requires:

An intention to destroy, in whole or in part, a national, ethnical, racial or religious group through the commission of such acts as killing or causing serious bodily or mental harm to members of the group; deliberately inflicting on the group conditions of life calculated to bring about its physical destruction in whole or in part; imposing measures to prevent births within the group; forcibly transferring children of the group to another group.

although it is interesting to note that the Statute of the ICTR does not require a nexus with armed conflict. Whilst the ICTY also has jurisdiction over grave breaches of the Geneva Conventions and war crimes, the fact that the Rwandan conflict is not characterised as an international conflict has resulted in the exclusion of these two crimes from its Statute. Instead, Article 4 of the Statute of the ICTR deals with violations of Article 3 common to the Geneva Conventions[26] and of Additional Protocol II.[27]

At this stage in the proceedings the ICTY has indicted 56 individuals and has 26 accused in its custody.[28] The ICTR has indicted 37 accused and has 31 accused in custody.[29] Both Tribunals have indicted a range of actors, including extremely powerful individuals such as the Bosnian Serb President, Radovan Karadzic, and General Ratko Mladic of the Former Yugoslavia. Perhaps, the most significant developments of late have been the first ever convictions for the offence of genocide. The ICTR has recorded the convictions of two high-profile individuals, the *Bourgmestre* of Taba, Jean Paul Akayesu,[30] and the former Prime Minister of Rwanda, Jean Kambanda.[31]

The ICTR found Akayesu guilty of the offences of genocide (including, commission of genocide and direct and public incitement to commit genocide), crimes against humanity (including extermination, murder, torture, rape and other inhumane acts). The Tribunal however, found that he was not guilty of the violations of Common Article 3 of the Geneva Conventions (including, murder and cruel treatment), and Article 4(2)(e) of Additional Protocol II (including, outrage upon personal dignity, in particular

---

[26] See *Geneva Convention for the Amelioration of the Condition of the Wounded and the Sick in Armed Forces in the Field*, 75 UNTS 31 ('*First Geneva Convention*'); *Geneva Convention for the Amelioration of the Condition of Wounded, Sick and Shipwrecked Members of Armed Forces at Sea*, 75 UNTS 85 ('*Second Geneva Convention*'); *Geneva Convention Relative to the Treatment of Prisoners of War*, 75 UNTS 135 ('*Third Geneva Convention*'); *Geneva Convention Relative to the Protection of Civilian Persons in Time of War*, 75 UNTS 287 ('*Fourth Geneva Convention*'). All these conventions entered into force on 21 October 1950,and as at 17 March 1999, there were 188 States Parties.

[27] *Protocol Additional to the Geneva Convention of 12 August 1949,and Relating to the Protection of Victims of Non-International Armed Conflicts*, 1125 UNTS 609; 16 ILM 1442 (entered into force on 7 December 1978), ('*Additional Protocol II*'). As of 17 March 1999, there were 145 States Parties.

[28] Information accessed from the ICTY Website (18 November 1998) located at the following URL: <http://www.un.org/icty/glance/fact.htm>.

[29] Information accessed from the ICTR Website (18 November 1998) located at the following URL: <http://www.ictr.org/english/factsheets/Detainees.html>.

[30] *Prosecutor v Jean-Paul Akayesu* [1996] ICTR-96-4-T. The decision dated 2 September 1998 can be accessed at <http://www.un.org/ictr/english/judgements/akayesu.html>.

[31] *Prosecutor v Jean Kambanda* [1997] ICTR-97-23-S. The decision dated 4 September 1998 can be accessed at <http://www.ictr.org/english/judgements/kambanda.html>. The accused had pleaded guilty to the four counts of genocide (including the commission of genocide, conspiracy to commit genocide, direct and public incitement to commit genocide, complicity in genocide), and to two counts of crimes against humanity (murder and extermination). He was sentenced to life imprisonment.

rape, degrading and humiliating treatment and indecent assault). It was deemed that the Prosecutor had not proven beyond a reasonable doubt that the acts perpetrated by Akayesu in the commune of Taba, at the time of the events alleged in the Indictment, were committed in conjunction with the armed conflict or that he had acted either for the Government or as a member of the armed forces under military command.[32] Akayesu has appealed his conviction.

On 5 March 1998, the trial chamber of the ICTY sentenced Drazen Erdemovic to 5 years' imprisonment after he pleaded guilty to violations of the laws or customs of war.[33] In May of 1997, the ICTY handed down a judgment in relation to Tadic.[34] The trial had begun exactly a year before and the defendant was charged with thirty-four counts, including, crimes against humanity, grave breaches of the Geneva Conventions and violations of the laws or customs of war. The Chamber found Tadic guilty on eleven counts of violations of the laws or customs of war and crimes against humanity.[35] Tadic was found not guilty on eight counts and all charges laid against him pursuant to the grave breaches of the Geneva Conventions were dismissed.[36] He was sentenced to 20 years imprisonment and both the Defence and Prosecution have appealed.[37]

It is interesting to note in relation to the previous discussion on the role that international criminal trials play in the development and clarification of international criminal law, why the Trial Chamber in the *Tadic* Case chose not to consider any charges under grave breaches of the Geneva Conventions. Even though the purpose of this article is not to conduct an in-depth examination into the *Tadic* decision, I believe that it is important to note that two of the three trial judges, constituting the majority, con-

---

[32] See above n 29, 259.

[33] *Prosecutor v Drazen Erdemovic (Sentencing Judgment)* [1996] Case IT-96-22-S. The judgment is accessible at: <http://www.un.org/icty/erdemovic/trialc/judgment/80305ms2-e.htm>. In this case, an earlier Trial Chamber, having accepted the accused's plea of guilty to the count of a crime against humanity sentenced him on 29 November 1996 to ten years' imprisonment: *Prosecutor v Drazen Erdemovic*, 108 ILR 180. Subsequently on 23 December 1996, he lodged an appeal against the Sentencing Judgement. The Appeals Chamber delivered its judgment on 7 October 1997. The Appeals Chamber remitted the case to a new Trial Chamber, holding, *inter alia*, that: (a) in the circumstances of the case, the accused's plea of guilty was not informed; and (b) duress does not afford a complete defence to a soldier charged with a crime against humanity and/or a war crime involving the killing of innocent human beings: it is admissible in mitigation, *Drazen Erdemovic v Prosecutor* [1996] Case IT-96-22-A, [18]. In view of the above, the Appeals Chamber directed that the accused be allowed to re-plead with full knowledge of both the nature of the charges against him and the consequences of his plea before another Trial Chamber, [20]. It was against this background that the 5 March 1998 sentence was pronounced.

[34] *Prosecutor v Dusko Tadic (Decision of Trial Chamber II, 7 May 1997)* IT-94-1-T; 36 ILM 908 ('*Tadic Judgment*').

[35] *Tadic* Judgment [693]-[765].

[36] *Tadic* Judgment [577]-[608].

[37] *Prosecutor v Dusko Tadic (Sentencing Judgment, 14 July 1997)* IT-94-1-S [74]-[75].

cluded that the status of victims as protected persons pursuant to the Geneva Conventions was not satisfied in this case.[38] Article 4 of the Fourth Geneva Convention supplies the definition of protected persons as those being persons who find themselves in the case of conflict in the hands of a party to the conflict or occupying powers of which they are not nationals.[39] Whilst other elements of this definition were satisfied, the majority of the Chamber concluded that the victims were nationals of the occupying power and thus were not protected persons. Where this will lead us in relation to further developments of international law is unsure, particularly considering the strong dissenting judgment rendered by Judge Gabrielle Kirk McDonald.[40] Judge McDonald opined that the victims of the accused were persons protected by the Geneva Conventions because the conflict, on the evidence that was presented, was sufficient to classify it as an international armed conflict.[41] The pending appeals will be interesting.

---

[38] *Tadic* Judgment, [608] (Stephen and Vohrah JJ). This conclusion was arrived at by the Trial Chamber pursuant to the earlier finding by the Appeals Chamber in *Prosecutor v Dusko Tadic (Jurisdiction)* 105 ILR 420, 453 ('*Appeals Chamber Decision*') to the effect that, 'in the present state of development of the law, Article 2 of the Statute, (which gives the Tribunal jurisdiction in respect of grave breaches of the Geneva Conventions) only applies to offences committed within the context of international armed conflicts,' [499].

[39] *Tadic* Judgment, [607]. During trial, the Trial Chamber was called upon to decide whether at 'all relevant times the victims of the accused were in the hands of "a Party to the conflict or Occupying power of which they are not nationals' [578]. The Trial Chamber, on an analysis of the factual position and the circumstances surrounding the conflict, found that the conflict at the relevant time was an 'internal conflict' and thereby the victims of the accused enjoyed protection of the prohibitions contained in common art 3, 'rather than the protection of the more specific grave breaches regime applicable to civilians in the hands of a party to an armed conflict of which they are not nationals'.

[40] In this regard mention must be made of the observation of the Appeals Chamber with regard to the United States *Amicus Curiae* brief, which submitted that the grave breaches provisions of art 2 of the Statute of the ICTY apply to armed conflicts of a non-international character as well as to those of an international character. Noting this submission with satisfaction, the Appeals Chamber remarked:

> This statement, unsupported by any authority, does not seem to be warranted as to the interpretation of Article 2 of the Statute. Nevertheless, seen from another viewpoint, there is no gainsaying its significance: that statement articulates the legal views of one of the permanent members of the Security Council on a delicate legal issue; on this score it provides the first indication of a possible change in *opinio juris* of States. Were other States and international bodies to come to share this view, a change in customary law concerning the scope of the "grave breaches" system might gradually materialize.

Appeals Chamber Decision, above n 38, 498.

[41] *Tadic* Judgment, [979]. Judge McDonald in a well-reasoned opinion differed from the majority on the issue of the status and role of the Bosnian Serb Army (VRS), the perpetrators of the atrocities in the area of Prijedor, *vis-à-vis* the Federal Republic of Yugoslavia (Serbia and Montenegro) (FRY). The majority had concluded that the latter had not exercised 'effective control' over the VRS, whereas, Judge Mcdonald found there was sufficient dependence by the VRS on the FRY and that the high threshold requirement set by the majority was not justified in the context of international humanitarian law.

More recently, the ICTY pronounced its judgment in the case of *Prosecutor v Zenjil Delalic et al.*[42] This is only the second judgment upon trial to be rendered by the ICTY, and the third judgment which imposed sentences upon the accused. For the first time since the decisions of the Nuremberg and Tokyo Military Tribunals the concept of command responsibility has been addressed.[43] On the question of the legal classification of the conflict in Bosnia and Herzegovina, the Trial Chamber concluded by stating that the conflict 'in Bosnia and Herzegovina must be regarded as an international armed conflict throughout 1992.'[44] This finding thus being in conformity with the dissenting opinion of Judge McDonald in the *Tadic* Judgment.[45] Pursuant to this critical finding the ICTY convicted an accused person for rape as torture. Rape as torture is charged as a grave breach of the Geneva Conventions and a violation of the laws and customs of war.

The final matter I would like to address is the practical difficulty involved in the gathering of evidence for international criminal proceedings. Here I will focus upon the ICTY as it is further advanced in proceedings in relation to this matter. Unlike the Nazi paper-chain, the ICTY has experienced problems with accessing vital evidence. Unlike the post-World War II scenario with investigators having access to mass graves and other sites – in many of the instances investigators associated with the ICTY have not been granted visas to visit the areas under question. Indeed the *Tadic* Judgment actually acknowledged that access to evidence in the territory of the Former Yugoslavia is difficult 'due in no small part to the unwillingness of the authorities of the Republika Srpska to cooperate with the International Tribunal.'[46] It is interesting to note that with the Rwandan experience not only is there assistance from the current Government, but many of the leaders of the massacres are no longer in power and are hiding in refugee camps. Thus it is more likely for them to be captured than those still in power in the former Yugoslavia.

Other challenges facing the Tribunals include the fear of many witnesses giving evidence, particularly those with family or friends still caught up in conflict. Testament to the newness of such a trial, decisions have had to be

---

[42] [1996] IT-96-21-T (Judgment of 16 November 1998). The four accused indicted in this case were tried together for grave breaches of the Geneva Conventions and violations of the laws and customs of war, including superior responsiblity for murder, torture, causing great suffering or serious injury, inhumane acts and participation in the unlawful confinement of civilians in inhumane conditions. The Trial Chamber's official summary of the judgment is currently available at: <http://www.un.org/icty/pressreal/statcel.htm>. However, the first accused *Zejnil Delalic* was found not guilty of grave breaches and war crimes and acquitted of the count charging him as a direct participant in the unlawful confinement of civilians. The other 3 accused received sentences of imprisonment ranging from 7 to 20 years.

[43] The Trial Chamber emphasised that 'not only military commanders, but also civilians holding positions of authority, are encompassed by the doctrine', ibid.

[44] Ibid.

[45] See above n 34.

[46] *Tadic* Judgment, [530].

made in relation to the protection of witnesses as well as rules developed in relation to the use of video conference linkages.[47] In particular there have been robust debates in relation to the process of preserving the anonymity of witnesses and how far this protection can go.[48] Consideration in such proceedings also had to be given to the role played by pre-trial media with the potential for the infection of testimonial evidence due to the mass publication of the event. Many of these issues, which appear challenging at the moment, will no doubt become an integral part of international criminal jurisdiction in the future.

The world is watching the *ad hoc* Tribunals – the development of the Statute for an International Criminal Court in Rome in June/July 1998, relied heavily upon these two international legal institutions. Not only did the ICTY and ICTR provide strong legal precedents in a technical sense during the Rome debates, the Tribunals' proceedings also proved that international criminal trials *can* work. The combination of demonstrating the legal capacity to try those accused of atrocities, as well as the political will of the majority of the international community to assist in this process, was a powerful driving force in creating the ICC. It is indeed fortunate that many of the matters that the ICTY and ICTR are currently grappling with, might be resolved by the time the ICC gets up and running. It will be naive to assume that the development of the ICC will result in the eradication of breaches of international humanitarian law or revolutionise human behaviour. On the other hand, the creation of such a court reflects the truism that crimes are not committed by abstract entities, but rather by individuals and that it is thus essential to develop an international system that punishes individuals. More than anything – the creation of the ICC is a symbolic first step towards a civilisation that cannot and will not tolerate devastating acts committed with impunity.

---

[47] See *Prosecutor v Dusko Tadic (Protective Measures for Victims and Witnesses Decision, 10 August 1995)* 105 ILR 599, [48] ('*Protective Measure's Decision*').

[48] See, eg, Christine Chinkin, '*Amicus Curiae* Brief on Protection Measures for Victims and Witnesses' (1996) 7 *Criminal Law Forum* 179, 182.

GEOFFREY J. SKILLEN

10. Enforcement of International Humanitarian Law

1. INTRODUCTION

The subject of the enforcement of international humanitarian law has troubled me greatly as a military legal officer. Historically, there has been extensive cynicism among my colleagues about the efficacy of international humanitarian law as it applies to the conduct of military operations. Take, for example, the words of Sir Arthur Harris, who retired as Marshal of the Royal Air Force at the end of World War Two. Sir Arthur had achieved great notoriety during the war as the commander of the RAF's Bomber Command, to the extent that he was popularly known as 'Bomber Harris'. After the War he concluded, that '[i]nternational law can always be argued pro and con, but in this matter of the use of aircraft in war there is, it so happens, no international law at all.'[1]

Lest it be thought that such views have only been confined to soldiers, and not shared by other members of the international law community, consider the following assertion from Sir Hersch Lauterpacht. '[I]f international law is the weakest point of all law, then the law of war is virtually its vanishing point.'[2]

While I do not share either of these views, I am conscious that many have done and continue to do so, and as a pragmatic practitioner, I am forced to wonder why. While there may be many and varied reasons, one of the weak points to which Lauterpacht may have been referring to is the matter of enforcement. Of course, one of the major points of difference between international law and domestic law is the absence of a systematic regime for the enforcement of international law. Nowhere has this absence been more pronounced than in international humanitarian law. In no case, I would argue, has the absence of a systematic enforcement regime contributed more to a lack of respect for the legitimacy of the law than has been the case with international humanitarian law.

---

[1] W Hays Parks, 'Air War and the Law of War' (1990) 32 *Air Force Law Review* 1, 2.
[2] Ibid.

Helen Durham and Timothy L.H. McCormack (eds.), The Changing Face of Conflict and the Efficacy of International Humanitarian Law, 205–216.
© 1999 *Kluwer Law International. Printed in Great Britain.*

What does history tell us about the enforcement of international humanitarian? To answer this question, we could look back as far as the Middle Ages,[3] but since time does not permit a history lesson of this kind, I will confine myself to the notable enforcement efforts since the end of World War II. In so doing, I will argue that these efforts have proved largely unsatisfactory, and that they require the international community to investigate new means of enforcement of international humanitarian law which will promote international respect for and observance of it. The most promising international initiative of this kind is the establishment of a permanent international criminal court, which is the focus of the final part of this chapter.

2. THE INADEQUACY OF NATIONAL AND INTERNATIONAL APPROACHES SINCE WORLD WAR II

Alleged war criminals have been tried under both domestic and, to a far lesser extent, under international jurisdiction on several occasions in the last 50 years. Domestic war crimes trials have been conducted in several countries, including Germany, Austria, the United Kingdom, and the Netherlands, France, Italy, the former USSR, Israel, Canada, the United States and Australia since 1945.[4] While the overwhelming majority of these trials were conducted in the immediate aftermath of World War Two, several states have experienced a more recent resurgence of interest in war crimes trials. Some of the more recent domestic trials have focussed on alleged atrocities from World War Two while others have involved alleged atrocities from more contemporary conflicts. For example, in response to the concerns of the presence of alleged Nazi War Criminals in Australia, the Commonwealth Parliament amended the *War Crimes Act* 1945 (Cth) in 1988 to enable the prosecution of the alleged war criminals in Australia for their conduct which answered the description of 'war crimes' committed

---

[3] The Trial of Peter von Hagenbach in Austria in 1474 is often cited as the first reported international war crimes prosecution. Hagenbach was tried by the allied states of the Holy Roman Empire for atrocities he committed in the town of Briesach. He was ultimately convicted of the crimes of murder, rape, perjury and other crimes against the laws of God and Man. See especially Timothy L H McCormack, 'From Sun Tzu to the Sixth Committee: The Evolution of an International Criminal Law Regime' in Timothy L H McCormack and Gerry J Simpson (eds), *The Law Of War Crimes: National And International Approaches* (1997) 37-9. See generally, Georg Schwarzenberger, *International Law as Applied in International Courts and Tribunals* (1968) 462-6; J W Bishop Jr, *Justice Under Fire: A Study of Military Law* (1974) 4; Cherif M Bassiouni, 'The Time Has Come for an International Criminal Court' (1991) 1 *Indiana International and Comparative Law Review* 1; Theodor Meron, 'Shakespeare's Henry the Fifth and the Law of War' (1992) 86 *American Journal of International Law* 1.

[4] See McCormack and Simpson, above n 3, 74–92 (various European states), 110–8 (Israel), 129–34 (Australia), 164–70 (Canada).

between 1 September 1939 and 8 May, 1945.[5] Although three prosecutions were launched in Australia under the Act in 1992, none proceeded very far. No convictions were recorded.[6]

Some of the more notable domestic war crimes trials conducted elsewhere in the world since World War Two include those of Adolf Eichmann in Israel in 1961,[7] Klaus Barbie in France in 1986,[8] and John Demjanjuk (allegedly 'Ivan the Terrible') which concluded in Israel in 1993.[9] Two new high public profile trials that have been instituted recently in Europe are: in Italy against former Nazi SS captain, Erich Priebke extradited from Argentina for his alleged participation in the murder of civilians in the Ardeatine Caves in Rome, and the recent conviction in France of Maurice Papon for collaborating in the transportation of French Jews to Nazi concentration camps.[10]

In addition to these trials, numerous others have been conducted under domestic jurisdiction using provisions that apply specifically to military forces. The best known modern example of a military war crimes trial is that of Lieutenant William Calley of the United States Army, arising out of the so-called 'My Lai' massacre. Lieutenant Calley was tried for the murder of at least 102 Vietnamese civilians by a military court martial convened under the authority of the United States Uniform Code of Military Justice.[11]

---

[5] Section 9 of the *War Crimes Act* 1945 (Cth) as amended by *War Crimes (Amendment) Act* 1988 (Cth).

[6] For an overview of the Australian cases see Gillian Triggs, 'Australia's War Crimes Trials: All Pity Choked' in McCormack and Simpson, above n 3, 129–34.

[7] *Attorney-General of the Government of Israel v Adolf Eichmann* (1962) 36 ILR 277 (Supreme Court of Israel).

[8] *Federation nationale des Deportes et internes et Patriotes contre Klaus Barbie*, reprinted in 90 RGDIP 1024 (1986). See generally Axel Marschik, 'The Politics of Prosecution: European National Approaches to War Crimes' in McCormack and Simpson, above n 3, 82–3.

[9] *State of Israel v John Demjanuk* Crim Case No 373/86 (District Court of Israel), overturned in *Demjanuk*, Crim App No 347/88 (Supreme Court of Israel, 29 July 1993), reprinted in Landau (ed), *The Demjanuk Trial* (1991). See also Jonathan M Wenig, 'Enforcing the Lessons of History: Israel Judges the Holocaust' in McCormack and Simpson, above n 3, 110–8.

[10] Paul Webster, 'Trial Probes French War Conscience', *The Age* (Melbourne, Australia), 8 October 1997, 11. Papon was found guilty of crimes against humanity and sentenced to 10 years imprisonment on 2 April 1998. The jury found him guilty of complicity in organising the round-up and detention of Jews during World War II, but acquitted him on charges of complicity in the deaths of the Jews, most of whom perished at Auschwitz: see Christopher Henning, '*Papon* Trial: Guilty of Crimes Against Humanity', *The Sydney Morning Herald* (Sydney, Australia), 3 April 1998, <http://www.smh.com.au/daily/content/980403/world/world6.html>.

[11] *United States v Calley*, 46 CMR 1131 (1971); aff'd 22 USCMA 534, 48 CMR 19 (1973). Lieutenant Calley was ultimately convicted for the murder of 22 Vietnamese civilians. For a comprehensive study of the case see Hammer, *The Court-Martial of Lt Calley* (1971).

I would observe at this point that many countries, including Australia, have provisions in their military legislation enabling the conduct of such trials. The Australian legislation is known as the *Defence Force Discipline Act* 1992 (Cth) and allows trials by military Tribunals for a wide range of offences, including murder, although the circumstances in which serious offences such as murder can be tried are restricted.[12]

What lessons can we learn from the history of national approaches to the prosecution of alleged war crimes? In short, I am of the view that national interests have outweighed the willingness to comply with international humanitarian law. War Crimes trials have only been convened when national political will has so dictated. Some commentators have suggested that trials will only take place 'where defeat and criminality coincide'.[13] Only a truly international forum can demonstrate the impartiality needed to guarantee that proceedings are taken when necessary and appropriate, regardless of political considerations.

Of course, we have already seen that there have been and are international Tribunals operating. In fact, there have been only four instances since World War Two of the creation of international Tribunals to try war criminals. These were the Nuremberg and Tokyo Tribunals immediately after World War Two and more recently the creation by the United Nations Security Council of the international criminal Tribunals to try crimes committed in the Former Yugoslavia[14] and Rwanda.[15]

A charter drafted in London between June and August 1945 by representatives of the United States, United Kingdom, USSR and France established the Nuremberg Tribunal.[16] It created the offences of crimes against peace (the planning and waging of a war of aggression), crimes against humanity and war crimes.[17] Twenty-four defendants were charged in all,

---

[12] Sections 61(1) and 63(1).

[13] Gerry Simpson, 'War crimes: A Critical Introduction' in McCormack and Simpson, above n 3, 5.

[14] The *Statute of the International Tribunal for the Prosecution of Persons Responsible for Serious Violations of International Humanitarian Law committed in the Territory of the Former Yugoslavia since 1991* is found in the *Report of the Secretary-General Pursuant to Paragraph 2 of Security Council Resolution 808 (1993)*, UN Doc S/25704 (1993); 32 ILM 1159. The Security Council formally approved the Statute and established the Tribunal by adopting Resolution 827, SC Res 827, 48 UN SCOR (3217th mtg), UN Doc S/RES/827 (1993); 32 ILM 1203 ('*Statute of the ICTY*').

[15] *Statute of the International Tribunal for the Prosecution of Persons Responsible for Genocide and Other Serious Violations of International Humanitarian Law Committed in the Territory of Rwanda and Rwandan Citizens Responsible for Genocide and Other Violations Committed in the Territory of Neighbouring States, Between 1 January 1994 and 31 December 1994*, UN Doc S/RES/955 (1994), 49 UN SCOR (3453rd mtg); 33 ILM 1600 ('*Statute of the ICTR*').

[16] *Agreement for the Prosecution and Punishment of Major War Criminals of the European Axis, (London Agreement)*, 8 August 1945, 82 UNTS 279. The Charter of the International Military Tribunal is appended to the Agreement ('*Charter of the IMT*').

[17] Charter of the IMT, art 6.

including one *in absentia*. Twenty-two were ultimately tried; of whom 3 were acquitted. Of the defendants convicted, 12 were sentenced to death.[18] Of course, many more defendants were charged and convicted for offences under the subsidiary law, Control Council Law No 10,[19] and by individual allied military tribunals.

The Tokyo Tribunal was established by a proclamation issued in January 1946 by the Supreme Commander for the Allied Powers, General Douglas MacArthur.[20] As was the case with Nuremberg, the crimes within the jurisdiction of the Tokyo Tribunal involved crimes against peace, war crimes and crimes against humanity.[21] Twenty-eight defendants were charged in all, of whom two died during the trial, and one could not be tried because of his incapacity to stand trial. Of the remaining convicted defendants, seven were sentenced to death, and those remaining were sentenced to undergo various terms of imprisonment.[22] As with Nuremberg, subsidiary trial processes were undertaken by individual allies against Japanese defendants.[23] Australia's original *War Crimes Act* 1945 (Cth) was enacted to allow Australian military tribunals jurisdiction over Japanese

---

[18] Roger S Clark, 'Nuremberg and Tokyo in Contemporary Perspective' in McCormack and Simpson, above n 3, 172. For other accounts of the Nuremberg trials see, G Ginsburgs and V Kudriavtsev (eds), *The Nuremberg Trial and International Law* (1990); Telford Taylor, 'The Nuremberg War Crimes Trials' (1949) *International Conciliation No 450;* R Woetzel, *The Nuremberg Trials in International Law* (1962); B Smith, *The Road to Nuremberg* (1981); B Smith, *Reaching Judgment At Nuremberg* (1977); Telford Taylor, *The Anatomy of the Nuremberg Trials, A Personal Memoir* (1992). On war crimes trials in the 1940s, see J Appleman, *Military Tribunals and International Crimes* (1954).

[19] *Allied Control Council Law No 10 Punishment of Persons Guilty of War Crimes, Crimes Against Peace and Humanity*, 20 December 1945, Official Gazette of the Control Council for Germany, No 3, Berlin, 31 January 1946 ('*Control Council Law No 10*'). The prohibition of crimes against humanity was subsequently affirmed by the General Assembly in its resolution entitled *United Nations General Assembly Resolution in Affirmation of the Principles of International Law Recognized by the Charter of the Nuremberg Tribunal*, 11 December 1946, UN GA Res 95, 1 UN GAOR (Part II) at 188; UN Doc A/64/Add.1 (1946), and thereafter confirmed in the *Principles of International law Recognized in the Charter of the Nuremberg Tribunal and in the Judgment of the Tribunal*, adopted at Geneva, 29 July 1950; 5 UN GAOR Supp (No 12) 11; UN Doc A/1316 (1950); (1950) 4 *American Journal of International Law (Supp)* 126. The twelve US Control Council Law No 10 trials are also discussed in Taylor, above n 18, 272-3. For Soviet prosecutions, see George Ginsburg, 'Moscow and International Legal Cooperation in the Pursuit of War Criminals' (1995) 21 *Review of Central and Eastern European Law* 1, 12. For Polish trials, see Appleman, above n 18, 267-345.

[20] *Charter of the International Military Tribunal for the Far East*, 19 January 1946, revised 26 April 1946 ('*The Tokyo Charter*'), reproduced in C Bevans, *Treaties and Other International Agreements of The United States of America 1776-1949* (1970) vol 4, 27.

[21] The Tokyo Charter, art 5.

[22] Clark, above n 18, 181–2.

[23] Perhaps the most famous US trial was that of General Yamashita in the Philippines. See *Re Yamashita*, 327 US 1 (1946).

defendants. In excess of 900 trials were conducted pursuant to this legislation.[24]

As is the case in relation to the domestic trials, several lessons can be learned from this experience. The first, and most often cited, is that the creation of the Tribunals and the conduct of trials represent an exercise of 'victors' justice', that is the trial and punishment by the victors of the vanquished, regardless of the merits of the case. The defence at Nuremberg argued that the same rules should have applied to certain alleged Allied transgressions which were claimed to have been as serious as the ones committed by those who were in fact tried.[25]

The two recently created Tribunals, namely the International Criminal Tribunals for the former Yugoslavia and Rwanda, were established for the specific purpose of trying offences committed during the course of recent events in those troubled regions. The Tribunal for the former Yugoslavia has jurisdiction to try 'serious violations of international humanitarian law' committed in the territory of the former Yugoslavia since 1991.[26] The specific violations are the grave breaches of the 1949 Geneva Conventions, 'violations of the laws and customs of war', genocide and crimes against humanity.[27] In the case of the Rwanda Tribunal, jurisdiction is limited to events occurring in Rwanda between 1 January and 31 December 1994.[28] Its jurisdiction encompasses genocide, crimes against humanity and violations of Common Article 3 of the 1949 Geneva Conventions and Additional Protocol II to those Conventions,[29] recognising that the conflict in Rwanda was of a non-international character. For each Tribunal the Statutes regulate the more important aspects of its operation, although the Tribunals have also created their own Rules of Procedure.

Regardless of the ultimate success or otherwise of the ICTY and the ICTR, several aspects of their creation and operation point clearly to the need to establish a permanent, standing international Tribunal to ensure that proper and consistent standards are applied.[30]

It can be argued cogently that the existence of a standing Tribunal, ready and able to sit in judgment on crimes committed during armed conflict, or in appropriate cases in situations short of armed conflict, would serve as a powerful disincentive against flagrant breaches of international humanitarian law. This could accordingly act as an effective means of promoting

---

[24] For a history of Australia's war crimes trials immediately following World War II see especially, Triggs, above n 6.

[25] Simpson, above n 13, 5.

[26] Statute of the ICTY, art 9(1).

[27] Statute of the ICTY, arts 2–5.

[28] Statute of the ICTR, art 8(1).

[29] Statute of the ICTR, arts 2–4.

[30] See generally, Timothy L H McCormack and Gerry Simpson, 'Achieving the promise of Nuremberg: A New International Criminal Law Regime?' in McCormack and Simpson, above n 3, 229-50.

respect for international humanitarian law. Such a body would make no distinction between war's winners and losers, and would operate during time of peace as well as war.

The *ad hoc* Tribunals were created to respond after the occurrence of events in those specific regions. Many in the international community have argued that political factors have acted as an influence on the decision to establish these means of enforcement of international humanitarian law, something which ought to have been determined judiciously and uninhibited by political considerations. Some commentators have asked the questions: if Yugoslavia, why not Chechnya? If Rwanda, why not Tibet? A permanent court, less prone to political constraints on the exercise of its jurisdictional competence, could help overcome these criticisms.[31]

Ad hoc bodies with limited subject matter, temporal and territorial jurisdiction do not have the opportunity to establish an extensive jurisprudence in relation to multiple conflicts over an extended period of time. The establishment of a permanent court could foster the development of consistency in matters such as general principles of criminal law, procedure and punishment.[32]

The United Nations Security Council, representing an elite group of States sharing common interests, without the involvement of the broader international community created all the four international Tribunals. In the case of the ICTY, there was no agreement with even the parties to the conflict for the establishment of the Tribunal. Although the criticism of inconsistency does not of itself constitute an argument against the validity of trials in the Former Yugoslavia, the criticism remains. Some perpetrators of atrocities in the Former Yugoslavia and in Rwanda will be tried before international tribunals while equally deserving individuals in other conflicts will not. The extensive international involvement, which was evident in the negotiations leading to the establishment of the International Criminal Court, could well answer this criticism.[33]

These are in my opinion, some of the more significant lessons that can be learned about contemporary efforts to try war criminals, in both domestic and international fora. It also suggests that there are a number of weaknesses, which can only be appropriately addressed if the permanent court is endowed with the characteristics necessary to ensure that the lessons of history are learned, and that the court enjoys both an adequate jurisdictional basis and the freedom to act when necessary, unencumbered by interference from any non-judicial considerations. With this in mind, I will now turn to a consideration of what appears to me to be the most critical

---

[31] Christopher Blakesley, 'Atrocity and its Prosecution: The *Ad Hoc* Tribunals for the Former Yugoslavia and Rwanda' in McCormack and Simpson, above n 3, 227.

[32] Ibid.

[33] Ibid, 227–8.

issues confronting the International Criminal Court (ICC), the Statute for which was adopted in Rome on 17 July 1998.[34]

3. KEY ISSUES FACING THE INTERNATIONAL CRIMINAL COURT

Three of the most significant issues which are yet to be resolved, and which would determine the efficacy of a Permanent international criminal court are: the extent of the Court's jurisdictional competence; the relationship between the Court and national jurisdictions; and the circumstances in which the Court's jurisdiction may be invoked.

3.1 *Extent of the Court's Jurisdictional Competence*

The court's jurisdictional competence, as defined in Article 5 of its Statute, extends to the crime of genocide, crimes against humanity, war crimes and, once the Statute is amended to include an acceptable definition, the crime of aggression.

An acceptable definition of the crime of genocide creates little difficulty because there is widespread acceptance of the definition in the Genocide Convention.[35] Since its opening for signature in 1948, the Genocide Convention has attracted 129 State Parties and has been referred to in various international judgments as now reflective of a peremptory norm of international law.[36] If anything, the agreed conventional definition, subsequently shown to be too restrictive, has resulted in atrophy by the international community in demonstrating its extreme reluctance to amend or update agreed treaty provisions. The high threshold *mens rea* requirement of 'intent to destroy, in whole or in part' an identifiable group of people has often been criticised because of the difficulty of proving this intent

---

[34] *Rome Statute of the International Criminal Court*, adopted by the United Nations Diplomatic Conference of Plenipotentiaries on the Establishment of an International Criminal Court on 17 July 1998; 37 ILM 1002. The whole of the Statute is located at <http://www.un.org/icc/romestat.htm> (Statute of the ICC). See generally, Jelena Pejic, 'Creating a Permanent International Criminal Court: The Obstacles to Independence and Effectiveness' (1998) 29 *Columbia Human Rights Law Review* 291.

[35] *Convention on the Prevention and Punishment of the Crime of Genocide*, opened for signature 9 December 1948, 78 UNTS 277 (entered into force 12 January 1951) ('*Genocide Convention*'), art 2. As at 17 March 1999, there were 129 States Parties.

[36] The International Court of Justice in the *Barcelona Traction Case* has recognised genocide as an obligation *erga omnes*, involving rights which all States have a legal interest in protecting. See *Barcelona Traction Light & Power Co Ltd (Belgium v Spain) (Merits)* [1970] ICJ Rep 3. See also *Application of the Convention on the Prevention and Punishment of the Crime of Genocide (Bosnia and Herzegovina v Yugoslavia) (Preliminary Measures)* [1993] ICJ Rep 3, 325-44 and *Military and Paramilitary Activities in and against Nicaragua (Nicaragua v US) (Merits)* [1986] ICJ Rep 14.

behind specific instances of genocidal acts.[37] A second major limitation of the definition relates to the exhaustive list of 'a national, ethnical, racial or religious group' the object of the genocidal activity. Pol Pot's reign of terror in the killing fields of Cambodia, which resulted in the death of more than two million people, fell outside the strict legal definition of genocide because the Cambodian victims were not covered by the exclusive list of targeted groups in the conventional definition. Despite this glaring example of the inadequacy of the accepted definition, the international community has refused to open up the list of groups, and this restricted formula is reflected in Article 6 of the Court's Statute. There is, however, general agreement that a number of inhumane acts should be characterised as crimes against humanity, when committed on a large scale or as part of widespread or systematic attack against a civilian population, with knowledge of the attack. There is no nexus to an armed conflict necessary for an act to be characterised as a crime against humanity. In fact, like genocide, crimes against humanity have been considered to be *jus cogens* or peremptory norms of customary international law by both the International Court of Justice[38] and by the Appeals Chamber of the ICTY.[39]

The Court's war crimes jurisdiction is invoked when crimes are committed as part of a plan or policy or as part of a large-scale commission. In international armed conflict it extends to the grave breaches of the 1949 Geneva Conventions[40] and to a number of other acts generally recognised as war crimes under customary international law. These acts are comprehensively listed in Article 8(b) (i) to (xvi). Some are drawn from Additional Protocol 1 to the Geneva Conventions,[41] while others are drawn from other sources. The structure of that part of Article 8 dealing with non-international armed conflicts is similar, in that it draws on Common Article 3 of the Geneva Conventions, and adds a number of other acts, some of which find their source in Additional Protocol II to the Geneva Conven-

---

[37] Antonio Cassese, *Human Rights in a Changing World* (1990) 75-8.

[38] See especially, the cases, above n 36, in relation to genocide.

[39] *Prosecutor v Tadic (Jurisdiction)* (Decision of the Appeals Chamber, 2 October 1995) 105 ILR 419, 453 [70].

[40] See *Geneva Convention for the Amelioration of the Condition of the Wounded and the Sick in Armed Forces in the Field*, 75 UNTS 31 ('*First Geneva Convention*'); *Geneva Convention for the Amelioration of the Condition of Wounded, Sick and Shipwrecked Members of Armed Forces at Sea*, 75 UNTS 85 ('*Second Geneva Convention*'); *Geneva Convention Relative to the Treatment of Prisoners of War*, 75 UNTS 135 ('*Third Geneva Convention*'); *Geneva Convention Relative to the Protection of Civilian Persons in Time of War*, 75 UNTS 287 ('*Fourth Geneva Convention*'). All these conventions entered into force on 21 October 1950, and as at 17 March 1999, there were 188 States Parties.

[41] See *Protocol Additional to the Geneva Convention of 12 August 1949, and Relating to the Protection of Victims of International Armed Conflict*, 1125 UNTS 3; 16 ILM 1391 (entered into force 7 December 1978) ('*Additional Protocol I*'). As at 17 March 1999, there were 153 States Parties.

tions.[42] It is not difficult to find fault with the extent of the Court's war crimes jurisdiction, but the result represents what was considered necessary to accommodate the diverse range of interests evident in those participating in the negotiations in Rome.

The inclusion of the crime of aggression in the Court's Draft Statute is intended to continue the tradition begun with the Nuremberg and Tokyo Tribunals, which tried the offence of 'crimes against peace.'[43] This provision is intended to impose individual criminal responsibility on persons in positions of national authority who plan or conduct a war of aggression against another State. The crime of aggression poses particular jurisdictional challenges – largely because of the political nature of the crime. Despite constitutional authority under the United Nations Charter for the United Nations Security Council to determine that an act of aggression has occurred,[44] the Council has never once made such a determination. Agreement on a definition of aggression will be extremely difficult to find. It is perhaps worth noting that it is exactly this failure to reach agreement on the definition of aggression that has been responsible for past unsuccessful attempts to create a Permanent International Criminal Court.[45]

3.2 *Relationship Between the Court and National Jurisdictions*

Many of the crimes to which I have referred can be tried under national jurisdictions. For instance, States Parties to the Geneva Conventions must enact appropriate domestic legislation to prosecute grave breaches of those Conventions. This leads to another vital issue that must be properly resolved: that is, the relationship between national jurisdictions and the international Court. In this regard the preamble to the Court's Statute makes clear that it is intended to be complementary to national jurisdictions, not to replace them.[46] For this reason, the term 'complementarity' has been coined.

Generally, it is accepted that the international Court will only operate when national jurisdictions have completely broken down, or are unable to operate, or, when, despite their ability to operate, they have failed to do so effectively. This is analogous to the experience with the conduct of war crimes trials under domestic jurisdictions, and the apparent lack of willingness to act effectively when national interests dictate otherwise. If the ICC had not been granted the ability to act when national jurisdictions have

---

[42] See *Protocol Additional to the Geneva Convention of 12 August 1949, and Relating to the Protection of Victims of Non-International Armed Conflicts*, 1125 UNTS 609; 16 ILM 1442 (entered into force 7 December 1978) ('*Additional Protocol II*'). As of 17 March 1999, there were 145 State Parties.

[43] Charter of the IMT, art 6.

[44] United Nations Charter, art 39.

[45] McCormack, above n 3, 61-2.

[46] Statute of the ICC, preamble para 3.

failed and the means to determine when this is so, then, the lessons of history would not have been learned and the efficacy of the Court would be diminished accordingly.

One key argument used by those who opposed the creation of the Court is that it represents an affront to State sovereignty. On the other hand, it has also been suggested that the existence of an international jurisdiction may have a highly desirable result, in that the performance of national jurisdictions will be improved with the knowledge that failure to act effectively may lead to action in the international Court, thereby embarrassing the State concerned. In any case, the creation of the Court will not diminish the constitutional authority of the United Nations Security Council. The option will remain for the Security Council to act pursuant to Chapter VII of the United Nations Charter and establish an *ad hoc* tribunal, whether or not the State concerned accepts that tribunal, if the Council believes the court is not adequate for the situation.

3.3 *Circumstances for the Invocation of the Court's Jurisdiction*

Finally, I address a matter, which I regard as being vital to the Court's success and to its ability to overcome the historical shortcomings that have been evident in the enforcement of international humanitarian law. I refer to the question of how the jurisdiction of the court is invoked – the so-called 'Trigger Mechanisms.' It matters little whether the court is endowed with an adequate jurisdictional basis, or whether it has been endowed with powers to punish, or what principles of criminal law it applies or what procedures it adopts, if there are practically insurmountable barriers to its operation in the first place.

This issue has not assumed the same magnitude in the case of the previous International Tribunals, given that they were all created after the event, and that, accordingly, the opportunity existed at the point of establishment to make provision for the mechanisms whereby the Tribunal could act. In the case of the ICC, the world was forced for the first time to grapple with this issue before, rather than after the event. In this regard, national interests were very much to the fore in the negotiations.

The Court's Statute provides that its jurisdiction may be invoked by one of three means, namely referral of a situation by a State Party, referral of a situation by the UN Security Council acting under Chapter VII of the UN Charter, or on the basis of an investigation by the prosecutor acting on his or her own initiative, in accordance with a number of preconditions laid down in Article 15. In addition, Article 12 establishes an overlay to the preconditions for the exercise of jurisdiction, by requiring that either the State on whose territory the alleged crime was committed or the State of nationality of the accused or suspect must be a State Party, or have agreed to accept the Court's jurisdiction for the crime in question. In the case of many non-international armed conflicts, this State will be one and the same, and could well act as an effective bar to prosecution.

On the positive side, Article 16, on the role of the Security Council, represents a substantial improvement over previous drafts of the Statute. It provides that the Council may request the court, by resolution adopted under Chapter VII of the Charter, not to investigate or prosecute a case for a (renewable) period of 12 months. Under the voting provisions in the Charter, such a resolution would require a majority of members of the Council, including the affirmative votes of all permanent members. This provision effectively means that a single permanent member of the Security Council cannot block the Court's proceedings unilaterally.

4. CONCLUSION

I have argued that the matter of enforcement of international humanitarian law is its greatest weakness; the absence of a systematic enforcement regime has contributed to a lack of respect for its legitimacy, and maybe even to a degree of cynicism about it. I have viewed the establishment of a Permanent International Criminal Court as representing an historic opportunity to put in place such a regime. However, the Court must have an adequate jurisdictional basis, there must be an acceptable understanding of the relationship between the court and national jurisdictions, and finally and most critically, the court must be allowed the freedom to act when appropriate and necessary, unrestricted by improper and irrelevant considerations. Only time will tell whether the Statute adopted in Rome in July 1998 will adequately meet these requirements, and whether the Court's establishment can be considered a success. However, the international community, having successfully concluded negotiations on the Rome Statute, now has the unprecedented opportunity to fully support the establishment of the Court and to work assiduously for its efficacy.

Index

International Humanitarian Law Series

KLUWER LAW INTERNATIONAL – THE HAGUE / LONDON / BOSTON